Pictorial
History of
Aircraft

Pictorial History of Aircraft

David Mondey

First published 1977 by
Octopus Books Limited
59 Grosvenor Street
London W1

ISBN 0 7064 0617 6

Produced by Mandarin Publishers Limited
22a Westlands Road
Quarry Bay, Hong Kong

Printed in Hong Kong

Drawings by Michael Badrocke

Contents

Introduction

From the moment that man evolved as a thinking animal, standing erect and two-legged like the birds, he must have envied their freedom of the air. Not only was their mode of travel fast, and seemingly effortless, but it enabled them to escape easily from four-legged predators. One can assume that this was the initial spur which drove men to seek ways of travelling in the air.

The earliest man-made airborne object was the kite, in use in China approximately 1,000 years BC. It is not known for certain when that nation first developed man-lifting kites, but there is evidence which suggests this to be some centuries before the birth of Christ.

Here, then, was the embryo flying-machine, but there were then none to appreciate the real significance of this vehicle which could be made to lift a man into the air and was used militarily for reconnaissance purposes.

The Italian, Leonardo da Vinci, famous primarily as an artist and sculptor, was the first to make a serious study of bird flight, leading men into the cul de sac of the ornithopter or flapping-wing aircraft. It was not until the beginning of the 17th century that a fellow countryman, Giovanni Borelli, proved it 'impossible that men should be able to fly craftily, by their own strength'.

At the beginning of the 18th century, on 8 August 1709 to be precise, the Jesuit priest Bartolomeu de Gusmaõ demonstrated a model hot-air balloon in the ambassador's drawing room at the court of King John V of Portugal. Present were the king, Queen Maria Anna, the papal nuncio Cardinal Conti, and other distinguished members of the court, noblemen and courtiers. Their evidence confirms that the principle of the hot-air balloon was understood and demonstrated almost three-quarters of a century before the first *Montgolfière*, created by the brothers Etienne and Joseph Montgolfier in France, took to the air on 5 June 1783.

In England, at the end of the 18th century, the Yorkshire baronet Sir George Cayley engraved on a silver disc a diagram relating the aerodynamic forces of lift, drag and thrust: on its reverse he sketched a fixed-wing glider. Five years later, having gained an understanding of the aerodynamics of the kite, he built and flew a model glider which had a fixed-wing of kite form, tail surfaces mounted universally to the fuselage pole to allow some measure of control, and a weight which could be moved to adjust the aircraft's centre of gravity. Within another five years he had constructed a full size glider which is generally believed to have carried a small boy in gliding flight.

Just past the mid-19th century a French naval officer, Félix du Temple, designed and built a model aircraft which, with a steam-engine for its power plant, became the first powered aeroplane capable of sustained flight.

And now we come to the last two decades of the 19th century, the moment when the pace of invention and development began to hot up. In 1884, Alexander Mozhaiski in Russia achieved the non-sustained ramp-assisted flight of a steam-powered monoplane. Then, in Australia, in 1893, Lawrence Hargrave invented the box-kite, a lightweight, stable structure with good lifting power. This was to have important influence during aviation's formative years.

In France, in 1890, Clement Ader's steam-powered monoplane, *Éole* (bat), became the first piloted powered aeroplane to raise itself from the ground, however briefly. While over the Channel in Britain, on 31 July 1894, Sir Hiram Maxim's steam-powered track-mounted giant biplane broke away from its restraining rails and was wrecked. And way across the grey North Atlantic, American scientist Samuel Pierpont Langley scored his first significant success on 6 May 1896 when his *No. 5* steam-powered model, which had a wing span of approximately 4·27 m (14 ft), flew for rather more than half-a-mile.

And while these mechanical events were capturing the imagination of those with the slightest interest in aviation the German, Otto Lilienthal, was quietly learning how to fly. With beautifully-constructed hang-gliders, which he could partially control by movements of his body, he achieved well over 2,000 flights. More importantly, he recorded his findings for all to study and was thinking seriously of attempting powered flight when, on 9 August 1896, he crashed in one of his *No. 11* gliders, and died the following day.

His work inspired the Scotsman Percy Pilcher in Britain and Octave Chanute in America. Pilcher, too, was mortally injured when the tail unit of his *Hawk* glider broke away and the machine crashed, on 30 September 1896, and he died two days later. The work of Lilienthal and Pilcher was known to Chanute who, besides designing and building a most successful biplane hang-glider, collected and collated a vast amount of information on aviation developments, which he produced as a book in 1894, entitled *Progress in Flying Machines*. This work, and Lilienthal's *Der Vogelflug als Grundlage der Fliegkunst* ("Bird Flight as a basis of Aviation") were the two primary sources of authentic information based on experimentation. They, and Octave Chanute in person, were the catalysts which started Orville and Wilbur Wright along the road to that historic day of 17 December 1903, when they achieved with their *Flyer* the first powered, sustained and controlled flight in history.

"Success", they telegraphed to their father, "four flights Thursday morning all against twenty-one-mile wind started from level with engine power alone average speed through air thirty-one miles longest 59 seconds inform Press home Christmas".

This realization of flight had taken some 3,000 years since an unknown Chinaman first discovered that a kite could be made to fly in the air. From 1903 it was to take only another 66 years to put two men on the Moon and bring them safely back to Earth. Such has been the speed of aviation progress, and much of this is mentioned in the pages which follow.

Strangely enough, the achievement of the Wright brothers did not result in newspaper headlines around the world. This was due to a combination of factors. First and foremost, American news editors would not accept the exaggerated report received from a free-lance journalist. Conviction that they were correct in their scepticism came in May 1904 when, at a demonstration for the press, the Wrights were able to achieve nothing better than a 60 ft (18 m) glide.

This was particularly ironic when one knows that approximately 17 months later they recorded a non-stop flight of 24 miles (30 km). And even then the world was still unaware of the miracle of powered flight.

The awakening came on a cold October day in 1906, when a rather tentative flight was made from the Bois de Boulogne, in Paris, by Alberto Santos-Dumont in his No. 14 **bis** aircraft. Although he was airborne for just under 200 ft (61 m), this flight was witnessed by so many people that it was hailed as, and for some time regarded as, the world's first powered and controlled flight by a heavier-than-air craft.

Europe became the centre of the new art of flight and the biplane **(1)** built by A. and H. Dufaux of Geneva, Switzerland, typifies the aeroplane that had evolved in continental Europe by 1909–10.

In Britain, progress had not been so rapid. A. V. Roe was the first national to fly an all-British machine, on 13 July 1909. His mount was a frail-looking triplane of his own design, its wings covered with brown paper, the aim being to achieve an ultra-lightweight structure that could be powered by a 9 hp J.A.P. engine. Instead of acclaim for his achievement, Roe was threatened with prosecution for endangering public safety.

Twelve days later the Frenchman, Louis Blériot, completed successfully the first cross-Channel flight. He landed on North Fall Meadow, near Dover Castle, after an eventful 37 minute flight from Les Baraques, near Calais. Britain's 'moat' was no longer an impregnable defence that could be policed by the Royal Navy. And in the light of this achievement, the case against Roe was quashed.

Among the first practical aircraft to equip the British Army was the Bristol Box-kite **(2)** of 1910, which gives an appreciation of the design lead then held by the more advanced French pioneers.

1

2

4

3

By the time that the aeroplane had attained reasonable reliability and controllability, World War I had started. As was to be expected, little time was lost in adapting this new vehicle for military use, although only a few far-sighted men could visualize it ever becoming a significant weapon. The majority of Army planners seemed to regard the aeroplane as an unnecessary complication to the art of war, delegating to it only the tasks of message carrying and reconnaissance.

It had not been appreciated in advance how vital was to be its contribution in the reconnaissance role. Soon it became necessary to use every means possible to prevent enemy aircraft from having unrestricted use of your airspace. So came the development of fighters to destroy hostile reconnaissance aircraft, or to escort ones own 'recce' machines: leading to bomber aircraft to destroy the bases from which they operated or the factories where they were built.

Typical of the more efficient fighter aircraft is this Hanriot HD1 (3). Note that it is of biplane configuration. Accidents with monoplane aircraft had suggested that a single wing was structurally unreliable, leading to widespread adoption of what was then the more robust biplane.

As the battle on the Western Front mounted in ferocity, so increased the demands on the combatant air forces. Early attempts to eliminate reconnaissance aircraft had been little more than knightly jousts, with opposing crews taking pot-shots at each other with revolvers or rifles.

But it was not long before aircraft were equipped with the far more lethal machine-gun. The main snag was that it could only be aimed properly and fired from a central mounting, which meant that the nearest target was your own propeller. Roland Garros, one of France's foremost pre-war sporting pilots, borrowed the

idea of fitting steel plates to the back of each propeller blade so that any bullet would be deflected before cutting its way through the wood.

He had considerable success with this device before a forced-landing behind enemy lines enabled the Germans to discover the secret of the forward-firing machine-gun. When ordered to copy the idea, Anthony Fokker devised instead an interrupter gear which 'timed' the bullets to miss the spinning propeller blades.

Typical of the more advanced fighter aircraft of 1917 is the French SPAD XIII **(4)**, of which many were flown also by the United States Air Service. That depicted carries the insignia of the US 94th Pursuit Squadron. Its 'Hat in Ring' symbolizes Uncle Sam's hat being thrown into the fighting ring.

Following page:
British designers and manufacturers had also worked hard to produce more effective aircraft. Army requirements had

been met by the Royal Aircraft Factory at Farnborough, Hampshire, where efforts had been concentrated initially on the evolution of an inherently stable aircraft. Ideal for unopposed reconnaissance sorties, it was at a great disadvantage when combat required evasive manoeuvres.

The British Admiralty had not been slow to appreciate that aircraft had much to offer to the Navy. This brought a variety of minds to bear, resulting in a wider range of types.

Among the Navy's suppliers was the Sopwith Aviation Company at Kingston upon Thames, Surrey, and typical of the company's excellent products was the Pup, with which the Royal Naval Air Service (RNAS) developed the concept of aircraft carriers. Shown on the ground and in the air **(5, 6)**, so efficient were these aircraft—often rated as one of the finest flying machines ever built—they were soon to be adopted by the Royal Flying Corps (RFC).

5

6

8

7

Bearing an unmistakable family likeness, but identifiable easily by its two-bay biplane wing, the later Sopwith Snipe (7) was another valuable addition to the Royal Air Force (RAF), which had been founded on 1 April 1918.

Designed around a new engine, the Bentley rotary, it was intended as an ultimate replacement for the superb Sopwith Camel, which had done so much to eliminate enemy air superiority. Unfortunately, it entered service in the closing stages of the war, too late to play a significant role.

But with the war's end, the Snipe became the RAF's standard fighter, some examples remaining in service until 1927. Snipes of No. 1 Squadron formed part of the original air control force in Iraq, a spectacular use of air power when the RAF was made responsible in 1922 for peace-keeping in that country, instead of traditional and far more costly to maintain ground forces.

Manoeuvrability was the primary requirement of those fighter aircraft involved in 'dog-fights', which developed on both sides of the Western Front as squadrons sought to prevent intrusion of their own airspace. This was completely the reverse of the inherently stable aircraft which Britain had tried so hard to perfect at the war's beginning.

Manoeuvrability required a compact and robust aeroplane of short wing span. But if the wing span was reduced too much, reducing also the wing area, then the amount of lift which it could develop was considerably less. This meant that manoeuvrability was gained only by increased take-off and landing speeds, a slower rate of climb and a lower operating height.

One solution to overcome these problems lay in the triplane wing, introduced initially on a fighter by the Sopwith Triplane. The impact of this aircraft on air fighting at the Western Front was such that the German Staff demanded an equivalent without delay, resulting in production of the Fokker Dr I triplane (8), which entered service in August 1917. Perhaps best-known of the many pilots who flew the type was Manfred von Richthofen—the 'Red Baron'—who was killed eventually while flying the Dr 1 425/17 on 21 April 1918.

Following the Fokker triplane into production was the same company's D VII (9), regarded as one of the best fighter-scout aircraft produced during World War I.

A single-bay biplane, powered by a 160 hp Mercedes D III or 185 hp BMW III six-cylinder in-line liquid-cooled engine, it was armed with two forward-firing Spandau machine-guns. Entering service soon after the death of Manfred von Richthofen, the unit which he had commanded, **Geschwader No. 1**, was among the first to be equipped with the type.

Proving easy to fly, being highly manoeuvrable and remaining readily controllable even at the operational ceiling of 22,900 ft (6,980 m), the D VII proved to be a formidable opponent. In fact, their potential was regarded so highly by Germany's adversaries that a term of the Armistice Agreement demanded that all Fokker D VII aircraft must be handed over to the Allies.

9

The Wright **Flyer** had been fundamentally a dead-end design, offering
no scope for development, but it should
not be thought that the Wrights had held
a monopoly of aircraft design in the
United States. Next in line of succession
was Glenn Curtiss, and because his
original creations had development
potential he should, perhaps, be
regarded as the country's foremost
pioneer. His **June Bug** biplane, powered
by a 40 hp V-8 engine of his own
design, won a trophy on 4 July 1908
after recording a flight of nearly one mile.
Naval aviation may be said to owe its
beginnings to Glenn Curtiss, and the
world's first really practical seaplane was
built and flown by him on 26 June 1911.

Impressed by the products of the
British Avro Company, established by
A. V. Roe, Curtiss paid for an engineer of
that company—B. Douglas Thomas—to
design a tractor biplane for him. This had
evolved by the beginning of World War I
under the designation JN-2.

But it was a development of this
aircraft, the JN-4 **(10)**, which was to be
produced in large numbers. A total of

1,412 JN-4A/Ds were built by the Curtiss Aeroplane & Motor Company, and an additional 1,310 JN-4Ds by other companies. Used as primary trainers the 'Jennies', as they were known affectionately, not only remained in service use until 1927, but were also the main mount of the first barnstormers, the men who popularized flying throughout the United States.

It has been quoted time and again that development of the aeroplane as a practical vehicle was boosted considerably by the two world wars. If by the term aeroplane one implies also its airframe, then this is not strictly true of the first major conflict.

A careful study of the aeroplane's structure which had evolved by 1918 reveals how little had been the effect of four years of combat. It is true that the airframe had advanced beyond the stick-and-string stage—just—but there was little sophistication. Heavy biplane structures, extensively braced and strutted, they demanded a great deal from the power plant, long before

receiving the added weight penalty of a substantial military load. Anthony Fokker commented that these aircraft had built-in headwinds.

The greatest development had come within the field of power plants, but for them to be able to carry aircraft, crew and weapons into the air, they had first to be started: not always a simple procedure.

The traditional method of starting an aircraft's engine was by means of the procedure known as hand swinging. With the ignition system switched off, a mechanic pulls the propeller through by hand to induce a combustible mixture of fuel and air into the cylinders. Then, with ignition on, a sharp pull on the propeller is usually sufficient to encourage the engine into life.

For aircraft like the Avro 504K (11), powered by engines of 100 to 130 hp, hand-swinging was—and very often still is—the only means available for starting the engine.

With more powerful engines it was sometimes possible to start them by

more than one man being involved in the procedure, two or three linking arms to provide a more hefty pull. Another expedient was the rope-and-glove technique, with a canvas glove being slid over one propeller blade. Attached to the canvas was a length of rope, enabling a team of men to give a good strong pull on the propeller for almost 180° of its rotation.

For engines of 200 to 300 hp, like that which powered the F.2A/F.2B Bristol Fighter (12), something rather more positive was necessary. This led to a device known as the Huck's Starter, the original being based on a Model T Ford. A special mechanical arrangement allowed an output shaft to be clutched-in to the engine of the vehicle. This shaft had at one end a metal dog which engaged with a similar dog secured to the propeller boss, allowing the propeller to be spun until the engine fired.

The mobility of the Huck's Starter enabled it to be driven from one aircraft to another, and most airfields soon had one of these indispensable devices available.

12

In the closing months of the war quite a number of new aircraft types were introduced into service by the combatant nations. Most of these benefited from the improvements in structure and power plant which the cut and thrust of active service had imposed. Typical was the Fokker D VII (9, page 13), which had gained a reputation second to none with the pilots of Germany's *Geschwader* I, II and III, as well as those of the many other *Jastas* which operated the D VII.

Such was this reputation that machines introduced subsequently were often regarded as being inferior without fair trial, and one of the aircraft to suffer by this comparison was the Pfalz D XII (12A). A good-looking single-seat biplane fighter, it was powered by a 160hp Mercedes D IIIa 6-cylinder in-line water-cooled engine, driving a two-blade wooden tractor propeller. Although it had a resemblance to the Fokker D VII, when it entered service in August 1918 it was considered a poor imitation until such time as reluctant pilots had gained some experience with the type. It was then found to be equal to the Fokker in many respects, and even superior in some manoeuvres. For example, its large horn-balanced ailerons on the upper wing imparted a high rate of roll, and its stable high-speed dive made it an excellent mounting for its two forward-firing Spandau machine-guns. Had it entered service some months earlier, the Pfalz might have gained for itself a reputation similar to that of the D VII.

Fixed Wing Flight

We all know from our own experience that aircraft do fly, but many people have no real idea why this is so. Some have tried to find the answers for themselves by obtaining what they considered a suitable book from the local lending library, only to discover that its explanations were studded with mathematical formulae which put it immediately beyond their understanding.

The aim here is to achieve the same result without any formulae or mathematics. As we work our way through this section *italics* will be used to pinpoint those words or phrases which are in common use by designers, engineers and those who work in the aviation industry, or who are concerned with the operation of *aircraft*.

The word aircraft is in italics because it is desirable to point out that there are two main streams of aircraft: *lighter-than-air craft*, which includes *airships*, *free-balloons* and *captive-balloons*; and *heavier-than-air craft* which includes *fixed-wing* aircraft and *rotary-wing* aircraft (dealt with separately in the next chapter) and, perhaps surprisingly, *kites*. There are, of course, a number of sub-divisions of both fixed-wing and rotary-wing aircraft, these relating to their use as, for example, *amphibians*, which can operate from and land on either water or land, and can also belong to one or other of the two main aircraft classes mentioned above.

Let us begin by considering the air which surrounds us, the air we breathe, and in which all classes of aircraft fly. It can be said that we live in an ocean of air and, in many ways, the behaviour of an aircraft in the air is similar to that of a submarine in water. The principal difference is that water is incompressible while, as we know by using a bicycle pump, air can be compressed. Until man created aircraft which could fly near to or faster than the speed of sound this factor was not very significant. It need not concern us at this particular moment.

Like water, air has density. Under normal conditions this is perhaps difficult to appreciate. But if you ride a bicycle along a road with the wind behind you, and then turn round and pedal back along that same road, you immediately become aware that something is holding you back. That something is not just simply the speed of the wind, it is the density of the air. Without it flight would be impossible, even for a bird. Its wings must have something against which to push; again, that something is density.

When experimenters wanted to see exactly how air flowed past different shapes they constructed *wind tunnels*. In them, air is drawn through the tunnel by a powered fan, and the shape to be examined is mounted in an area known as the *test section*. If smoke is injected into the *airstream* it is possible to see how it moves around the model or component under test. It is possible also to mount the model in such a way that the forces acting upon it as a result of the airstream can be measured and so help, to some extent, in deciding on the final *configuration*, or shape, of the aircraft under design.

If we had a wind tunnel available to us at this moment we could mount a piece of stiff card in it so that the edge facing the airstream – *leading-edge* – is higher than that at the rear, or *trailing-edge*. If the test section of our wind tunnel is horizontal, and the airstream coming from the left as we observe the behaviour of our piece of card, then the measuring instruments will show that there is a force at right angles to the airstream trying to *lift* the card. It will be possible to measure also the resistance of the card to the horizontal airstream flowing past it, called *drag*. These are two of the important forces which we must understand. Lift, beneficial, the designer's aim is always that this should be as great as possible. Drag, undesirable, every effort is employed to reduce this to an absolute minimum.

If we put a flat plate into our wind tunnel, with one of the large, flat faces pointing directly at the oncoming airstream, then our drag measurement will be very high. If we can also inject smoke, we will see that the airstream begins to lose its smooth lines some way ahead of the plate, that having passed around its edges it attempts to change direction, and then becomes broken up into eddies and swirls. This shows drag at its very worst and every attempt is made to achieve the reverse of this by utilising a smooth *streamline* section. If we substitute in our wind tunnel a streamline shape which has exactly the same cross-sectional area as that of our flat plate, we shall find on test that our drag measurement is only a fraction of the former test. If our streamline shape is well designed a smoke injection will show that the airstream is flowing smoothly over the model, clinging to and following its surface without any attempt to break away.

But you haven't got a wind tunnel! Hold a piece of stiff card between the thumb and finger, raise the leading-edge in relation to the trailing-edge, and then swing your arm quickly through the air. You can actually feel the forces of lift and drag. Try the effect of increasing and decreasing the angle which the card makes to the oncoming airstream. This angle is called the *angle of attack*. The nearer the angle approaches to zero the less will be the effects of both lift and drag. As you increase the angle you should be able to discern that lift increases faster than drag: and then suddenly this situation changes, the lift dropping to zero and the drag continuing to increase. This is because our card is beginning to approach the condition of the flat plate that we tested by discussion a little earlier. If our piece of card was an aircraft's wing, we would describe such a condition by saying that the wing had *stalled*. Let us now talk more specifically about an aircraft's wing, or *aerofoil*. If we were to cut a section cleanly through an aircraft's wing, at right angles to the *main spar* around which the wing is constructed, the resulting shape would be called an *aerofoil section*.

Aerofoil Section

We have discovered already that we can produce lift from a flat-section wing. Experimenters soon found they could get far more lift from an aerofoil section which had a pronounced curve on the upper surface. This is an effect due to the density of the air. If we look at the illustration, it will be noted that the airstream is represented by a series of short, 'fat' dashes moving parallel to each other. Those which pass over the *upper-surface* of the aerofoil have to travel much faster than those moving beneath the *lower-surface*. The vertically-ruled paper shows, visibly, that the upper-surface molecules of air have had to go faster to travel the arc of the aerofoil which is, clearly, a greater distance than the flat under-surface. To do this they have had to stretch out – to lengthen themselves – and, like a piece of stretched elastic, have narrowed in section. This narrowing means they are less strong or – put another way – they have lost pressure. Conversely, the under-surface molecules of air have tended to slow, to maintain the status quo between upper and lower surface molecules, and they have become compressed, increasing their pressure. Thus, in effect, the aerofoil is sucked up into the low pressure area above the wing, and pushed up by the high pressure beneath.

Because, generally speaking, air and water act very much alike you can easily test this to your own satisfaction. Turn on a water tap so that you have a fairly powerful and smooth flow, and then insert a knife blade at an angle into the flow. The water pushes it away, like the airflow on the flattish under-surface of an aerofoil. Now present the convex surface of the bowl of a large spoon into the stream of water and – surprise, surprise – it is drawn into the stream, the water stream clinging to its surface like the airflow over the upper-surface of an aerofoil.

Back again to our real aerofoil, experimenters discovered that by drilling a series of equidistant holes in a straight line from leading-edge to trailing-edge, in both upper- and lower-surfaces, and connecting a highly sensitive manometer to each hole, they were able to measure the distribution of lift. Approximately three-quarters came from the reduced pressure over the upper-surface,

the remaining quarter from the increased pressure beneath the lower-surface. The pattern of pressure distribution around the aerofoil is much what you would expect if you have begun to appreciate the principle of lift. That is to say, that the maximum reduced pressure above the wing is just aft of the leading-edge, falling away to nothing at the trailing-edge, and the same applies also to the under-surface of most aerofoil sections. Incidentally, the distance from the wing leading-edge to the wing trailing-edge is termed the *wing chord*.

We need now to carry out another experiment with our piece of flat card in the wind tunnel. If we adjust its supports to secure the card at mid-chord of each end, we shall soon discover that the lift force generated by the airstream will attempt to rotate the card, the leading-edge trying to go back and over the top. If we move the supports so that they are nearer to the leading-edge we shall find, by trial and error, that there

Airflow past various shapes (a) Flat plate (b) Ball (c) Streamlined shape

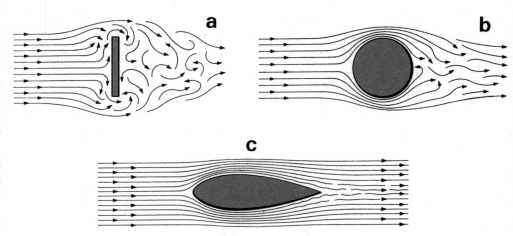

is a position when the nose will start to dip. With a certain degree of patience, assisted perhaps by adding a small balance weight to the leading-edge, we should be able to find a position for the supports that will allow the card to 'fly' in the airstream in balance. If we were then to draw a line from one support to another, along the length of the card, it would define a position parallel to the leading-edge which for that particular card, under the specific test conditions which applied, would be known as its *centre of pressure*.

It would seem logical, from all of the foregoing, that the thicker the aerofoil section the greater the lift. This is fundamentally true but, unfortunately, as the lift increases so does the drag induced by the thicker aerofoil. This is the first case where we discover that there are compromises which have to be accepted, according to the role of the aircraft which is being designed. A fast, lightweight fighter will usually be found to have a slim-section aerofoil, a slow cargo aircraft will have one of comparatively fat-section.

To permit comparison between the characteristics of various aerofoil sections, one of the basic factors is known as *thickness/chord ratio*, derived from a measurement of the maximum thickness of the aerofoil expressed as a percentage of the wing chord. Thus, we find that the McDonnell Douglas Phantom II interceptor has a thickness/chord ratio of its aerofoil which averages 5 per cent, while that of the Lockheed Hercules cargo aircraft averages about 18 per cent, these figures bearing out what has been stated above. The accepted compromises give the Phantom speed (1,450mph, 2,330km/h) at the expense of useful load (27,000lb, 12,247kg), while the Hercules has a cruising speed of only 386mph (621km/h) with a useful load of around 100,000lb (45,360kg). This is, of course, an over-simplification, without taking wing area into account, but serves well to illustrate the points above.

If we now return to our flat card, which let us call an aerofoil, let us imagine that it has been found capable of lifting a weight of 1lb (·45kg). If we now attach a weight of 1lb (·45kg) at the centre of pressure of the aerofoil, its angle of attack will remain unchanged because the aero-foil is in balance. In other words, when the centre of pressure and the *centre of gravity* (weight) coincide, the aerofoil is *in equilibrium*. If the centre of gravity (CG) is forward of the centre of pressure, then the aerofoil – or aircraft to which it is attached – becomes *nose-heavy*. Conversely, if the CG is aft of the centre of pressure, then the aircraft is *tail-heavy*.

Stability
We have already discovered three of the forces which act upon an aircraft in flight: lift, drag and weight. Before we can put our imaginary aircraft into steady flight we need one more balancing force. This fourth force we call *thrust*, and if an aircraft is to remain in level forward flight the forces of lift and weight must be equal, to keep it at a constant *altitude*, or height. Similarly, the forces of thrust and drag must be equal for it to continue in steady forward flight. Perhaps you find this latter statement a little difficult to accept. Consider carefully that if the thrust is greater than the drag, then the aircraft must be acceler-ating and is not in balanced flight. If the thrust is less than the drag then, by the same token, it must be decelerating. Only when thrust and drag are equal can the aircraft be travelling steadily forward at a constant speed.

Lift
(a) Lift diagram **(b)** Airflow over wing in normal flight **(c)** Airflow at point of stall, high angle

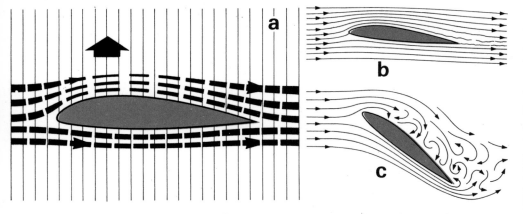

Let us now turn to the subject of *stability*, which is the inherent ability of the aircraft to maintain itself in stable level flight. This assumes that engine power remains constant and that the pilot takes no action to change the aircraft's *heading*, or direction, or the altitude at which it is flying.

For the purpose of understanding inherent stability you must first appreciate that an aircraft can move in three *axes*. All three of these run through its centre of gravity. That which is parallel to the wings is called its *lateral axis*, and is concerned with up and down *pitching move-ments* of the aircraft, like those of a ship heading into waves. The axis which runs through the centre of the fuselage, fore and aft, is termed the *longitudinal axis*, and is concerned with *rolling movements*. The third axis is known as the *vertical axis*, and passes vertically through the aircraft's centre of gravity. This is concerned with *yawing movements*, which are changes of the aircraft's heading to either *port* (left) or *starboard* (right).

If an aircraft starts to pitch as the result of a gust of wind lifting the nose, you must appreciate that as a result of its inertia the entire aircraft will continue, at first, to follow its original course. This means that the wings are at once positioned in a greater angle of attack, which automatically creates additional lift, tending to bring the nose up still higher. Similarly, the *tailplane* or *stabiliser*, the horizontal surface of the tail unit, is placed at a greater angle of attack, and as the aircraft continues to travel forward the tailplane, due to its long lever arm, has sufficient moment, or movement of force, to stabilise the situation, the tail coming up to level off the aircraft. The reverse occurs should the nose drop, the moment of the tailplane being sufficient to bring the tail down to eliminate the nose-down situation. It must be appreciated that the area of the tailplane is critical if it is to be able to do its job properly, as is the length of the fuselage. It follows that an aircraft with a long fuselage will generally have a tailplane of smaller area than an aircraft with a short fuselage.

Before we consider stability in the longitudinal axis, which is concerned with restoring a level attitude of flight when, for one reason or another, an aircraft dips a wing, it is desirable to take a quick look at how the wing is attached to the *fuselage*, or body structure. If you take a head-on view of the aircraft you will find that in the majority of cases the *wing root*, which is the point of the wing's attachment to the fuselage, is lower than the *wingtip*. The resulting angle which the wing makes to a horizontal surface is called its *dihedral angle*, and this is an important feature in the maintenance of longitudinal stability.

If, for instance, an aircraft's port wing dips, then the whole aircraft rolls to port. Immediately this happens the lift on the starboard wing is decreased, the lift on the port wing increased and the aircraft's roll is arrested. It then, momen-tarily, continues to fly forward with the port wing low. This means that the lift is no longer per-pendicular, but inclined to port, yet the weight force remains perpendicular to the Earth's sur-face. The resulting combination of the inclined lift force and perpendicular weight force causes the aircraft to begin to slide sideways to port, this motion being referred to as *sideslip*. As soon as the sideslip begins, the resulting sideways airflow gives increased lift to the lower wing due to its dihedral angle, helps push down the upper wing,

and also reacts on the side of the airframe structure, the combined effect being to roll the aircraft back to level flight.

The third axis is concerned with directional stability, that is stability about the vertical axis. If for any reason the nose of the aircraft is deflected to port or starboard, we start with the same premise as in the two former cases, namely that initially the entire aircraft continues to follow its original flight path. But, if the nose has been deflected to port, it will be yawing – or flying crabwise – several degrees to port. This motion exposes the entire side of the airframe to the airstream and, in particular, the fin and rudder components of the tail unit. The fin, especially, has a primary role in controlling directional stability, and its area in relation to the length of the fuselage is as critical as that of the tailplane.

We have discussed briefly the three axes of an aircraft's motion, and the design features which help to give it as much inherent stability as is desirable for its particular role. Those who have been fortunate enough to fly an aircraft, or have flown in close proximity with other aircraft, will be fully aware that an aircraft's movements in the air cannot be defined precisely by three rigid axes. In fact they blend, so that the aircraft becomes a living thing in the air, moving gracefully in, perhaps, all three axes simultaneously. Its movements are most akin to those of a fish in water.

So we see how designers have been able, over a period of time, to evolve aircraft which have sufficient stability built into their basic structure to reduce the pilot's work load to some extent. This inherent stability must not, however, interfere with the pilot's ability to control the aircraft easily, so that it will adopt the attitude and heading that he wishes it to take.

Pilot Control
So that he can direct the aircraft wherever he

Control axes
(a) Pitch (b) Roll (c) Yaw

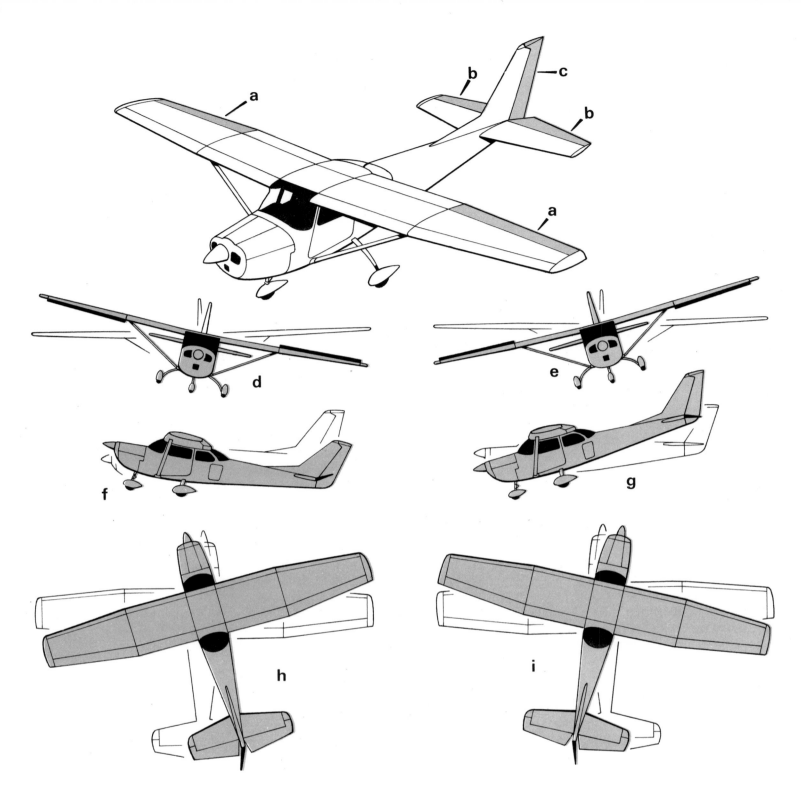

Control surfaces
(a) Aileron (b) Elevator (c) Rudder
(d) Roll-left (e) Roll-right
(f) Nose-up pitch (g) Nose-
down pitch (h) Yaw-left
(i) Yaw-right

wishes it to go, the pilot has two basic flying controls. The first is the *control column*, known commonly as the joystick or 'stick', the name joystick emphasizing perhaps better than any other single aviation word the feeling of the pioneer pilots who had succeeded in conquering the air. The control column is used to control pitching and rolling movements. The second control, the rudder bar – or more frequently today the rudder pedals – is used to initiate turning movements about the vertical axis.

Let us now look more closely at these controls, taking them in the same order in which we examined the three axes of motion: pitch, roll and yaw.

Control in pitch is the function of the *elevators*, movable, hinged control surfaces affixed to the trailing-edge of the tailplane. The movement of this surface is initiated by the pilot's control column. When this is in a central, or neutral, position, the elevator is similarly neutral, then

being virtually an extension of the tailplane and adding to its total area. When the control column is pulled back towards the pilot, the elevator is moved upward. When the airstream meets this raised surface the air becomes compressed and pushes against it. Since the control surface is temporarily immovable, the control column being held back by the pilot, the tail of the aircraft is forced down, bringing the nose up into a climb. Similarly, if the control column is pushed forward the tail unit will rise and the nose point downward.

Roll control is achieved by surfaces at the trailing-edge of each wing, normally adjacent to the wingtip, which are called *ailerons*. They, too, are connected to the pilot's control column. Moving the column to the right, or turning the control wheel often attached to the column to the right, raises the starboard aileron and drops the port aileron. The resulting effect of the airstream is to push the starboard wing down and the port wing up, initiating a rolling movement to starboard. Similarly, moving the control column to port initiates a roll to port. The earliest aircraft did not have ailerons, but adopted the system of roll control which had been used by the Wright brothers in their successful *Flyer*, namely *wing warping*. This method of lateral control was possible because the early aircraft had extremely flexible structures, so it required no great feat of strength from the pilot to operate a control column which caused the tip of each wing to be warped, or twisted, in opposite directions, the subsequent effect of the airstream on the distorted wingtips being equivalent to the effect described for ailerons, which eventually became standard.

Control of yaw is the function of the *rudder*, which is another movable surface attached to the trailing-edge of the fin. It is operated by a rudder bar, or rudder pedals, in the pilot's position, the pilot controlling the rudder by using his feet. It is, on the face of it, a very simple control: push the right foot forward and the rudder moves to starboard. The immediate effect of the airstream is to try and push the rudder out of the way, which forces the entire tail unit to port and consequently the nose swings to starboard. It is important to appreciate that if the rudder alone is used to make a turn, then the resulting movement would be an uncomfortable, flat turn. If a little aileron control is used in conjunction with the rudder, the resulting combination of bank and turn results in a pleasant, controlled movement.

Trim and Servo Tabs
In the case of a small aircraft the load imposed by the slipstream on these control surfaces is comparatively small, so that the pilot has no manual difficulty in operating the controls. However, as aircraft became bigger and faster, it became increasingly difficult for the pilot to cope with the forces acting upon the control surfaces. Much thought was expended on finding some means of overcoming the problem simply. One solution was the development of control surfaces with *horn balances*, so that the horn containing the mass balance extended into the airstream when the surface was moved in the opposite direction.

The action of the airstream on the projecting horn, plus the balance force, was sufficient to take some of the load off the pilot's control. The main disadvantage of the horn-balanced control surface is that the balance area is at one end of the surface, tending to twist the surface and initiate a phenomenon known as *flutter*.

An improvement on this idea is the inset hinge control surface, which can be easily modified to achieve a graduated degree of balance. Its disadvantage is that it is more difficult and costly to construct.

At a later period came *trim tabs* and *servo tabs*, originating from the practical action taken by early aircraft riggers to correct a tendency for a control surface to adopt a non-neutral position. Thus, if an aircraft habitually flew port wing low, a small piece of cable taped to the upper-surface trailing-edge of the port aileron would cause the aileron to be deflected down and the wing to be lifted up. Trial and error adjustments with longer or shorter pieces of cable enabled the conscientious rigger to trim the aircraft so that its pilot could boast of being able to fly 'hands off'. At a later stage of development small strips of duralumin were attached to the trailing-edge of control surfaces, and these could quite simply be bent on the ground to provide variations of adjustment to achieve the same result.

From there it was but a short step to controllable trim tabs, adjustable by control wheel from the pilot's cockpit, enabling the aircraft's trim to be adjusted in flight. This was especially useful in respect of trim in pitch, for an aircraft fully laden with fuel often needs re-trimming throughout a flight as the fuel is consumed and the aircraft's CG shifts fore or aft, according to the disposition of the fuel tanks. Variable trim devices were particularly valuable for World War II military aircraft, since the varying changes of CG, resulting from consumption of fuel and the disposal of military stores, often left the pilot with a tiring control load which he would otherwise have had to maintain until the aircraft returned to its base.

Servo tabs have the task of helping the pilot to operate the related control surface, being so linked mechanically that when the servo tab is

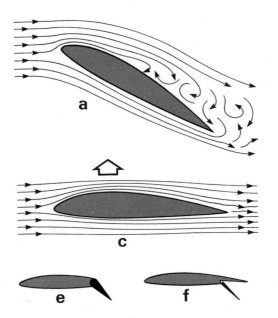

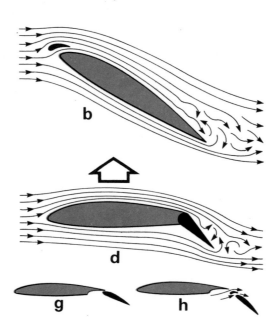

Flaps and slats
(a) Airflow at high angle of attack
(b) Airflow improved by the addition of a leading edge slat
(c) Airflow in normal horizontal flight (d) Addition of plain flap giving increase in both lift and drag (e) Plain flap (f) Split flap (g) Fowler flap (h) Double-slotted flap

moved in one direction by the pilot's control, the control surface moves in the opposite direction. The aerodynamic force on the tab aids the pilot to move the control surface.

It is an ironic fact that the more slowly an aircraft is flown the more unsafe it is. Think back to what was said at the beginning of this section regarding the lifting powers of an aerofoil. We spoke only of the fact that an aerofoil moving through the air was able to create lift. The question of the velocity of the airstream passing over the aerofoil was not mentioned.

If, for example, an aircraft's wing can develop sufficient lift at 100mph (161km/h) to support the aircraft at its maximum take-off weight, then clearly the wing will be unable to develop the same amount of lift at, say, 80mph (129km/h). There will even be a point lower down the speed scale where the lift is insufficient for the aircraft to take to the air. If we assume that we are dealing with a fairly modern aircraft, with retractable landing gear, then immediately it is airborne and maintaining *flying speed* the landing gear can be retracted. The considerable reduction in drag as a result of the landing gear being out of the way will unbalance the thrust/drag relationship and the aircraft immediately accelerates. If, instead, the engine is throttled back, we shall discover that we can maintain flying speed at a somewhat lower airspeed. The reduction in parasite drag enables the aircraft to be flown at a greater angle of attack, increasing the lift, but resulting in a lower flying speed. There is a speed slightly below the flying speed, known as *minimum control speed*, which is the lowest practicable speed at which the aircraft can be flown and controlled. If the airspeed falls still lower, until the lift generated by the wings is insufficient to keep the aircraft in the air, then as the smooth airflow breaks up the wing becomes stalled, and the speed at that moment in time is the aircraft's *stalling speed*.

If this situation occurs at height it presents little problem. In most aircraft the nose drops smoothly, and as the aircraft dives towards the ground the speed builds up until full flying speed is attained and lift generated. It is when this situation occurs near the ground, particularly during the phase of take-off or landing, that serious problems are caused. What has been done to remedy such a problem?

Slots, Slats and Flaps

The first important development came as long ago as 1919, when the *Handley Page slot* was designed and introduced. It consists of a small auxiliary aerofoil surface mounted at the leading-edge of an aircraft's wing. This is known as a *slat*, and many of these devices are constructed to operate automatically, opening at low speed and closing again for high-speed flight. When the slat opens, it leaves a gap between it and the leading-edge of the main aerofoil, this gap being known as the *slot*.

Experiments with aerofoils had shown that lift increased as the wing's angle of attack increased. This was true only to an angle of about 15 degrees. Beyond this angle the lift fell off, and as the angle increased still further the turbulence of the airstream over the upper wing became so violent that all lift was destroyed and the wing stalled. The use of Handley Page slots was so effective that angles of attack of up to 25 degrees could be maintained and at the same time the wing's lift was increased. This meant that adequate lift could be obtained at considerably slower speeds.

This very significant increase in aerofoil efficiency is brought about by the effect of the slot, which splits the airflow at the wing leading-edge. This reduces still further the above-wing pressure, with the result that the airstream flows back smoothly over the entire upper surface of the wing in the region which has slots. Early applications tended to limit slots to the outer wing panels, primarily because the ailerons were located on the wing trailing-edge in this area and the smooth airflow improved also aileron control. It is quite common today to see *full-span* leading-edge slats, these extending from wing root to wingtip. But the introduction of slots was only the first stage in improving an aircraft's flight characteristics in the low-speed regime.

The ability to approach for a landing at as low a speed as possible was apparent to all. Clearly, that speed must be somewhat faster than the minimum control speed to ensure that the pilot has complete control of the aircraft at a critical stage of flight. Slats, if fitted, would bring the speed range lower by increasing lift. What else could be done to improve the situation? It was soon discovered that the addition of a hinged *flap* at the wing trailing-edge could have a considerable effect on lift. Furthermore, when the flap was lowered to its design maximum position it made a significant increase in drag, which brought landing speeds down still more.

Do you remember that quite early in this section it was mentioned that deep-camber aerofoils were the most suitable for weight lifting at lower speeds; conversely, that thin-section aerofoils were best for high-speed flight, but produced less lift? If you look at the sectional drawing of a wing, with the trailing-edge flap retracted, you will see that it has the appearance of a thin-section high-speed aerofoil. The same wing, with the trailing-edge flap extended, has the upper surface profile of a thick-section high-lift wing. The extended flap has, in effect, changed the wing's camber. Even a simple flap is able to increase the lift of a wing by about 50 per cent.

Improved flaps, such as split flaps, offered lift increases of up to 70 per cent. But the Fowler type flap, which has the benefits of the split flap when retracted and, because it moves aft as well as down when it is deployed, virtually increases wing area and camber, very nearly doubling its lift.

There is another aspect of low-speed flight which is worth mentioning at this point. Will you try and imagine an aircraft in level flight at a speed slightly less than its minimum control speed. Yet, it can continue to fly because the speed has not dropped to stalling speed. But in such a situation it is possible only to maintain level flight, for the use of control surfaces will increase drag and, without additional engine power being available, can bring the speed quite quickly down to a stall. In the case of lateral control, you will remember that to bank for a turn to port the starboard aileron is lowered to lift that wing. Under the abnormal slow speed situation, the increased drag on the starboard wing caused by the lowered aileron is sufficient to initiate a flat turn to starboard. This emphasises the importance of establishing a minimum control speed, above which it is possible to avoid such freak situations; not that it is usual to fly even private aircraft under such conditions.

Problems

Let us now consider a few of the insidious problems which beset early designers of aircraft. They were problems that were very difficult to resolve because the power plants then available had only limited output. Given any particular engine, the tendency was to build around it the largest possible aeroplane, which meant that from the outset the performance was somewhat marginal. This sort of performance demanded a high degree of piloting skill, and the natural pilot with a sympathetic understanding of what he was asking the aircraft to do could achieve comparative miracles. The amateur pilot with limited training was in difficulties from the start. Today the amateur can cope far more easily because most aircraft have a reserve of engine power and modern light aircraft are equipped with devices which make the piloting of such an aircraft more akin to driving a car.

trailing-edge of a wing. It was a little puzzling to find that while under normal flight conditions the majority of them trailed smoothly aft, as was expected, those at the wingtips gyrated in corkscrew fashion. Research showed eventually that the airflow was also cascading away in a corkscrew fashion, increasing drag considerably. The motion was caused by the high-pressure undersurface air at the wingtip taking the shortest round-the-wingtip path to the low-pressure area above the wing, inducing a swirling motion of the local airflow which trailed off in a corkscrew fashion as the wing passed through the air, these being known as *wingtip vortices*.

Research into the problem showed that for a wing of any given area, the most efficient was that with the greatest span and the narrowest chord – known as a *high aspect ratio* wing. Conversely, a wing of the same area with wide chord and narrow span is known as a *low aspect ratio* wing. The higher the aspect ratio the smaller the wingtip vortices, and the lower the induced drag, which will perhaps help you to understand why aircraft like sailplanes have wide-span narrow-chord wings.

There is, however, one drawback to the high aspect ratio wing. Generally speaking, each square foot of such a wing will be structurally heavier, to provide adequate strength, than each square foot of a low aspect ratio wing. Here is another case where the designer has to arrive at a compromise to suit the particular aircraft being designed.

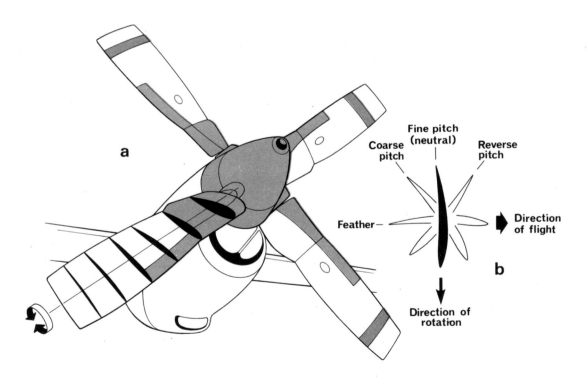

Propellors
(a) Propellor showing blade sections and twist (Lockheed C130 Hercules) **(b)** Pitch change—blade rotation

a

Coarse pitch
Fine pitch (neutral)
Reverse pitch

Feather

Direction of flight

b

Direction of rotation

We have seen already that the wide-chord deep-section aerofoil has the best low-speed high-lift characteristics. Unfortunately, it suffers also from a great deal of *induced drag*: that is drag caused by the particular structural design. It was not easy at first to discover why this should be so, but one of the early techniques to study airflow around the wing was to attach streamers to the

Another problem facing early designers was that of *parasite drag*, the drag induced by components that make no contribution to lift. Unfortunately, the easiest structure to build – that of the biplane – had interplane struts, bracing struts and wires that created enormous drag. So much so that a famous designer referred to one well known type of biplane transport as

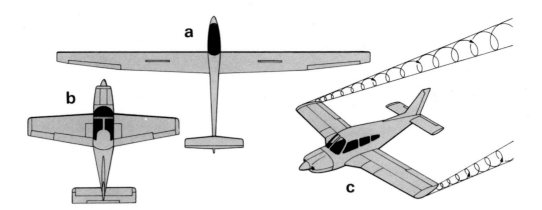

Aspect ratios
(a) Sailplane—high aspect ratio
(Gros Astir) (b) Lightplane—low
aspect ratio (Victa Airtourer)
(c) Generation of wing-tip
vortices

'having built-in headwinds'. Another major source of drag was the landing gear, with struts, bracing, wheels and axle all helping to limit performance. No wonder that the pioneer designers talked hopefully of creating aircraft that were virtually flying wings, all lift-inducing and free from drag.

It just wasn't possible to find such an easy solution, and the evolution of the modern aeroplane was comparatively slow. Streamlining of struts and wires, adding fairings to landing gear struts and wheels, and other structural refinements of this kind represented the first and quickly achievable stage. It took rather longer to evolve such improvements as retractable landing gear; the *cantilever monoplane wing*, free from bracing struts and wires; and neatly-cowled engines. And by the time that these improvements became general, the power plants themselves had become so much more reliable and were capable of developing more power per unit weight, that there were sudden and almost dramatic improvements in aircraft performance.

There are still a couple of drag problems that we should mention. When designers and engineers were busily streamlining fuselages, wings, tails units and cowling their power plants in the years 1919 to 1933 they assumed, quite reasonably one would think, that having arrived at the best possible shape for each of their separate assemblies it would follow that, when they were all put together, they would have achieved the most perfect streamline structure. They hadn't. They discovered a new phenomenon to which they gave the name of *interference drag*, caused by the clash of airflows from adjacent streamline structures. Gradually they learned to overcome this, by the skilful blending of shapes to avoid such areas, and by the use of *fillets* to smooth the airflow around attachment points.

Skin Friction

The other form of drag is caused by the air flowing over the aircraft's structure, and is referred to usually as *skin friction*. You will appreciate that air flowing over a rough surface will induce more drag than if that surface is smooth. Which explains why many high-performance aircraft have their skin surfaces polished as smoothly as possible. And when

composite structures of wood and fabric or metal and fabric were displaced by all-metal aircraft, it must seem surprising to learn that skins were attached to the inner airframe structure by domed rivets. Perhaps it shouldn't be too surprising, for metal ships had always been put together with domed rivets! However, the effect of domed rivets on skin friction was appreciated eventually, and flush riveting then became the rule. Today, *bonded structures*, which use special adhesives to attach skins to the inner airframe structure, are becoming commonplace, ensuring a very smooth surface to offer minimum resistance to the airflow.

Even under these comparatively ideal conditions, there will be a layer of air in contact with the aircraft's surfaces which has relatively little motion: above that there will be another layer of air travelling slightly faster, and so on, until a point is reached where the airflow is at the velocity at which the aircraft is travelling. This thin stratum of air is known as the *boundary layer*, and because there are mixed layers which are travelling at different speeds, a degree of turbulence is created which causes drag. It is most pronounced where the airflow is travelling at maximum speed, close to the leading-edge of an aerofoil surface. In recent years there have been a number of *boundary layer control* (BLC) experiments and applications to locally remove this turbulence, so that the airflow can pass closely and smoothly over the related surface.

Propeller Operation

Have you ever given any serious thought as to why a propeller, turned by an engine, is able to move an aircraft forward? The fact is that each blade of a propeller is of aerofoil section: as the propeller is rotated by the engine and the blades driven through the air, they behave in exactly the same way as any other aerofoil and develop 'lift'. Except, of course, that in the majority of cases this 'lift' is almost horizontal and the aircraft is drawn forward. When the propeller is forward of the engine the term *tractor propeller* applies; when the engine is forward of the propeller it becomes, rather inaccurately, a *pusher propeller*.

Like a wing, each propeller blade is mounted at a certain angle of attack, known as the *blade angle, pitch angle* or, simply, *pitch*. If you examine

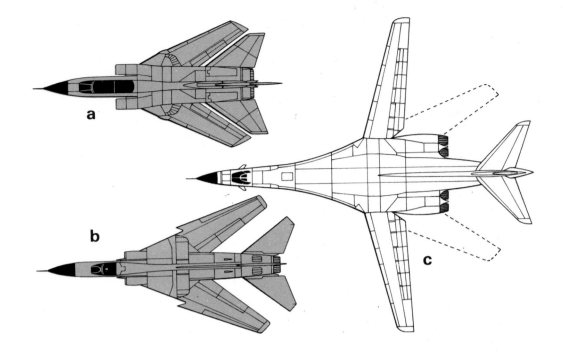

Variable geometry aircraft
(a) Panavia MRCA Tornado
(b) MiG-23 Flogger (c) Rockwell
International B1

a propeller blade carefully you will find that this angle is not constant. Quite clearly the angle is at its greatest near to the propeller's *hub*, and smallest at the blade tip. This is essential because all parts of the propeller blade must advance uniformly forward, despite the fact that the tip of the blade travels further – and therefore faster – than the blade section near to the hub.

A propeller which has its blades set at a fine pitch angle travels a lesser distance forward for each revolution than one with the blades set at a coarse pitch angle. The fine pitch angle allows the engine to develop more revolutions per minute (rpm), is ideal for take-off and climb conditions, but means that the engine consumes more fuel for each mile flown. It is like driving a car in bottom gear. A coarse pitch angle is not very satisfactory for take-off and climb, but once the aircraft is airborne and at its optimum height gives the best speed and fuel economy.

For the aircraft designers this was another compromise problem: what was the best pitch angle for any particular application? Compromise it remained until development of the *variable-pitch propeller*, which could be set at low pitch for take-off, and could then be moved to a coarse pitch setting, by hydraulic or electric power, for cruising flight. The ultimate is the *constant-speed propeller*, which can be set to allow the engine to operate at its most efficient rpm under all flight conditions. When the engine is under load the pitch fines off to maintain rpm, and as the load comes off, so the blade pitch will coarsen to hold the rpm steady. A *reversible-pitch* setting is available on many constant-speed propellers to reduce the aircraft's landing run, and in multi-engine applications it is usual to allow a *feathered* setting. This means that in the event of engine failure the propeller blades of that engine can be set so that the leading-edge faces directly into the airstream; the blades therefore

cause the minimum amount of drag and, in addition, prevent the airstream from turning the propeller (*windmilling*). Windmilling not only creates drag but can obviously cause further damage to an engine which has failed.

Now we have learned something of how an engine and propeller can move an aircraft through the air, and how the aeroplane itself can stay in the air and be controlled by its pilot, it is desirable to look at one or two points dealing with how the aircraft gets into the air and lands again.

Landplanes have two main types of under-carriage: *tailwheel type landing gear*, with the main units at the forward end of the aircraft and the tailwheel aft; *tricycle type landing gear*, with the main units slightly aft of the aircraft's CG and a nosewheel at the forward end of the fuselage. Before we can watch our imaginary aircraft take off there is one other point to note. The wings of an aircraft are usually attached to the main structure at a slight positive angle, known as the *angle of incidence*. This means that in relation to a centreline extending the length of the fuselage, the wing's leading-edge is set slightly higher than its trailing-edge. This angle of incidence *must not* be confused with angle of attack.

If we now look at an aircraft with a tailwheel type landing gear which is ready for take-off, we shall note that because the aircraft's tail is on the ground, and because the wing is set at a positive angle of incidence, the resulting angle of attack of the wing is quite large. This can impose unnecessary drag and prolong the take-off run.

With his machine aligned for take-off, the pilot opens the engine's throttle and the aircraft moves forward, slowly gaining speed. As soon as this is high enough for aerodynamic forces to react on the tail unit, the pilot eases the 'stick' forward, putting the elevators down, which causes the tail to lift. The 'stick' is then brought back a fraction to balance the aircraft, continuing to run forward on its main wheels with tail in the air. The angle of attack of the wing has now been reduced considerably, and so has the drag, so the rate of acceleration increases. When flying speed is attained the 'stick' is moved smoothly back, moving the elevators up, the tail down, increasing the angle of attack of the wings and, consequently, the lift, and the aircraft becomes airborne. Take-off with tricycle landing gear is rather different, for the aircraft is already virtually in flying position and the pilot does not have the same problem of getting the tail off the ground to attain a position of minimum induced drag.

Landing

When it comes to making a landing, the aircraft with the tricycle landing gear scores again. It can be flown almost onto the runway and immediately the main wheels touch it will, unless prevented, pitch forward on to the nosewheel. Even if the landing speed is high it is less likely to 'float' off again because the wing is at a minimum angle of attack. On the other hand, the aircraft with tailwheel landing gear needs, ideally, to be at its stalling speed at the precise moment when main wheels and tailwheel meet the runway in a *three-point landing*. If the speed is much above

pressibility, the word used to describe the condition imposed on an aerofoil at this critical speed, had shown that a thin-section aerofoil and especially a *swept wing*, one in which the angle between the wing leading-edge and the fuselage centreline was less than 90 degrees, postponed the build-up of shock-waves. Research suggested that such a wing should allow the aircraft to pass smoothly from *subsonic* (below the speed of sound) to *supersonic* (above the speed of sound) flight.

This proved to be true, but a swept wing is fundamentally a high-speed wing, not the best for the lift and control characteristics we have seen to be desirable for take-off and landing conditions. This meant another compromise situation, to select a wing giving the best possible results throughout an aircraft's *flight envelope* (performance range). The ideal was a wing that was unswept or only slightly swept for low-speed conditions, and which could be swept to a desirable maximum for high-speed flight. This has led to the complex *variable-geometry wing* (swing-wing) of such aircraft as the General Dynamics F-111 tactical fighter and Europe's internationally-built Tornado multi-role combat aircraft (MRCA).

Modern technology has done much to enhance

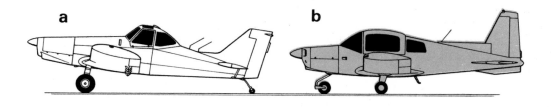

Undercarriages
(a) Piper Pawnee—tail wheel undercarriage (b) Grumman American Traveller—nosewheel undercarriage

the stall the increased angle of attack resulting from the three-point landing will generate plenty of lift and the aircraft will tend to 'float' off again. This is, indeed, the pupil pilot's nightmare!

Supersonic Flight

High-speed fighter aircraft being dived in combat during World War II occasionally travelled so fast that the airflow over the wing's upper surface was approaching the speed of sound (about 760mph, 1,223km/h at sea level, falling to about 660mph, 1,062km/h above 36,000ft, 10,970m, depending upon temperature). Under such conditions the air no longer flows smoothly over the wing, but is compressed ahead of the wing leading-edge, causing *shock-waves* of such energy that, unless the aircraft is specially constructed, the structure can be broken up by the force of these waves. Many wartime pilots lost their lives when wings or tail units were torn away from their aircraft.

Men discovered eventually how to build aircraft to fly faster than sound. Among the basic requirements is a robust structure, an engine of adequate power and a special wing. German wartime research into the problems of *com-*

the safety of all classes of aircraft currently in production. In the main this stems from the very considerable increases in lift and stability which the latest techniques have made possible. Even many lightweight private aircraft have specially-designed wing leading-edge and wingtip features to increase lift and reduce drag. By introducing cambered wingtips, trailing-edge flaps and drooped ailerons, that is ailerons which can serve partially as flaps and yet be used differentially for roll control, these aircraft have the sort of performance that would have made the pioneers gasp in amazement. Yet it is to them that we owe thanks for these innovations.

So next time you fly off on holiday, try and sit so that you can see the aircraft's wing. If it happens to be a Boeing 747, don't imagine the wing is dropping to pieces as you come in to land. Each wing has variable-camber and Kreuger leading-edge flaps, triple-slotted trailing-edge flaps, high-speed and low-speed ailerons and *spoilers* (drag-inducing devices used frequently to supplement ailerons) on the wing upper surface. Quite a bag of tricks! But these are the technological improvements which make it, and other giant aircraft like it, so safe in which to fly.

Rotary Wing Flight

You may recall, from the introduction to this book, that the earliest man-made heavier-than-air craft were the kites, which the Chinese had invented and were flying about 1,000 years before the birth of Christ.

It would seem also that this nation first discovered, almost certainly without appreciating its significance, the basic concept of rotary-wing flight. This knowledge comes from the fact that hundreds of years ago little children in China were playing with a rotary-wing toy. It is believed to have been constructed of cork and bamboo, the rotary-wings being made of feathers. When spun it would fly into the air.

Rather more sophisticated toys of this kind can be seen today, usually made of plastic or metal, and set spinning by a spring-loaded device which sends them climbing high into the air. The principle by which they climb links these toys, separated by much more than a thousand years, for it is fundamentally the same.

The first serious study for a rotary-wing aircraft is that of Leonardo da Vinci who, at the beginning of the 16th century, sketched a machine which had a rotating spiral plane. This, he believed, would enable it to 'screw' its way upward in the air.

There were to be many similar but impractical proposals, for although man had not then discovered how to fly, the advantages of being able to take off and land vertically were readily apparent. It was not until 1842 that a small model helicopter with rigid rotor blades was flown successfully in Britain. Designed by W H Phillips, it was steam-powered, the rotor being driven by steam jets at the tips of the blades.

It took another 65 years, four years after the Wright brothers' success at Kitty Hawk, before the first true free flight by a man-carrying rotary-wing aircraft was recorded. This was achieved by a very basic twin-rotor helicopter, designed and built by the Frenchman Paul Cornu, at Lisieux, France, on 13 November 1907. Brief though its flight was, little more than an up and down affair, it confirmed that flight by a rotary-wing aircraft was possible. It required only time for development and refinement to produce the remarkable safe, versatile and valuable aircraft which are now commonplace around the world.

It should not be too difficult for us to learn how it is possible for a helicopter to fly. We discovered in the last chapter the basic principles of flight, and you will probably remember one of the earliest lift/drag experiments, when it was suggested you took a piece of stiff card in your hand and swung your arm through the air.

Each blade of a helicopter's rotor is of aerofoil section and, basically, it acts similarly to an aircraft's propeller. Turned by an engine, each of the aerofoils is driven through the air and generates lift. This is the basic fact only. To understand the inherent safety of a rotary-wing aircraft, and how the pilot of such a machine is able to control and direct its course through the air, requires rather more detailed study.

Torque Reaction

Pioneer designers of helicopters had discovered at an early stage that there were what appeared to be one or two insuperable problems. The first is concerned with what is known as *torque reaction*, which is the tendency of any power source to turn in the opposite direction to the mechanism which it is driving. An easy way to experience this force is to hold an electric drill in the hand. Immediately it is switched on you will find that the body of the drill tries to turn in the opposite direction to that in which the rotor of the AC motor is turning.

This explains why the first successful helicopters had more than one rotor. By having two rotors turning in opposite directions, the problem created by torque reaction was overcome. Unfortunately, there was no easy solution for aircraft with a single rotor, and we shall see in due course how this has been resolved.

The first successful helicopter flight was simply up and down. There was no provision to enable the aircraft to fly forward. The successful flights which followed that of the Cornu helicopter were with twin-rotor aircraft. Attempts to achieve

Hinge axes
(a) Flapping hinge (d) Drag hinge
(c) Pitch change hinge

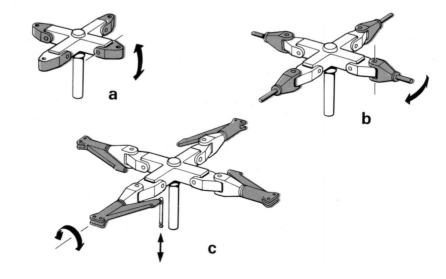

forward flight with a single rotor invariably ended up with the aircraft keeling over to one side, and it took some time to discover why this should be so.

Autogyro

Credit for finding the answer to this problem goes to the Spaniard, Juan de la Cierva, who in the early 1920s developed the world's first practical *autogyro*. This is an aircraft which has an unpowered rotary wing to provide lift when the entire machine is propelled forward conventionally by an engine and propeller. The rotary wing merely replaces, or supplements, the normal fixed wing, but confers one important safety characteristic, as we shall discover later.

De la Cierva was intrigued by the potential of a rotary wing, believing that it could do much to improve the safety of aircraft at low flying speeds. He had discovered that an unpowered rotor in which the blades were set at a small positive angle of attack would not only continue to rotate (*autorotation*) automatically in an airstream if once set in motion, but that they would also contribute lift.

To prove his theory he used a conventional fixed-wing aircraft, with a single unpowered rotor mounted on a pylon above the aircraft's fuselage. When the pilot was ready to take off a number of assistants applied their muscles to a rope wound round the rotor shaft, setting the rotor spinning. If his theory and experiments were correct, it would continue to rotate as the machine moved forward and became airborne.

Unfortunately, the aircraft did not become airborne but tipped over to one side. Subsequent attempts had precisely the same result. It was clear to de la Cierva that there must be a very good reason why this was happening. Indeed, there was. As soon as the rotor was set in motion it began to develop lift. As the aircraft moved forward the rotor autorotated, and due to the forward speed developed even more lift. On one side of the aircraft the rotor blades were advancing into the airstream; on the other side they were retreating from the airstream. You will be able to understand, from reading the last chapter, that the advancing blades were reacting to a higher velocity airflow than the retreating blades and, in consequence, were developing more lift. It did not take de la Cierva long to discover this

factor; it took far longer to find the answer. His important pioneer researches contributed much to the understanding of the problems of the rotary wing, work which eventually helped to make possible a practical single-rotor helicopter.

The Flapping Hinge

His solution to the unequal lift developed by the advancing and retreating blades comprised what is known as a *flapping hinge*. Each blade is attached to the *rotor hub* by a hinge which allows a limited amount of up and down movement. As the advancing blade gains lift it is the blade itself which rises, at the same time reducing its effective angle of attack. As it retreats the converse action takes place, equalising the lift on both sides of the rotor so that, for the first time, an aircraft with a single rotor became practical.

Because the rotor of de la Cierva's autogyro was unpowered he did not encounter the problem caused by torque reaction. But having solved the problem of unequal lift, he was able to fly his aircraft, which he called an *Autogiro*, and aircraft which incorporate de la Cierva's patents are still given this name.

To enable a rotor to autorotate it must have its blades set at a small angle of attack, usually about 2 degrees. If the angle is much greater than this figure, then the drag generated by the blade is too great for autorotation to continue. You will recall that, with any aerofoil, as the angle of attack increases so does the drag. At a lesser angle than 2 degrees the rotor will continue to autorotate, but does not generate sufficient lift to keep the aircraft in the air.

Tests with the de la Cierva *Autogiro* proved how valuable a rotary wing could be, even if unpowered, for it was found that an aircraft so fitted could be flown at speeds as low as 25mph (40km/h) before the lift generated by the rotor was insufficient to maintain level flight. Even when that point was reached, comparing with the moment when a fixed-wing stalled, the rotor continued to turn, generating a certain degree of lift, and the aircraft came down in a steady glide. If the aircraft lost all forward speed, the rotor continued to turn and the machine came down vertically and safely.

This work done by de la Cierva was of vital importance in the evolution of a true helicopter, an aircraft able to take off and land vertically and to hover stationary in the air. It inspired other designers and the first practical helicopters began to emerge in the late 1930s.

Twin-Rotor Craft

In 1936 the Breguet Company in France flew a helicopter with two contra-rotating rotors. In the same year the Focke-Wulf Fw 61 helicopter made its first flight. It, too, had twin rotors, but these were mounted on outriggers on each side of the aircraft. They, also, rotated in opposite directions. In Britain in 1938 Weir also flew a helicopter with contra-rotating rotors.

This seeming passion for twin-rotor designs was not as a result of endeavours to lift a heavy payload. On the contrary, two rotors were an embarrassment, their weight and that of their

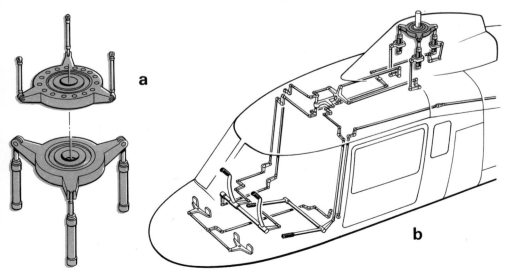

Helicopter controls
(a) Swash plate rotor control
(b) Basic control linkage of Augusta A109

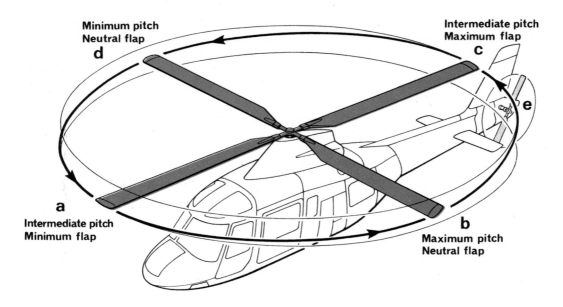

Minimum pitch
Neutral flap
d

Intermediate pitch
Maximum flap
c

e

a
Intermediate pitch
Minimum flap

b
Maximum pitch
Neutral flap

Blade rotation of helicopter in
forward flight
(a) Blade at front (b) Retreating
blade (c) Blade at rear
(d) Advancing blade (e) Tail rotor

control systems being such that the payload which could be lifted was very marginal. The truth of the matter was that no one had then discovered how to overcome the problem of torque reaction. Contra-rotating rotors, whether mounted separately or on a common shaft, were the only insurance against torque reaction, which would make the aircraft uncontrollable. Additionally, these early twin-rotor helicopters relied, in the main, on conventional tail unit surfaces to provide control in the pitch and yaw axes.

The Sikorsky Helicopter

The problem was resolved in 1939 by Igor Sikorsky in America. His VS-300 helicopter prototype introduced a small vertical rotor, carried on an extended tail boom, which developed sufficient thrust to neutralise the torque reaction of the power plant. This meant that Sikorsky's aircraft needed only a single rotor to provide lift, and it was recognised at once that the VS-300 represented the first successful single-rotor helicopter, one which was capable of development into a really practical vehicle. This, indeed, proved to be true, and the Sikorsky Company has continued to be a major constructor of helicopters to this day.

We are now in a position to learn how the modern helicopter is able to perform such amazing feats, and to appreciate what an important contribution it is able to make in today's world-wide aviation scene. First we must take a closer look at the rotary wing which has been developed from the early work of de la Cierva and Sikorsky.

Clearly, the rotor blades used by the pioneers in this specialised field were fairly simple aerofoils. As explained earlier, de la Cierva attached his blades to the rotor hub with a simple flapping hinge. In the case of the early autogyros this was quite adequate because the rotor was unpowered. With the development of powered rotors it became necessary to pay more attention to the design of the rotor blade and hub.

Generally speaking, rotors are of fairly large diameter in relation to the overall size of the aircraft to which they are fitted. This means that there is a very considerable difference in the velocity of the aerofoil at the blade root by com-

parison with that at the tip. In order that the lift shall remain fairly uniform throughout the length of the blade, it is usual to ensure that the camber of the aerofoil at the root is greater than that at the tip. This means that the slower-velocity deep camber at the root develops approximately the the same lift as the high-velocity thin-section camber at the tip, preventing the blade from bending.

Because the flapping hinge attachment of the rotor blade is intended to reduce lift, and consequently drag, on the advancing blade, the tendency is for this advancing blade to accelerate. The converse applies for the retreating blade: it tries to decelerate. If suitable provision were not made to counteract this, the blades would be subjected to a bending action and resulting stress. This is overcome by having what is known as a *drag hinge*, which allows the blades a certain amount of freedom in the plane of rotation.

Changes of Pitch

There is one other complication so far as the blades are concerned. The rotor blades of a helicopter are set normally at a fairly large angle of attack, this being somewhere about 10 degrees on average. It is obviously essential for the pilot to be able to control this angle: if the 10 degree setting is for a maximum *rate of climb*, he will need to reduce this angle, or the rotor's speed, if he wishes to achieve hovering flight. He needs to be able to reduce it to about 2 degrees in the event of an engine failure, so that autorotation will continue and he will be enabled to bring the helicopter in to a safe landing.

This change of angle of attack is achieved through the medium of a *pitch change bearing* which allows the blades to be turned to adjust their setting. However, it must be remembered that the rotor is turning independently of the airframe. The problem is how to control the rotor from the cockpit.

It is achieved through the medium of a mechanism known as a *swashplate*, which comprise two plates in contact with each other. The lower one is stationary and the controls from the cockpit are attached to it: the upper one turns with the rotor and has affixed to it linkage to the rotor blades.

Pilot Control

The pilot's control column is connected to the swashplate in such a manner that when he pushes it in any particular direction the swashplate is tilted in the same direction. When the pilot's *collective pitch lever* is operated it raises or lowers the bottom section of the swashplate bodily, without tilt in any direction, and this in turn raises or lowers the upper section of the swashplate by exactly the same distance. This means that the *connecting rods* (linkage) between the upper swashplate and each blade arm are moved an equal distance, and all the rotor's blades are *collectively* (simultaneously) reset to the same angle. There is also a direct linkage between the collective pitch lever and the helicopter's power plant, so arranged that when the lever is moved to increase the pitch of the rotor blades the power output of the engine is increased. This provides the additional power demanded by the new, coarser setting of the blade pitch, and the overall thrust from the rotor is increased.

There is another lever in the cockpit which looks rather like the control column of a fixed-wing aircraft. This is the *cyclic-pitch lever* and it

circle, the pitch angle will be steadily reducing. This means that the blades at the forward end of the aircraft are producing minimum or near minimum lift, while those at the rear will, according to the height of the swashplate, be developing something between minimum and maximum lift. The result is that the rotor disc tilts forward until it adopts the same angle as that of the upper swashplate, and the helicopter as a whole flies forward. The entire fuselage adopts the same angle so that the aircraft develops a nose-down attitude in forward flight and, conversely, a tail-down attitude when it is flying backward.

Hovering Flight

In fact, the helicopter will fly in the direction in which the cyclic pitch lever is moved. If, when the aircraft is in flight, it is retained in a central position then, theoretically, the helicopter will hover motionless in the air.

Unfortunately, hovering flight is not quite so easy as one might imagine. The air in which the helicopter is flying is seldom still: not only may there be a near vertical airflow, up or down, there can also be a wind stream blowing in one direction

Rotor head of Augusta A109 helicopter

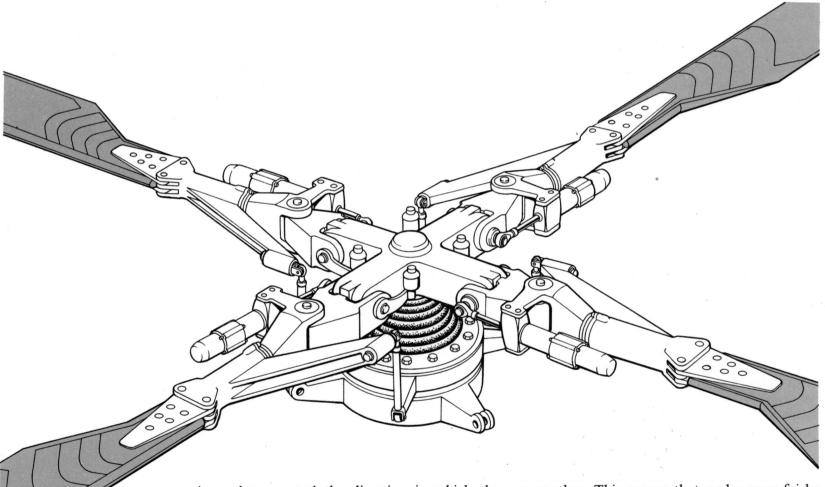

is used to control the direction in which the helicopter will fly. If it is pushed forward it raises the lower half of the swashplate at its aft end, and the upper swashplate takes up the same position. The resulting effect on the blades needs careful consideration. Take a blade which is directly over the aircraft's nose, and which is at or near to a minimum pitch setting. As it rotates it will, via its pitch-change connecting rod, be steadily increasing its pitch angle until it has completed 180 degrees of its turn, when it will be facing aft. As it progresses back to the beginning of the

or another. This means that under even fairly ideal conditions it needs a fair degree of skill on the pilot's part to maintain the aircraft in steady hovering flight.

He has, in all, four controls to fly the helicopter. In addition to the collective-pitch and cyclic-pitch controls mentioned already, there is a twisting-grip at the end of the collective-pitch lever that controls the power output of the engine which is used primarily for starting and to make small adjustments to engine/rotor *rpm* (revolutions per minute) during flight.

The fourth control is used to initiate movements about the helicopter's vertical axis, comprising foot-operated pedals similar to the rudder pedals of a fixed-wing aircraft. Their function is, however, very different, for a helicopter does not usually have conventional tail surfaces. Instead of moving a rudder, to initiate a change of heading, the pilot's foot pedals in a rotary-wing aircraft alter the pitch-setting of the blades of the anti-torque rotor at the tail. An increase in pitch is caused by moving the left pedal forward, this increasing the thrust of the anti-torque rotor and a turn to port is initiated. When the right-hand pedal is moved forward the pitch and thrust is reduced and the torque induced by the main rotor initiates a turn to starboard.

When a pilot wishes to make the aircraft hover he needs to 'juggle' the four controls more or less simultaneously. If we assume the helicopter to be hovering at a constant altitude, imagine that a wind from port starts to drift it to starboard. The pilot will immediately move the cyclic-pitch control to port to offset the drift. Increased drag will need a little more power, and more power on the main rotor increases the torque. Which means the pitch setting of the tail rotor needs increasing. This reduces the rpm of the main rotor and more power is needed to maintain altitude, involving the adjustment of the collective-pitch lever. These circumstances can occur as normal under good flying conditions, requiring a fair degree of skill and concentration from the pilot. You will understand the ability which is needed to carry out a typical helicopter rescue operation, requiring the aircraft to hover above a storm-tossed vessel while a rescue cable and crew-man is lowered to secure and winch-up an injured seaman.

This is but one of the kinds of operation which has made the helicopter such an invaluable member of the heavier-than-air family of aircraft. They are used for agricultural spraying and dusting; ambulance services; handling of unusual cargo; inspection of power lines, oil and gas pipes; servicing of oil and gas rigs offshore; surveys; fire-fighting; wildlife conservation; logging operations; sorting out traffic jams; and rescuing holidaymakers; to mention but a few of the tasks which are routine to helicopters and their pilots.

Military usage of rotary-wing aircraft is no less versatile, but their ability to operate into and from virtually any type of terrain, irrespective of natural barriers, has made them of vital importance to modern military forces whether they be land, sea or air services. This is especially true of guerrilla warfare where the role of traditional aircraft has been reduced.

The requirements of these services has hastened the development of helicopters with new capabilities. Of primary importance has been the ability to lift heavy loads, to speed the transport of combat troops, weapons and supplies to forward areas. This resulted initially in a reversion to twin-rotor machines, for it was easier and quicker to use two established rotors than to design and then resolve the structural and aerodynamic problems of new high-lift large-diameter rotors.

Turboshaft Engines

Since that time there have been many advances in the technology of rotors and rotor hubs. But the development of turbine power plants has brought considerable improvement in load carrying capability. A turbine engine is smaller and lighter in weight than a piston engine of the same power output. The turbine engine used in a rotary-wing aircraft is known as a turboshaft, the turbine driving the main and tail rotors through related gear boxes, with take-offs for electric and hydraulic power.

Because of their small size and light weight, it has proved possible to mount one or more of these turboshaft engines externally, above the cabin. This has not only provided more internal space, but the reduced weight allows the carriage of increased payload, either in the form of more cargo, or more fuel to increase range.

There have also been attempts to evolve new kinds of rotary-wing aircraft, many aimed at producing a single-rotor helicopter which did not suffer the complications imposed by torque. One solution was the provision of a small *pressure-jet* at the tip of each rotor blade, for with no drive shaft from a fuselage-mounted power plant there is no induced torque. It would appear to be an attractive solution, for it eliminates the weight and complexity of conventional power plant, gearboxes, drive shafts and tail rotor. Unfortunately, blade-tip pressure-jets of this kind are heavy on fuel, excessively noisy and the supply of fuel to the pressure-jets creates difficult problems in the design and construction of suitable rotor blades. This is because each blade must have two ducts, for the fuel and compressed air which is mixed and burned to produce thrust at its tip. Another kind of jet, known as a *pulse-jet*, has been tried for the same purpose, as have *rocket-engines* and *cold-jets*, these latter being driven purely by compressed air.

Tilting Wings

There have been attempts also to develop new types of helicopter which would be able to overcome the comparatively slow speed and small payload capability of most rotary-wing aircraft. Practically all of the successful research designs have resulted in prototype aircraft with either tilting power plants at the tips of a fixed wing, or tilting wings to which the power plants are mounted. In both types it means that the rotors/propellers operate as conventional rotors for vertical take-off, and are tilted progressively so that lift is transferred from rotor to fixed-wing as forward speed increases. When the wing is providing all the lift in forward flight, the rotors are then being used as conventional propellers.

There is still a long way to go before the helicopter will have the lift capability of the large fixed-wing transport: it is unlikely that it will ever have the same speed capability. But even at its present stage of development the helicopter has the ability to carry out unique tasks. There is every reason to believe that new technology will continue to offer increasing standards of performance which will extend the range of activities of the helicopter.

Between the World Wars

The end of World War 1 brought an appropriate moment for the creation of civil air routes, primarily of a domestic nature, because long range and a worthwhile payload were not then very good travelling companions. The potentially lucrative inter-continental route between London and Paris was perhaps the easiest to bring into being, and was first flown regularly from 8 February 1919. The passengers on these first services were limited to military personnel, as civil aviation had not then been authorized in Britain.

But others were setting their sights on far more ambitious routes than the handful of miles which separated Britain and France. Already there were several teams anxious to be first across the North Atlantic, spurred on by a £10,000 prize offered by the **Daily Mail**. The first private attempt was that made by Harry Hawker and McKenzie Grieve, ending in the ocean some 1,000 miles (1,600 km) from their starting point. Miraculously, they ditched safely near a steamer and both were rescued.

Then, on 14 June 1919, a gravely overloaded Vickers Vimy, crewed by Capt John Alcock and Lt Arthur Whitten-Brown, trundled into the air at St John's, Newfoundland **(13)**, to land 16 hr 27 min later at Clifden, Ireland (Eire). The first non-stop crossing of the North Atlantic had become a reality.

13

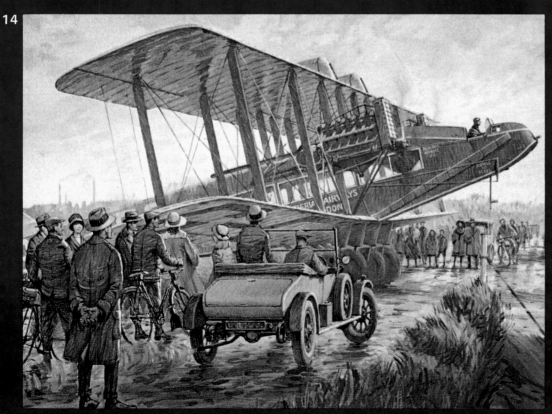

14

Soon after the excitement of the Vimy's success had died down, Air Transport & Travel Ltd initiated the first regular London-Paris scheduled passenger service on 25 August 1919, operated from Hounslow aerodrome in a converted de Havilland D.H.4A. Handley Page Transport, flying from Cricklewood, was soon to follow AT & T's lead, utilizing for their service Handley Page 0/400 and V/1500 heavy bombers, which had also been converted for civil use. The other British pioneer airlines were The Instone Air Line and Daimler Airways.

When the latter company began operations on the London-Paris route in April 1922, they were equipped with de Havilland D.H.34s, a specially designed airliner, which could accommodate nine passengers and carried a steward to serve refreshments.

But it was soon clear that there were nowhere near enough passengers for the British airlines to operate economically, leading to Government intervention and formation of Imperial Airways. This great company was to blaze air lanes around the world, and in so doing created standards of service and safety for others to emulate.

A typical scene of this early period is caught by the skill of artist Kenneth McDonough whose picture **(14)** depicts a Handley Page W.8b Royal Mail airliner of Imperial Airways taxiing across Plough Lane, adjacent to Croydon Airport.

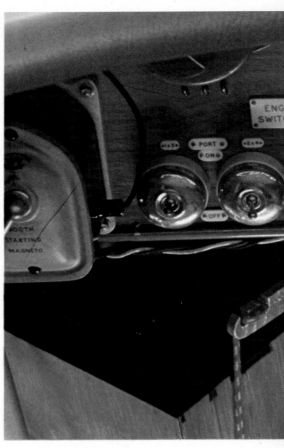

This view of the instrument and control panel of the Vickers Vimy **(15)** shows there was no advanced instrumentation or navigational aids in the great pioneering days of long-distance flight in the twenties and thirties.

There were no meteorological services to warn the pilot of what weather he might expect to find on his route. He had no radio with which to seek even elementary assistance — or psychological comfort — in dealing with problems that might beset him. He had no navigational equipment beyond a very simple compass, the accuracy of which might be suspect.

16

17

Preceding page:

One aeroplane which was to have a great impact on civil aviation was on a very different scale to the 12-seat Handley Page W.8b: namely, the little two-seat Moth designed by Geoffrey de Havilland. Powered by a 60 hp Cirrus engine, this flew for the first time in February 1925.

It was an immediate success, and the Air Ministry ordered it into production for use by flying clubs, this action starting a boom in private and club aviation which spread around the world. Three years later the company developed its own 80 hp Gipsy engine, designed by Frank Halford, which gave the Moth an airspeed of 95 mph (153 km/h).

Then, in the early 1930s, an improved Tiger Moth was evolved, to serve with the RAF from 1932 to 1945 as the standard elementary trainer of Flying Training Command. It remained in service with the RAF Volunteer Reserve until 1951. Many have since become privately owned, and an unusual seaplane conversion is shown in the illustration **(16)**

The majority of the aircraft types which had been produced until the mid-1930s were of biplane construction. Indeed, at the outbreak of World War II in 1939, many of the world's air forces still retained aircraft of biplane configuration in front line service.

But the first signs of change had become apparent long before 1939. Many of the racing seaplanes designed to participate in the Schneider Trophy Contests were monoplanes, proving that it had become possible to build a clean and comparatively lightweight structure capable of withstanding speed-imposed stresses considerably higher than any experienced by aircraft in civil or military service. To qualify this, the average speed of the world's twelve fastest fighter aircraft was around 166 mph (267 km/h), while the Supermarine S.5 which had won the contest in 1927 had recorded a speed of just over 281 mph (452 km/h).

In Germany, Hugo Junkers had brought to practicality the cantilever monoplane of all-metal construction, using corrugated metal skins to carry some of the structural load. It was but a short step to the Junkers Ju 52/3m **(17)** of 1931, one of the world's best known transport aircraft.

Utilizing similar constructional techniques to those pioneered by Junkers, the Ford company in America had been a little earlier with a somewhat similar three-engined transport aircraft. The main difference lay in wing configuration, that of the Junkers 52 being low-wing, whilst that of the Ford Tri-motor **(18)** was high-wing.

It was to prove even more enduring than the Ju 52, and among the pioneering flights achieved by this great aeroplane one must mention the epic flight over the South Pole on 28 November 1929.

Unbelievable though it may seem, it is still possible to find isolated examples of the 'Tin Goose'—as the Tri-motor became known—operating commercial services, which is not too bad for an aircraft evolved in 1926. Many of the transport aircraft of that period took a long time to get from A to B, but their longevity shows clearly that a great deal had been learnt about building durable structures.

This page:

In the United States in 1933 was recorded the maiden flight of a strange looking civil airliner. Strange looking, that is, by comparison with the high-legged corrugated-metal Ford Tri-motor. Known as the Boeing 247 **(19)**, it was to demonstrate also that it was full of strange new ideas. Strange then, perhaps, but they were to revolutionize the design of civil transport aircraft.

A well-streamlined low-wing monoplane, powered by two engines, it was able to retract its landing gear in flight to reduce drag. Variable pitch propellers gave maximum efficiency for take-off and cruising flight: in emergency the fine pitch setting would allow the Model 247 to climb with full load on the power of only one engine. Trim tabs on the control surfaces brought reduction of aerodynamic loading on control surfaces, enabling an automatic pilot to fly the machine for long periods. And to overcome the old hazard of ice accretion on flying surfaces, a de-icing system was introduced for leading-edges of the wings and tail unit.

When the Boeing 247 entered service with United Air Lines (UAL) in March 1933, it reduced US transcontinental flight time to under 20 hours for the first time. Furthermore, it offered completely new standards of comfort for its ten passengers.

So severe was the impact on the revenue of the competing Transcontinental & Western Air (TWA), that it became essential for them to operate an aircraft that was at least as good if they were to stay in business. The relationship between UAL and the Boeing Company was such that TWA realized it was a waste of time to try and buy from Boeing. Instead, they approached the Douglas Aircraft Company to build a contender for the 247, resulting in the Douglas DC-1 which flew for the first time on 1 July 1933.

The 14-seat DC-2, which followed shortly after, shook the aviation world when one owned by KLM, and flown by Captains Parmentier and Moll, won the handicap section of the London—Melbourne McRobertson Air Race. And in America its successor emerged, the 21-seat Douglas DC-3 **(20)**, destined for immortal fame whether known as DC-3, C-47, Dakota or 'Gooney Bird'. This wonderful aeroplane has served honourably and valiantly, and still continues to serve, with air forces and civil operators around the world.

20

21

22

21A

While the Douglas DC-3 was busy establishing itself as the champion of US domestic routes, with no less than 80 per cent of all scheduled airlines using the type by December 1941 — and recording a 100 per cent safety record during 1939–40 — other operators were thinking hard about the Pacific and North Atlantic routes.

Britain's Imperial Airways had pioneered flying-boat services that linked the home country with Australia, India, New Zealand and South Africa, and points between and around. America had concentrated on the Pacific Ocean, a Martin M.130 **China Clipper** recording an inaugural mail flight across the central Pacific from San Francisco to Manila. France and Germany had achieved links between the old and new worlds via the South Atlantic to Rio de Janeiro.

The only stumbling block was the North Atlantic, plagued by weather that posed severe navigational problems and a west-east airstream inimical to all east-west crossings. Although America, Britain and Germany succeeded in flying between Europe and the United States by various experimental means during the 1930s, it remained for America to inaugurate the first regular passenger service across the North Atlantic on

8 July 1939, using 42-ton Boeing Model 314 flying-boats (**21**).

The use of the expression '42-ton flying-boat' gives little impression of the true size of the Boeing Model 314, known more usually as 'Boeing Clippers'. This resulted from their individual names, such as **Yankee Clipper**, bestowed upon them by Pan American Airways.

A total of twelve were built, six as 314s with 1,500 hp Wright Double Cyclone engines, and a subsequent six 314As with increased passenger accommodation and 1,600 hp engines.

With a crew of 6–10 and a maximum of 77 passengers, the 'Clippers' proved rugged and reliable, both on Atlantic and Pacific routes. Early in World War II three of Pan American's 'boats' were sold to British Overseas Airways Corporation (BOAC), who used them on the Atlantic route throughout the war.

A visual impression of the size of these majestic flying-boats is given by the accompanying photograph (**21A**) which looks along a part of the 152 ft (46·33 m) wing span.

Simultaneously with the between-wars development of civil aircraft had come similar advances in the military aeroplanes

that equipped the world's air forces.

New standards had been imposed by the seaplanes which had been created to decide final ownership of the Schneider Trophy. In America, the combination of Curtiss D.12 in-line liquid-cooled engine, which reduced frontal area, Curtiss-Reid propeller and streamlined Curtiss racer had so very nearly tipped the scales in their favour.

C. Richard Fairey (later Sir Richard) was so impressed by the D.12 engine that he acquired licence rights to use it, this powering a new aircraft designated Fairey Fox. When demonstrated to the RAF, this day bomber not only proved 50 mph (80 km/h) faster than any other bomber aircraft in service, but could also show a clean pair of heels to any contemporary British fighter. Richard Fairey's far-sightedness shocked designers in the United Kingdom, rather like that from an unexpected bucket of cold water, giving new impetus to the development of more potent fighter and bomber aircraft.

One result was the Hawker Hart (**22**), which flew for the first time in June 1928. When these aircraft were deployed in the 1930 air exercises they, too, were to prove embarrassing, for the 'defending' Siskin fighters were not fast enough to intercept them.

23

24

25

The last biplane fighter to serve with the RAF, the Gloster Gladiator (23) had flown for the first time in September 1934. A fast and highly manoeuvrable single-seat fighter, it virtually represented the ultimate in aerodynamic efficiency for an aircraft of biplane configuration.

In retrospect, it seems strange that Glosters did not utilize a monoplane structure for their private venture project which produced the Gladiator. Their Gloster VI monoplane racing seaplane. built for the 1929 Schneider Trophy Contest, but withdrawn due to engine trouble, had established a little later a world speed record of 336 mph (540 km/h) and demonstrated a maximum speed of 351 mph (565 km/h).

But Glosters were not alone in this respect, for manufacturers the world over seemed reluctant to turn their backs on the biplane configuration which, for so many years, had made it possible to build robust aircraft well able to cope with the stresses and strains of service use.

It was not surprising, of course, that the Fairey Swordfish torpedo-bomber (24) which had flown for the first time in April 1934, was of biplane configuration. With ailerons on both the upper and lower wings, leading-edge slats and generous wing area, the Swordfish was highly manoeuvrable. It had also a wide speed range, between about 50 and 135 mph (80 to 217 km/h), which meant, according to Terence Horsley, author of **Find, Fix and Strike**, that in the Swordfish an ''. . . approach to the carrier deck could be made at stagger-ingly low speed, yet response to the controls remained firm and insistent. Consider what such qualities meant on a dark night when the carrier's deck was pitching the height of a house.''

Known more generally as the 'Stringbag', this was not only a legendary aeroplane in respect of its exploits, but also in terms of longevity, for they were to remain in operational service until after VE-Day, outpacing aircraft which had been built to replace them.

But to even the most unambitious designers it was clear that the days of the biplane were numbered. In continental Europe, Britain and far away America, new sleek lines began to appear as routine on drawing boards. Their originators knew not only that the structures they proposed were capable of

catering for the higher standards of performance demanded by more far-sighted and realistic military planners, but also that there would no longer be automatic prejudice against a monoplane configuration. The Schneider Trophy Contests, which by 1931 had raised circuit speeds to 340 mph (547 km/h), and the winner of which had set a world speed record of 407 mph (655 km/h), had shown that no longer were drag-inducing configurations necessary to ensure robust structures.

First of these exciting new fighters was named Hurricane (25), a design originating from the drawing board of Sydney Camm at Hawker Aircraft. It

26

retained the well-known Hawker fuselage structure of fabric-covered tubular steel, and all except early production aircraft had all-metal stressed-skin wings set in a low-wing configuration. Power plant was the Rolls-Royce Merlin, derived from the P.V.12, 'R' and 'sprint' engines which that company had developed to contend the Schneider Trophy.

By the outbreak of World War II, RAF Fighter Command had a total of 18 squadrons of Hurricanes, compared with only 9 squadrons of Spitfires.

Following upon R. J. Mitchell's successful design of the Supermarine S.5, S.6 and S.6B, the trio which had won the Schneider Trophy outright for Britain, it was only to be expected that the company would utilize their hard-earned knowledge to develop a new eight-gun

fighter to meet the requirements of the Air Ministry.

It, too, was designed around the Rolls-Royce Merlin engine, and first flight of the prototype was made on 5 March 1936, some four months after that of the Hurricane. Named Spitfire (26), the first squadron to become equipped with the type in July 1938 was No. 19, based at RAF Duxford.

In the United States there had been no similar development of advanced aircraft. On the contrary, the nation's traditional policy of isolation, plus an acute shortage of funds for the procurement of any new military equipment, had brought stagnation. Furthermore, a long drawn

out Army/Navy battle, on the issue of which service was the most able to defend the nation in the event of attack, had produced an atmosphere that was not conducive to the development of any-thing but ill-feeling.

The Army, however, did produce one officer who was a firm believer in air power. William 'Billy' Mitchell (1879–1936) joined the Army as a private during the Spanish-American War and worked his way through the ranks. He was introduced to aviation during World War I. By 1918 he was in command of a joint US-French force of almost 1,500 planes. Thereafter his outspoken advocacy of a separate US Air Force led to his court-martial. His ideas lived to inspire the creation of one of the greatest air forces in the world.

27

The United States Army Air Corps
(USAAC) retained many devotees of
General 'Billy' Mitchell in its ranks. It was
this officer who had fallen foul of the
establishment by his continued avowal
that air power had made sea power
obsolescent. Fortunately for America,
those who believed in air power were not
to be deterred by opposition, and
managed eventually to bamboozle a small
order for a strategic bomber, having
developed a convincing argument to the
effect that this particular aircraft was
really a defensive weapon.

Built as a private venture by the
Boeing Company, their Model 299
prototype flew for the first time on 28 July
1935. Less than a month later, on
20 August 1935, this aircraft made a
remarkable 2,100 mile (3,380 km)
non-stop flight to Wright Field for its
official tests. Then came apparent
disaster for Boeing in October, when the
299 crashed on take-off, it being discovered subsequently that the control-
locks had not been released before the
take-off run.

But the performance of the prototype
had been heartening, and eventually
13 aircraft were ordered in January 1936.
These were given the designation Y1B-17
when they entered service, between
January and August 1937, and one of
these early examples is seen in the
contemporary colour photograph **(27)**.

Soon after introducing the B-17 Flying
Fortress into service, the USAAC
planned to demonstrate its capability by
'intercepting' the Italian liner **Rex**
725 miles (1,167 km) out in the Atlantic.
The exercise was a great success, three
B-17s making a spot-on rendezvous with
the liner. Unfortunately, this caused new
ill-feeling between Army and Navy, and
the USAAC found itself ordered to limit
maritime patrols to 100 miles (160 km)
offshore. And to cut the air force down to
size, it was pointed out quite ruthlessly
that the 'enormous' sum spent on a few
big and useless bombers was poor
planning: a far greater number of small
fighter aircraft could have been bought
for the same sum.

As a result of the tension created, the
procurement of additional urgently
needed Flying Fortresses was delayed: to
the extent that when the United States
realized that strengthening the defence of
its Pacific bases was a priority requirement, there were nowhere near sufficient
available. In fact, when war in the Pacific
seemed inevitable, only 35 B-17s could
be deployed there.

It was the Japanese attack on Pearl
Harbor, on 7 December 1941, which
brought the United States into World
War II, and which soon had production
lines turning out B-17s **(28)** like hot
cakes. By the war's end, nearly 13,000
had been built.

28

30

31

British bomber procurement had not suffered from the restrictions imposed in the United States. Past experience had left little doubt in the minds of British planners as to the most likely targets, and aircraft like the Vickers Wellington **(29)**, with a range in excess of 2,500 miles (4,023 km) with a 1,000 lb (453 kg) bomb load, had been covered by an Air Ministry specification of 1932. There was also the Armstrong Whitworth Whitley of slightly later vintage, which had a range of 1,650 miles (2,655 km) with 3,000 lb (1,361 kg) of bombs, and the Handley Page Hampden, also of 1932, which could carry 2,000 lb (907 kg) of bombs over a range of 1,885 miles (3,034 km).

It was however the Wellington, known more usually as the 'Wimpey', which proved to be the backbone of Bomber Command in the early years of the war. It retained this position until the first of the long-range four-engined bombers began to enter operational service.

Mk XVI versions could do even better, carrying 4,000 lb (1,814 kg) of bombs.

It was to prove a nightmare for German fighter defences, being too fast to be intercepted, and their loss rate was to prove the lowest of any aircraft utilized by Bomber Command. So successful was the Mosquito bomber, that fighter and reconnaissance versions were very soon put into production.

Meanwhile, in the background, the big four-engined strategic bombers were evolving. In the lead was the Short Stirling, emanating from an Air Ministry specification of 1936. The first successful prototype made its first flight on 3 December 1939.

Next was the Handley Page Halifax, also originating from a 1936 specification, which called for a twin-engined heavy bomber. When the proposed Rolls-Royce Vulture engines were not available, the design was changed to use instead four

29

Seeming very different from any conception of a bomber aircraft was the de Havilland Mosquito **(30)**. Not only did its size suggest that it would carry a bomb-load inferior to that of the slightly larger Bristol Blenheim IV (1,320 lb: 599 kg), but the fact that it was of all-wood construction, had no defensive armament and so relied upon speed to evade airborne adversaries, made it something of a non-starter so far as military planners were concerned.

When the prototype made a demonstration flight, official observers were staggered to discover that it possessed the agility of a fighter, could perform upward rolls on the power of one engine, had a level speed of nearly 400 mph (644 km/h), and could carry a maximum bomb-load of 2,000 lb (907 kg). Later

Rolls-Royce Merlins. Developing successfully, it shared with the Avro Lancaster the major burden of the night offensive against targets in occupied Europe.

Most famous of the three was the Avro Lancaster **(31)**, originating from the unsuccessful twin-engined Avro Manchester, which was also evolved to an Air Ministry specification of 1936. Powered by the new Rolls-Royce Vulture engine, it was withdrawn from service when recurrent trouble with the power plant proved to be a major problem. Like the Halifax, it was redesigned for a four-engine Merlin installation, but was re-named Lancaster. The only British bomber capable of carrying the 22,000 lb 'Grand Slam' bomb, it was of great importance in the latter stages of the war.

32

33

34

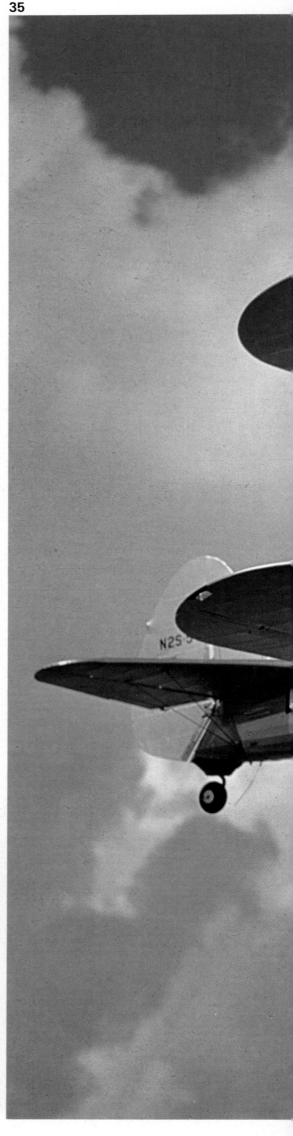

Preceding page:

In America, the need for a major strategic bomber had also been recognized by the advanced and dedicated planners of the USAAC. Unfortunately, the procurement of such a weapon was delayed until well beyond the eleventh hour, at a time when even the dumbest of dumb-bunnies was reasonably certain that the US was unlikely to avoid the spread of war taking place in Europe.

It was not until August 1940, after evaluation of competing designs from Boeing, Consolidated, Douglas and Lockheed, that Boeing and Consolidated were instructed to initiate prototype construction.

The Boeing aircraft promised to be the most important, and a mock-up was inspected by the air force in April 1941, at which time the company was urged to make all possible haste with the two XB-29 prototypes. Almost simultaneously a test batch of 14 YB-29s were ordered, and production contracts for 250 B-29s **(32)** were placed in September 1941, an additional 250 in January 1942, and in excess of 1,000 more by September 1942. Never had such large orders been placed for an unproven aircraft, the first proto-type of which did not fly until 21 September 1942.

In fact, the B-29 was very different from any aircraft which had been planned before. Not only was it required to carry a 2,000 lb (907 kg) bomb-load over a range of 5,333 miles (8,583 km), it was expected also to do this at a speed of 400 mph (644 km/h). In addition, armour protection, self-sealing fuel tanks, heavy defensive armament and the ability to uplift a 16,000 lb (7,257 kg) bomb-load over a shorter range were requirements of the specification.

When the B-29A entered service, it could demonstrate a range of 5,380 miles (8,658 kg), a maximum bomb-load of 20,000 lb (9,072 kg), and met the requirements in respect of armour protection and self-sealing tanks. Defensive armament comprised up to twelve 0·50-in machine-guns and one 37 mm cannon.

The accompanying illustrations **(33, 34)** give some appreciation of the size of this aeroplane, production of which became the largest single aircraft programme of World War II.

This page:

Like air forces around the world, that of the United States retained aircraft of biplane configuration for primary flying training. One of the most popular in America was the Stearman Kaydet **(35)**, first produced as a private venture by the Stearman Aircraft Corporation in 1934. Although Army reaction was slow initially, a total of almost 5,000 were built for the air force, in addition to others for the US Navy and for export. Power plant of the Kaydet's many versions differed somewhat, ranging from a 215 hp Lycoming R-680-5 to a 280 hp R-680-11.

For a primary flying training role the biplane proved ideal, being extremely manoeuvrable and with a high degree of controllability, even at low flying speeds. This meant that pupil pilots could make their first approaches and landings at speeds which gave them time to think.

While the European nations were busy preparing for World War II, a conflict which seemed inevitable having regard to events in continental Europe, the isolationist policy of the United States was still very much to the fore.

In the long-drawn-out battle between Army and Navy, it was the latter service which was able to exert the most influence on military policy decisions. In consequence, there had been a tendency for the Army to have to make do with the equipment it possessed. Naval planners considered that they could ensure the security of America's coastline, and with no national intention of joining in other people's quarrels, there was no real need for the Army to have any very startling attack aircraft. The only real danger to America lay in the Far East, which meant that procurement policy was concerned primarily with long-range transport, bombardment and logistic support.

In Europe, short- and medium-range aircraft were the most vital concern, particularly fighters and medium-range fast bombers. And when it seemed that national production capacity was likely to prove inadequate, both France and Britain turned to American manufacturers.

As a result of this approach, US designers and engineers began to produce new generations of aircraft, often sub-contracting production to other companies when their own capacity was at full-stretch. Thus, Boeing at Seattle was able to boast a line up of Douglas A-20s **(36)**.

36

The Douglas A-20 was an original design, but by the time the US Army placed its first contract in July 1939, production of several hundred of these aircraft for the French and British air forces was well under way.

In RAF service this aircraft is well remembered as the Boston (37), the original Boston Is serving as trainers, while Boston IIs were all converted as Havocs for the night fighter or intruder role. Boston IIIs, IVs and Vs served as light day-bombers, many replacing Blenheims in squadron service.

By direct purchase, and later by Lend-Lease, many US aircraft came into RAF use, including the Brewster Buffalo, Boeing Flying Fortress, Consolidated Catalina and Liberator, Curtiss Tomahawk and Kittyhawk, Douglas Dakota, Lockheed Hudson and Ventura, Martin Baltimore and Marauder, and North American Harvard, Mitchell and Mustang, amongst others.

The Mustang was of particular interest, for this was not merely an anglicized version of an existing type, but was designed to meet a British specification for an eight-gun fighter. It was to prove a vital aircraft to the United States Army Air Force (USAAF) in the European theatre, particularly when long-range fighters were needed to escort 8th Air Force bombers on daylight sorties that penetrated deep into enemy-held territory.

Germany had long been preparing for war in Europe, building up an air force, training its personnel in Russia.

The primary task envisaged for this air force—the Luftwaffe—was to be what we then called an Army co-operation role; today, such operations would be classed as close-support. Working closely in conjunction with, and acting as the spearhead of, fast-moving, well-armed and armoured ground forces, it was considered that this combination would prove to be the most effective for the kind of war which would be fought in Europe.

German participation in the Spanish Civil War showed that this concept was right, and provided a wonderful opportunity for the testing of weapons and military techniques under real operational conditions.

Among the first German machines to see service in Spain was the Messerschmitt Me 109 (38), designed by Willy Messerschmitt, and now regarded as probably the most outstanding German fighter aircraft of all time.

Like the Supermarine Spitfire, it was to remain in front-line service throughout the European phase of the war, and was developed progressively from the 254 mph (570 km/h), and 36,100 ft (11,000 m) service ceiling of the Me 109E, first major production version, to the 452 mph (727 km/h) and 41,000 ft (12,500 m) service ceiling of the Me 109K.

Both the Hurricane and Spitfire were powered by the Rolls-Royce Merlin in-line liquid-cooled engine. The small frontal area of this type of engine offered advantages for high-speed fighter aircraft, and it is significant that four great fighters—Hurricane, Spitfire, Me 109 and Mustang—all had in-line engines.

There were two notable exceptions, both conspicuously successful aircraft, which had radial air-cooled engines: the

38

39

German Focke-Wulf Fw 190 and Japanese Mitsubishi A6M Zero.

Before the war America had concentrated on the development of powerful and reliable radial air-cooled engines, accounting for the rather barrel-shaped appearance of many of her early wartime aircraft, including products of Boeing, Brewster, Curtiss, Grumman and Seversky. Some of these aircraft, and particularly those intended for US Navy service, were designed to have a dive-bombing capability.

Germany's Junkers Ju 87 **Stuka** dive-bomber **(39)** is reputed to have originated because Germany's Ernst Udet had been so impressed by American dive-bombing techniques. When first introduced into action in the Spanish Civil War the performance of the Ju 87 had not been impressive. When used in conjunction with armoured columns the **Blitzkrieg** was born, and Stukas spearheaded the attacks in Poland and France, the scream of their wind-driven sirens adding to the terror and confusion they caused, particularly to columns of civilian refugees.

German aircraft such as the Junkers Ju 87 and Messerschmitt Me 109 had been developed clandestinely, their pilots training at the Luftwaffe's pre-war base in Russia.

Bomber aircraft, such as the Dornier Do 17 and Heinkel He 111 cut their teeth in Lufthansa service, both ostensibly high-speed transport aircraft. Their use on Lufthansa international routes provided excellent crew training, with services to London and Paris allowing familiarization over routes which would one day have to be flown under far more difficult conditions.

The Heinkel He 111 **(40)**, powered by Daimler-Benz engines, was well known to the citizens of Britain during 1940–41, the note of its unsynchronized engines remembered still, and especially by those who lived in Birmingham, Coventry and London. It remained in service throughout the war, although gradually becoming obsolete, but was able to record a wide range of activities. These included torpedo-bomber, pathfinder, glider tug, V-1 missile launcher, paratroop and cargo transport.

37

40

Ernst Heinkel was not concerned only with conventional aircraft, such as the He III, but was both far-sighted and unafraid to experiment. Learning of the research on jet propulsion being carried out by Dr Pabst von Ohain at Göttingen University, he engaged the doctor and his assistant, Max Hahn, to continue their experiments at Marienehe. By September 1937 von Ohain was bench-running a hydrogen-fuelled turbojet engine, but although he was unaware of it, Frank Whittle in England had attained this goal five months earlier.

It was, however, the combined efforts of von Ohain and Heinkel that recorded the world's first flight of a turbojet-powered aircraft, when the Heinkel He 178 powered by an HeS 3b engine made its first successful flight on 27 August 1939.

Despite this early lead, it was not until almost three years later, on 18 July 1942, that the prototype of Germany's first operational turbojet aircraft, the Messerschmitt Me 262, made its maiden flight. There were to be further delays before it entered service, for Adolf Hitler insisted it should be developed as a fighter-bomber, and it was not until 3 October 1944 that the first unit began operations. The Me 262 **(41)** illustrated is in the Museum at Munich, surrounded by aircraft of other ages.

Development of a British turbojet-powered aircraft was to occupy a very similar time scale. Although Frank Whittle (later Sir Frank) had run the world's first aircraft turbojet engine on 12 April 1937, it was not until March 1938 that he received an Air Ministry contract to produce a flight engine.

The airframe to be wedded with this power plant was contracted with the Gloster Aircraft Company on 3 February 1940, designated by its AM specification number E.28/39. This flew for the first time at RAF Cranwell, on the evening of 15 May 1941, and proved to be a remarkably trouble-free machine considering the experimental nature of both engine and airframe.

At this time the German industry had a lead of 21 months, but before the E.28/39 had flown Glosters had already received an order for 12 twin-engined fighters to Air Ministry Specification F.9/40. Named Meteor **(42)**, the fifth prototype (DG206/G) was to record the first flight of the type on 5 March 1943, and they began to equip the RAF's No. 616 Squadron on 12 July 1944. Meteors became operational in August with 616 Squadron, and recorded their first 'kill' of a V-1 flying bomb on 4 August 1944.

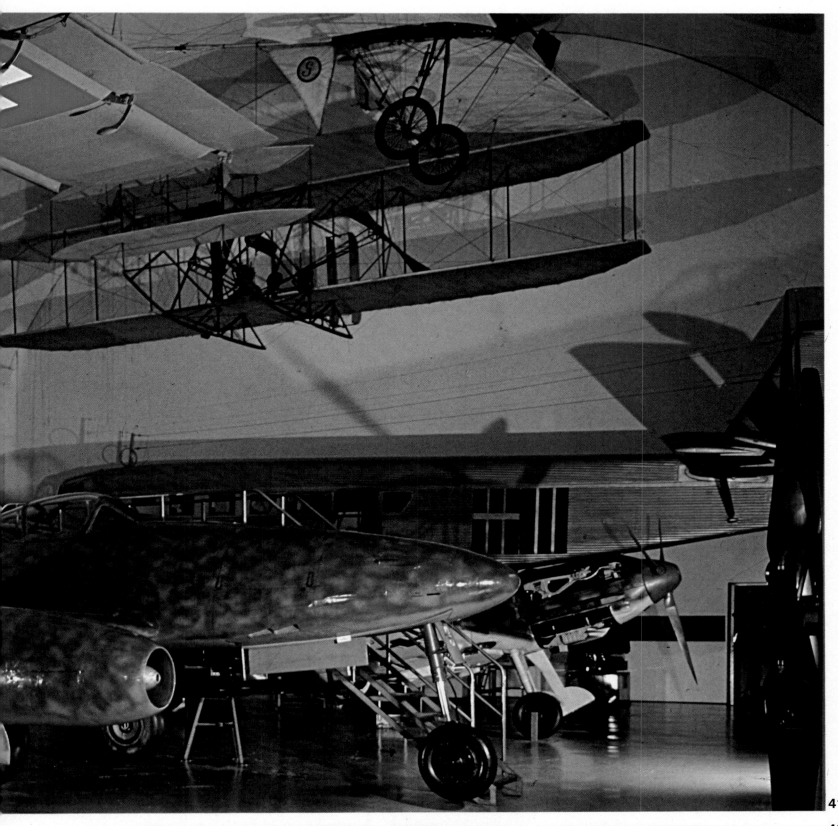

41

42

Not very long after the end of World War II, in mid-1948 to be more precise, the temperature of the Cold War between East and West dropped an alarming number of degrees. It was occasioned by the Soviet Union closing surface routes to Berlin,

During the eleven months duration of this attempt to force the occupying American, British and French troops out of the German capital, the entire population of West Berlin—some two million people—plus the occupying forces, were sustained from the air. Even bulk supplies of such materials as flour and coal were carried in vast quantities, but barrels of petrol were considered far from ideal loads by the crews involved.

USAF transport aircraft were heavily engaged: the C47, our old friend the DC-3 in military guise; the C-54 Sky-master, a military version of the Douglas

Post-War Military Aircraft

DC-4; the C-74 Globemaster, a development of the C-54; and the Fairchild C-82 Flying Boxcar, the only one of the four designed especially as a military transport. This experience showed the need for purpose-built heavy transport aircraft, and among the first to be evolved was the Douglas C-124 Globemaster II **(57)**, based on the C-74, and similarly powered with radial air-cooled engines. Large cargo volume was provided by the aircraft's deep fuselage, and clam-shell nose loading doors and a built-in ramp facilitated the rapid loading of cargo.

Fairchild's C-123 Provider **(58)** bore no relationship to the same company's Flying Boxcar. Instead, it evolved from a cargo glider designed by Chase Aircraft in 1949. When flown by that company as a powered aircraft, in April 1951, it became designated XC-123A.

Two years later, when Chase had been acquired by the Kaiser-Frazer Corporation, the USAF cancelled the contract for its production and gave it, instead, to Fairchild. This forward-looking company immediately began development of the basic design, introducing a large dorsal fin, and some examples had wider-track landing gear for improved stability on the ground and underwing pod-mounted auxiliary turbojet engines to augment the output of the conventional piston-engines.

Many C-123s served in Vietnam for the airlift of troops and cargo. Some, like the one illustrated, were transferred into the service of the Vietnam Air Force.

With the introduction of turboprop engines to civil transport aircraft, demonstrating daily the many advantages of turbine power plants, it was inevitable that the USAF would soon specify this power source for future military transports.

This moment came with the issue of a specification for a Logistic Carrier Supporting System, and the Douglas Aircraft Company's design was ordered into production for the Military Air Transport Service (MATS). Designated C-133 Cargomaster **(59)**, the first of these was delivered to MATS on 29 August 1957.

Later production versions had four 6,500 shp Pratt & Whitney T34-P-7WA turboprop engines, the gross take-off and landing weight of these aircraft being 282,000 lb (127,913 kg). They accommodate a crew of ten, plus 200 troops and their equipment, or 13,000 cu ft (368·12 m³) of cargo. Special clam-shell rear doors permit the carriage of operational Inter-continental Ballistic Missiles (ICBMs) without the need to disassemble them.

Lockheed's C-130 Hercules had been designed to meet the same turboprop transport requirement as the Douglas C-133. They serve the USAF in a wide variety of roles, including the conventional transport of troops and cargo, with DC-130Es for Remotely Piloted Vehicle (RPV) launch and control; WC-130Es for weather reconnaissance; KC-130Fs with flight refuelling capability; HC-130Hs for air search, rescue and recovery; HC-130Ns for the recovery of space capsules; KC-130R tankers; and LC-130Rs with wheel/ski landing gear for Arctic operations. C-130 Hercules served many other air forces throughout the world.

Lockheed followed with the C-141 StarLifter, a four-turbofan transport which went into operational service with MATS (now Military Airlift Command: MAC) on 23 April 1965. MAC's 14 C-141 squadrons comprised the primary airlift capability in 1971, providing supplies to US forces in Vietnam on a daily basis.

Grand-daddy of them all, of course, is Lockheed's C-5A Galaxy (46) with four 41,100 lb thrust General Electric turbofan engines, 220,967 lb (100,228 kg) payload, and maximum range with this payload of 3,749 miles (6,033 km).

46

All this talk about long-range civil and military transports of landplane configuration should not suggest that water-borne aircraft no longer exist, nor that attempts to develop new aircraft within this category died a natural death immediately after World War II.

Prior to the war the German company of Dornier had developed a particularly graceful three-engined flying-boat, the Do 24, the first prototype of which (D-ADLR) flew for the first time on 3 July 1937. Built by various manufacturers, they performed valuable wartime service on sea-air rescues.

Spain acquired twelve of these aircraft in 1944 for sea-air rescue in the Mediterranean. Designated HR.5, some continue in service, as shown by the aircraft on the right of the illustration (47). That filling the background of the picture is a Grumman Albatross, which is of rather later vintage.

The Glenn L. Martin Company of Baltimore, Maryland, had been building aircraft for the US Navy since the early 1920s. In 1937 they began design of a new flying-boat which was to be contemporary with the Consolidated PBY Catalina, many of which served with the British Royal Air Force during World War II. One of their best remembered actions was that performed by Catalinas of Coastal Command's Nos. 209 and 240 Squadrons, which respectively spotted and shadowed the German battleship **Bismarck** after naval forces had lost contact.

Martin's new boat, the PBM Mariner (48), first went into service during 1941. Most were employed on long-range maritime patrol or anti-submarine warfare (ASW), but twenty were equipped as 20-seat transports with standardized British/US equipment. A large number, of course, were used for sea-air rescue duties, and of the 631 built many continued in this role for twenty years. The Mariner will always be remembered for its graceful appearance, and was easily recognized by its gull-wing and inward-canted endplate fins.

But the days of water-borne aircraft were virtually numbered so far as long-range transport was concerned. Aircraft like Britain's post-war Saunders-Roe Princesses were cocooned and forgotten while awaiting more powerful engines that would convert them into Queens of the air. By the time that suitable engines were available, economists had proved that landplanes could accomplish the same duties faster and more cheaply.

Flying-boats for maritime patrol were to remain in service for some years, but specialized adaptations of landplanes had proved more versatile. Navies investigated a number of water-borne craft, such as the Convair Sea Dart for a strike role and various flying-boats as transports.

One ambitious project was the Martin P6M SeaMaster **(49)**, surely the most advanced flying-boat ever built. Intended to fulfil a mine-laying and reconnaissance role, this 100 ft (30·48 m) span all-metal

49

50

craft had a swept monoplane wing, with four turbojet engines mounted in pairs in nacelles on the upper surface of the wing. Its combat radius of 1,500 miles (2,415 km) could be extended by flight refuelling, and other advanced features included a pressurized flight deck and ejection seats for all four crew members.

Although the SeaMaster was capable of a speed in excess of 600 mph (960 km/h), service trials established that newly developing carrier-based aircraft had virtually outdated those which operated independently from the surface of the sea.

As the war neared its end, high-speed aircraft began to be challenged by a new enemy, one called compressibility. Pilots of high-performance fighters, such as the American P-38 Lightning and British Typhoon, had discovered that when approaching maximum speed in a dive their aircraft would often shudder violently. This was sometimes so severe that wings and tail units broke away from the main structure and many pilots lost their lives.

By testing models in supersonic (faster than sound) wind tunnels, aerodynamicists discovered that as the speed of sound was approached the previously smooth airflow over the wings began to break up into shock waves, causing the violent buffeting. Solution of the problem was speeded post-war when Allied scientific teams found documents which showed German researchers had discovered that thin-section swept wings (i.e. with the leading-edge of the wing forming an angle of less than 90° to the rear of the fuselage) could delay the onset of buffeting.

The Bell Aircraft Company was requested to build for the USAF a series of robust rocket-engined research aircraft. Flown by Major Charles 'Chuck' Yeager, the X-1 was the first to exceed the speed of sound in October 1947. Later, in 1953, he flew the X-1A (50) at 1,650 mph (2,655 km/h), proving that a properly designed aircraft would have no difficulty in entering supersonic flight.

Forty-five degrees of wing sweepback was responsible for North American's private-venture fighter being known as the Sabre 45. It had been developed from the highly successful F-86 Sabre, but was two years in project design before the company were awarded a USAF contract for two YF-100 prototypes.

It emerged as a sleek-looking aeroplane, the first of the USAF's 'Century-Series' fighters (F-100 and upwards), and the first operational fighter in the world capable of supersonic speed in level flight. It was used to set a new world speed record of 755·149 mph (1,215·29 km/h) on 29 October 1953.

Designated as the F-100 Super Sabre (51) they began to equip Tactical Air Command (TAC) in late November 1953. F-100Cs could carry a total of 6,000 lb (2,721 kg) of weapons on underwing hard points and demonstrated a speed of Mach 1·25. On 20 August 1955 one of these aircraft raised the world speed record yet again, this time to 822·135 mph (1,323·09 km/h).

The F-100 was to give valuable service during the early stages of the Vietnam War, and continues in service with a number of NATO nations.

Once called the 'missile with a man in it', the Lockheed F-104 Starfighter certainly provides breathtaking performance. Its initial rate of climb is 40,000 ft (12,192 m) a minute, representing about 450 mph (724 km/h) —upwards!

Its needle-nosed fuselage wrapped tightly around a powerful turbojet engine is illustrated clearly in the picture (52).

The Starfighter arms many NATO nations, and its 20-mm Vulcan gun and ability to deploy two or four Sidewinder air-to-air missiles make it a formidable adversary.

51

52

54

As research continued, the problems of flight at speeds in excess of Mach 1 (the speed of sound, approx 760 mph: 1,223 km/h at sea level) faded into the background. It was no longer a question of building an aircraft to slip cleanly from subsonic to supersonic flight, but how to cope with the airframe temperatures generated by kinetic heating as speeds climbed higher and higher. It was to be overcome by using titanium and stainless steel construction, the airframe 'skinned' with Iconel X nickel alloy steel to withstand temperatures ranging from +1,200°F to −300°F. When temperatures in excess of this upper limit were encountered it became necessary to cover the entire airframe with an ablative coating, like a missile's nose-cone, which burns away at about 530°F to maintain the temperature of the structure well below the design figure of 1,200°F.

Last of the rocket-engined aircraft, which terminated the high-speed research programme, was the North American X-15-A2 **(53)** which, in October 1967, carried Major 'Pete' Knight of the USAF more than fifty miles above the Earth's surface, earning him an astronaut's wings. More than that, it flashed him through the air at an almost unbelievable 4,534 mph (7,297 km/h), before he made a conventional—if fast—landing.

Design of a high-performance turbojet-powered fighter for the USAF had begun in 1944. But as we have already seen, German research had shown that swept wings were vital for high speeds and structural integrity.

It was decided, despite the inevitable delay, to redesign this fighter to incorporate such wings, and it was not until 1 October 1947 that the prototype of this new North American fighter took to the air, to be designated eventually as the North American F-86 Sabre **(54)**.

Within days of that flight, 'Chuck' Yeager had confirmed that a robust swept-wing design could exceed the speed of sound, and in the Spring of 1948 the Sabre exceeded Mach 1 in a shallow dive, the first USAF fighter to do so.

Communist plans having failed to make any headway with the confrontation on West Berlin, the next move was war in Korea. Here the Sabre was to win high esteem when in combat with Russian MiG-15 jet-fighters. The first recorded combats came on 17 December 1950, when four MiGs were destroyed.

Major variants of the F-86 included the F-86F with modified wing leading-edge to improve high-altitude manoeuvrability (2,540 built) and F-86D all-weather fighter (2,504 built). Many F-86Ks, also an all-weather fighter, served with NATO units in Europe. Though no longer serving with the USAF, they still equip some 20 of the world's air forces.

56

57

Armaments of the F-86 consisted of six 0·5-inch (13-mm) Browning machine guns plus 2,000-lbs (910-kgs) of bombs or sixteen 5-inch (130-mm) rockets.

The USAF's first multi-seat all-weather interceptor-fighter, the Northrop F-89 Scorpion, entered service in July 1950.

Intended as a home defence weapon for utilization by Air Defence Command (ADC), the Scorpion was powered by two turbojets which in the F-89D version gave an initial rate of climb of 8,360 ft (2,548 m)/minute—more than 1½ miles (2·4 km) a minute! Service ceiling was 49,200 ft (14,995 m).

The F-89D was certainly a potent weapon, for it carried an armament of twenty-six 2·75 in folding-fin rockets in a pod on each wingtip. The illustration (67) shows test firing of these rockets over the Californian desert during the summer of 1952.

heads of the missiles also 'lock-on', and the pilot is then instructed to fire his weapons. This action can be taken to destroy a target without it ever being seen by the pilot, except as a 'blip' on a radar screen.

We have seen already that when designers wanted to create an aircraft which could be flown faster than the speed of sound, one of the primary requirements was a swept wing of special aerofoil section.

Clearly, this is a specialized wing configuration which is most efficient in high-speed flight and, consequently, not ideal for the slow speeds associated with the critical manoeuvres of take-off and landing. For those flight regimes an unswept wing of 'fat' aerofoil section generates more lift.

Designers concluded that a wing which was unswept for take-off and landing, and which could be changed to a swept

ducks when air power was deployed effectively, it had shown also that the aircraft carrier was a very important weapon of war. As a result, the US began to build up a large carrier fleet. The wartime development of turbine engines and nuclear weapons meant that comparatively small aircraft would be able to operate from such vessels, and yet pack a punch.

In 1949 the Douglas Aircraft Company completed a design study for a carrier-based attack bomber known as the Skywarrior (58), which received the designation A3D, changed subsequently to A-3. When it entered service in March 1956 it was the largest aircraft produced for carrier operation, with a wing span of 72 ft 6 in (22·07 m) and a gross weight of 73,000 lb (33,112 kg).

When used operationally, however, during the Vietnam War, the Skywarrior's primary utilization was as a carrier-based electronic reconnaissance aircraft.

58

This page:

Contemporary with Lockheed's Star-fighter was the English Electric, later British Aircraft Corporation (BAC) Lightning (56), designed by W E W Petter who was responsible also for the design of Britain's first jet-bomber, the English Electric Canberra.

It was a significant aircraft for the RAF—its first single-seat fighter able to exceed the speed of sound in level flight. Not only is it capable of flight at Mach 2, with a ceiling of 60,000 ft (18,290 m), but it is also what is known as an integrated weapons system.

This means that once its search radar has located the target it can be 'locked-on', feeding information to an on-board computer which provides steering information. When the Lightning is within missile-firing range, the homing

position for high-speed flight, would be a valuable compromise. Tests showed this to be true, and a number of aircraft have been developed with variable-geometry wings

In America, General Dynamics evolved the world's first operational fighter to have variable wing sweepback, this receiving the designation F-111 (57). Since this aircraft's introduction into service, both tactical fighter and strategic bomber versions have been developed.

F-111As of the USAF's Tactical Air Force wings saw operational service in the closing stages of the Vietnam war, not only proving to be highly effective, but recording also the lowest loss rate of any USAF aircraft deployed in Southeast Asia.

If World War II had demonstrated effectively that battleships were sitting

59

Experience had shown also that one of the most valuable categories of aircraft were those able to fulfil close-support and interdiction roles. The Korean War had proved that when aircraft were in operation on the other side of the world, an aircraft carrier provided an ideal operational base, with most facilities of a land airfield. These two reasons explain why the US Navy drew up the specification for just such an aircraft to equip Navy and Marine attack squadrons.

Douglas met the requirement by a comparatively simple low-cost lightweight aircraft, providing the Navy with one that was almost half the weight of that contemplated in the original specification.

The first of these A-4 Skyhawks (59) were manufactured by Douglas and entered service in 1956: the later company of McDonnell Douglas—formed by a merger in 1967—were still building new advanced-version A-4s in 1974.

A single-seater with a maximum level speed of 675 mph (1,086 km/h) and the ability to carry up to 10,000 lb (4,535 kg) of assorted weapons on external strong points, the A-4 proved to be of primary importance during the Vietnam War.

While Douglas was busy with the Navy's Skyhawk, the McDonnell Aircraft Corporation began development of a high-performance attack two-seater, also for the US Navy. During the development period the specification was changed, requiring provision of air-to-air armament, and leading to a versatile multi-mission two-seater able to operate as a land- and carrier-based fighter/fighter-bomber.

Known as the F-4 Phantom II, it entered service with the Navy in December 1960, and trials for suitability in a ground-attack role led to USAF versions which entered service in 1963. Armament of the Phantom includes Sparrow and Sidewinder missiles, with the ability to carry a total of 16,000 lb (7,250 kg) of mixed weapons.

Readily identified by the dihedral on the outer wing panels and the sharp anhedral of the tailplane, Phantoms serve also with the RAF, the Luftwaffe, and the air forces of Iran, South Korea, Israel, Japan, Turkey, Greece and Spain.

Illustrated is a Luftwaffe RF-4E (60), a reconnaissance fighter version. It is a photograph which demonstrates clearly how effective a good camouflage scheme can be.

60

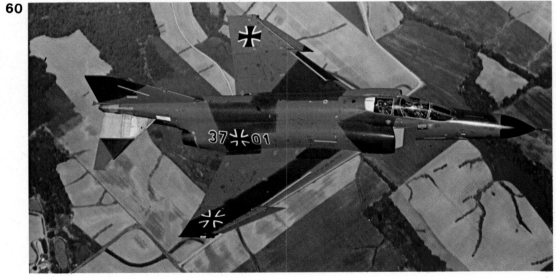

62

Chance Vought Inc were winners of a design competition to provide the US Navy with a carrier-based supersonic fighter. Clearly, such a category of aircraft was a designer's nightmare, for the kind of wing that was needed for the low approach speeds of deck landings seemed unlikely to be suitable for supersonic flight. The solution was novel: a two-position variable-incidence wing that gave good controllability at low speeds.

Designated as the F-8 Crusader, the first F-8As began to enter service in March 1957. Most-built version was the F-8E, which had armament comprising four 20 mm cannon and carried four Sidewinder missiles. Late production F-8Es had underwing pylons for the carriage of a wide range of attack weapons.

A total of 42 F-8E(FN)s were supplied also to the French Navy for service on the carriers **Clemenceau** and **Foch**, and these had additional aerodynamic modifications to the wings to permit them to operate from these smaller vessels.

The large incidence of the wing for take-off and landing is seen clearly in the illustration of an F-8E **(61)**, while the in-flight photograph of the F-8J **(62)** shows the incidence of the wing in flight.

61

63

It is interesting to note that most of the American attack aircraft evolved in the 1955–65 period were for Navy or Marine use, underlining the continuation of the 'floating aerodrome' policy.

In 1964 Ling-Temco-Vought (LTV), resulting from the merger of Vought with Ling-Temco Electronics, were the winners of a US Navy competition for the design of a new lightweight attack aircraft. One requirement was that initial production aircraft had to be in service by 1967, and LTV gained by basing the new design on the successful F-8, which promised speedier production and cost savings.

No longer requiring supersonic capability it was possible to dispense with the variable-incidence wing, and fuselage length was reduced also. Designated A-7 Corsair II, the first A-7As **(63)** were delivered to squadrons in October 1966 and were in operation in Vietnam in 1967.

Evaluation of the Corsair prior to its introduction into Naval squadron service had shown the potential of the design, and in October 1966 the USAF ordered A-7D Corsairs **(64)**, this illustration giving an excellent appreciation of the external armament carried by modern attack aircraft.

64

65

66

Successful testing of the Gloster-Whittle E.28/39 at RAF Cranwell in 1941 had left no doubt that new and excitingly powerful turbine engines would be developed eventually. When America was advised of the new power plant, the General Electric Company began to build engines based on the Whittle design, subsequently developing and initiating original design.

As we have already seen, the new engines had been utilized to power a whole new generation of fighter aircraft, the very first of which had been Bell's P-59 Airacomet, which flew for the first time on 1 October 1942.

One project which started a few months after the first flight of the P-59 was the design and production of the first swept-wing jet bomber to be produced in quantity for any air force. This was the Boeing B-47 Stratojet (65), powered by six underwing turbojets. So thin and flexible were the wings of this revolutionary medium bomber that, when the aircraft was on the ground, they drooped to give an appearance of anhedral. When loaded and in flight, however, they were seen to be set at a conventional dihedral angle. This flexible wing was strong enough for the Stratojet to use a low-level 'lob-bombing' technique, with the bomb being released during a zooming vertical climb, and the aircraft dis-engaging by completing a fighter tactic, the Immelmann turn.

Friction between the Eastern and Western powers had been greatly intensified during the period of the Berlin Airlift, an operation which cost valuable lives and a great deal of money. It served only to prove to the Soviet Union that the Western Allies were prepared to face grave problems or any cost if it would maintain peace. Two years later came the next major confrontation, with the beginning of war in Korea in mid-1950. The question in most minds then was: can this escalate into the third world war?

Undoubtedly it could have done, but by that time Russia had already demon-strated an ability to deploy atomic weapons. Thus came about the nuclear deterrent policy, with both East and West capable of annihilating attack. So unthinkable is an all-out nuclear war that, to this day, the deterrent threat has proved adequate to prevent a major conflict.

One of the keystones of America's deterrent policy was to be the Boeing B-52 Stratofortress (66). This strategic heavy bomber, with a wing span of 185 ft (56·39 m) and powered by eight turbojet or turbofan engines, was capable of delivering nuclear weapons on any target in the world. Their value was proven in 1962 when Soviet missile sites were discovered on Cuba. Faced with a full-scale nuclear alert, a percentage of Strategic Air Command's B-52's were kept airborne around the clock. When opposed by such determination, the Russians dismantled the sites and shipped the missiles back East.

Preceding page:

To enable aircraft like the B-52 to remain airborne for long periods it is necessary for them to take on additional supplies of fuel while in flight. This technique of flight-refuelling had originated from quite early days, the US Army Air Service pioneering the idea in 1923.

When three B-52 Stratofortresses completed a 45 hour 19 minute round-the-world flight in 1957, they had been refuelled en route three times by KC-97 tankers. These tanker aircraft had been developed from the Boeing-built C-97 Stratofreighter and at a later date the Boeing C-135 turbojet-powered Strato-lifter also became available as the KC-135 Stratotanker.

At the opposite end of the scale, aircraft like the Douglas A-3 Skywarrior have also been modified to serve as tankers, able to supply range-extending fuel to fast fighters, while other suitable aircraft have been converted to provide helicopters with the facility of an airborne filling station.

The US services make considerable use of a 'Flying-Boom' refuelling system, developed by Boeing, which is controlled by an operator who 'flies' the boom into a suitable position for the receiving aircraft to connect with it. The illustration shows an F-4E **(67)** approaching the 'Flying-Boom'.

An Air Ministry specification was drawn up in 1948 to equip the RAF with a force of long-range medium jet-bombers which, armed with conventional or nuclear weapons, would provide a modern striking force.

Known as the 'V' bomber programme, it initiated production of the Vickers Valiant—withdrawn from service in 1965; the Avro Vulcan; and Handley Page Victor. B.1 versions of this latter aircraft were delivered to the first operational squadrons in April 1958, and when superseded by Victor B.2s were converted to flight-refuelling tankers.

In Britain a different technique of flight-refuelling has developed, known as the drogue and probe method. The tanker trails a hose with a conical drogue at its end. Into this the thirsty aircraft pushes a rigid probe, an automatic valve then

effecting a fuel-tight seal.

The illustration **(68)** shows a Victor tanker using the probe and drogue system to suckle an RAF Buccaneer low-level strike aircraft.

This page:

Asmall nation seeking a particular class of aircraft has to evaluate whether it can be built or bought most cheaply. The former decision applies usually only when large numbers are involved, or there are prospects of sales to other nations.

The vast productive capacity of the American aircraft industry has made it possible for them to build new aeroplanes at comparatively low prices, and as a result this country has sold large numbers of aircraft to a worldwide market in the years since World War II.

When Spain was needing a general-

purpose amphibian for patrol and rescue duties, the requirement was met by buying a supply from Grumman Aircraft in America. This company had designed and built such an aircraft for the US Navy, known as the Albatross.

The illustration **(69)** shows a line-up of these aircraft in Spanish service, in which they have the designation AN-1 Albatross.

When a moderate number of aircraft are required, an alternative means of procuring them is by licence production. By payment of a licence fee, the designing company passes on the drawings and know-how, enabling the foreign company to build the requisite number of aircraft without having to face any unknowns or astronomical develop-ment costs.

The Northrop Corporation in America had designed a relatively simple light-weight fighter to US Government requirements for supply to friendly nations under the Military Assistance Program (MAP). Spain elected to manufacture her own version of Northrop's F-5, and Construcciones Aeronautica SA (CASA) was contracted by the Spanish Air Force to construct, under licence, 36 single-seat fighters and 34 two-seat fighter/trainers, these having the respective Spanish designa-tions of C.9 and CE.9. Built by CASA's factories at Getafe and Seville, the first ten entered service in June 1969.

Illustrated is a reconnaissance version developed by Northrop as the RF-5A, and built in Spain under the designation CR.9 **(70)**. Ports in the nose are for the four installed reconnaissance cameras.

The adjoining country of France, however, has a flourishing and forward-looking aircraft industry of its own which, in the years since the end of World War II, has produced some remarkable aircraft.

Avions Marcel Dassault (now known as Dassault/Breguet Aviation following a merger with the pioneering company of Breguet, founded by Louis Breguet in 1911) was responsible for design of the Mirage delta-wing all-weather high-altitude intercepter, of which the prototype first flew on 17 November 1957.

The delta-wing configuration was chosen because it not only provides a very rigid and enduring airframe structure, capable of supersonic flight, but the large wing area provides excellent performance and handling at high altitude.

Since that time a whole family of Mirage aircraft have been developed. The Mirage 5 ground-attack version, which flew for the first time on 19 May 1967, retains the delta-wing configuration of the parent Mirage. Illustrated is the Mirage 5V (71) being built for Venezuela.

Although the Mirage was established as a successful design, Dassault began the private-venture development of a new single-seat multi-mission fighter in the mid-1960s.

Designated as the Mirage F1, it differs from the basic family likeness by dispensing with the delta-wing configuration in favour of a swept wing and conventional all-moving tailplane. Advanced aerodynamic features of this wing enable the F1 to take off on an interception sortie in only 2,100 ft (640 m), even when

73

71

72

operating from unprepared strips.

It is a formidable aeroplane, armed with two 30 mm cannon, able to deploy Sidewinder missiles, to carry up to 8,820 lb (4,000 kg) of weapons externally, and to fly at Mach 2·2 (approx 1,460 mph: 2,350 km/h at 40,000 ft: 12,000 m). Illustration (72) shows the Dassault/Breguet production line of F1s.

In Britain, the delta-wing configuration chosen by Dassault for the Mirage was used by A. V. Roe and Company when they designed their contribution to the RAF's 'V' bomber programme.

This wing configuration was chosen by Avro for the same characteristic which had appealed to the French manufacturer. In addition, its use for a large bomber aircraft meant that the depth of the wing section would be adequate to contain fuel and bomb-load without any external drag.

The Avro Vulcan (73) flew for the first time on 30 August 1952, entering service in mid-1956, and despite a subsonic speed was regarded as one of the world's most redoubtable bomber aircraft. Confirmation of the excellence of the structural design is given by the fact that

Vulcans were still in RAF service in 1974, and there was talk of converting some aircraft for a strategic reconnaissance role.

Following page:
Supermarine, builders of the S.6B seaplane and Spitfire fighter, were to evolve a new interceptor for the RAF in the post-war years. Instead of the delta-wing chosen by Dassault for the Mirage III at a slightly later date, Supermarine elected to use the swept wing and conventional tailplane, to which the French manufacturers reverted. The resulting aircraft, the Supermarine Swift F.1, entered service with the RAF in 1952, but proving unsuitable as an interceptor only 36 aircraft (F.1s and F.2s combined) were built.

Developed from the interceptor was the Swift F.R.5 (74), a fighter-reconnaissance aircraft which was to see five years of service with the RAF before being replaced by the Hawker Hunter F.R.10 in 1961. In the F.R.5 Swift an extended nose carried three cameras, and armament comprised two 30 mm Aden guns, with provisions for bombs or rockets which were carried on underwing hard points.

One of the great technological achievements of World War II was radar. Intended originally for the detection and location of enemy aircraft, as it became developed it was to prove also a remarkable device for accurate navigation, the interception of enemy aircraft by night, and the blind bombing of ground targets.

It was discovered, however, that under certain circumstances it was possible for low-flying aircraft to escape detection. To exploit this weakness in an enemy's defences, the British Admiralty sought a carrier-based low-level strike aircraft. Blackburn Aircraft were chosen to build this aeroplane, the prototype of which flew for the first time on 30 April 1958.

Ten years later, the type was chosen by the RAF to close the gap in its ranks caused by the vacillations of successive governments, resulting in the Hawker Siddeley Buccaneer (75).

The type continues in RAF service, a significant strike aircraft which uses terrain-following techniques for low-level attack, and which is able to deliver nuclear or conventional bombs and rockets, as well as Bullpup or Martel missiles.

An important newcomer to the American military aviation scene in 1976 was the Fairchild A-10A (76). Unlike the dual-role Alpha Jet, the single-seat A-10A is a specially-designed close-support aircraft, and a most distinctive aeroplane for the spotter because of its unusual power plant installation, each of the two 9,065 lb (4,112 kg) thrust engines being pylon-mounted to the upper rear fuselage. Designed and built by the Fairchild Republic Company, it was also selected — like the YF-16 and YF-17 — as the result of a competitive prototype evaluation to provide a close-support aircraft for the USAF. A comparatively slow aircraft, it is designed around its formidable General Electric 30 mm seven-barrel cannon which has a maximum rate of fire of 4,200 shells per minute.

In addition to this impressive armament, the A-10A has eight underwing and three underfuselage stores pylons that can accommodate a maximum external load of 16,000 lb (7,247 kg). This can include general purpose, retarded, incendiary, cluster and laser — or optically-guided bombs, flare launchers, chaff or jammer pods, and Maverick TV-guided air-to-surface missiles. Entering service with the USAF in early 1976, current production planning calls for a total of more than 700 aircraft.

76

Design Revolution I Engines

As long ago as 1680, when the Italian Giovanni Borelli's *De motu animalium* was published posthumously, it gave as his opinion that man would be unable to fly by his own muscle power. The statement remained true for almost three hundred years, for it is only in recent times that a small number of individuals or groups have constructed ultra lightweight aircraft of special design, capable of being flown by one (sometimes two) people using pedals to drive a propeller. Despite the fact that the aircraft have been built from advanced materials such as polystyrene foam – to give rigidity and light weight – with balsa wood, plywood and transparent plastic covering, plus a minimum of essential metals and other woods, the distances they have been flown at the time of writing, in the summer of 1976, have no significance in terms of real flight. In fact, Borelli's statement is still fundamentally true, for he was speaking of free, unlimited flight, like that of the birds.

The problem of finding a suitable *power plant*, or engine, to propel a heavier-than-air craft was to remain virtually unsolved until the beginning of the 20th century. True, men had been experimenting during the 19th century with models driven by the power plant which was responsible for the first great industrial revolution to spread across the face of the civilised world – the steam engine. But however suited the steam engine might be for industrial and agricultural applications, and for transport by land or sea, it could hardly be considered the ideal power source for an aircraft.

The Internal Combustion Engine

The first important milestone came in 1861 when the German Nicholas Otto originated the four-stroke cycle of operation for an internal combustion engine. Since this is the basic principle upon which the majority of *piston engines* (one in which a piston/s within a cylinder/s transmits the power produced by combustion to a crankshaft) operate, even to this day, it is well worth explaining just how such an engine works.

You will see that we have four diagrams: in each there is a *cylinder* or tube and at the upper closed end of the cylinder (*cylinder head*) two valves which open and close to allow the free passage of gas. That on the left is called the *inlet valve*, which allows a combustible mixture of gas to flow into the cylinder; that on the right is the *exhaust valve*, which allows the burned gases to flow out of the cylinder. Inserted in the cylinder

head, between the valves, is a *sparking plug* which ignites the combustible mixture. Within the cylinder is a *piston*, its upper end closed, which is free to move up and down within the cylinder. The section beneath the cylinder is the *crankcase*, in which the *crankshaft* rotates. The crankshaft, as shown in the drawings, has two *webs* and a *crankpin* to which a *connecting rod* is affixed. This latter component is connected also to the piston so that as the piston *reciprocates* (moves up and down) in the cylinder, the reciprocating motion of the piston is converted into a rotary motion of the crankshaft. Missing from the very simple single-cylinder engine we have sketched is the *valve gear*, which opens and closes the valves at the right time, the *carburettor*, which supplies accurately metered proportions of air and fuel to provide a combustible mixture, and a *flywheel* to help to keep the crankshaft rotating smoothly. We are now able to examine the basic Otto cycle.

Look first at figure (a). You will note that the inlet valve is open, the exhaust valve closed, and the piston is at the top of its *stroke* (the distance which it travels up and down within the cylinder) which position is known as *top dead centre*. If we assume that the engine is running the mass of the flywheel will keep the crankshaft turning. This, in turn, will cause the piston to be drawn down in the cylinder, making the close-fitting piston suck in a fuel/air mixture. This is called the *induction stroke*.

Now look at figure (b). The piston has reached its lowest position in the cylinder, known as *bottom dead centre*, and has started on its way up the cylinder again, still being impelled by the

Four-stroke cycle (a) Inlet (b) Compression

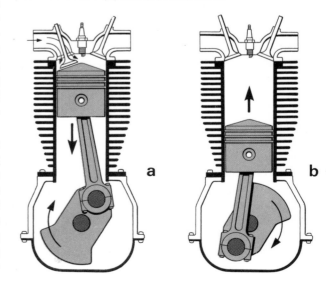

a   b

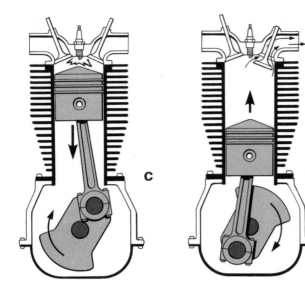

c

d

energy stored in the flywheel. Note carefully that both the inlet valve and exhaust valve are closed. The mixture which has been drawn into the cylinder during the induction stroke cannot escape, and is compressed by the piston as it rises. This is known as the *compression stroke*.

In figure (c) you will see that both valves are still closed, that the piston is again at top dead centre and that the sparking plug has just fired and initiated burning of the fuel/air mixture. As this burns it generates a large volume of hot gas, forcing the piston down the cylinder, in what is called the *power stroke*.

Figure (d) shows the last stroke of the Otto four-stroke cycle. The inlet valve is closed, the exhaust valve open, and the piston is at bottom dead centre. As the piston travels up the cylinder the burned exhaust gases are driven out of the exhaust valve in what is called the *exhaust stroke*. When the piston reaches top dead centre the inlet valve opens and the cycle recommences.

Note that only one of the four strokes is powered, three of them unpowered. This explains why it is unusual (except in motor-cycles) to find a single-cylinder engine. In such an engine there is only one power stroke for two revolutions of the crankshaft. A two-cylinder engine, with the crankpins of the crankshaft *horizontally opposed* (opposite to each other, or separated by 180 degrees) has two power strokes per two crankshaft revolutions. Similarly, a four cylinder engine produces four power strokes per two crankshaft revolutions.

Note also that we have considered only the basic Otto cycle. There are refinements, such as *valve lead* and *valve lag* (opening and closing of valves before and after piston dead-centre positions), and variations of *ignition timing* (the moment when the spark is initiated in a cylinder), to produce maximum engine power.

The combination of the Otto cycle and the petrol engine invented by Gottlieb Daimler in 1885 marked the beginning of a new, compact power source. It was seized upon first by the automobile enthusiasts, and as a result of the spur of competitive road racing events, was developed rapidly into a reliable power source.

The Wright Engine

When the Wright brothers reached that stage in the development of their aircraft when they were almost ready to buy the power plant, they expected to be able to pick one up quickly, 'off the shelf', at a motor engineer's. They were greatly disappointed to discover that no suitable engine existed. All were far too heavy, a facet of engine design of little significance where road transport was concerned.

The Wrights had reached a point in the evolution of their *Flyer* where they considered they could not afford to accept an indeterminable period of delay in obtaining a suitable power plant. With characteristic initiative and determination they designed and built their own four-cylinder *in-line* water-cooled engine, developing about 12*hp* (horse power) for a weight, including fuel and oil, of approximately 200lb (90.7kg), representing a weight of 16.67lb (7.56kg) for each horse power produced.

In-line Engine

The Wrights' engine was, as mentioned above, of the type known as an in-line engine. This means that the four cylinders are in a line, one behind another, and mounted on top of the crankcase. The cylinder at the front is traditionally numbered as 1; in a four-cylinder engine the rearmost is No. 4. Because the cylinder at the front masks the cylinders behind it from the effects of cooling air, it was usual for early in-line engines to rely upon a water-cooling system. This evolved from the type of system common in motor cars, the circulation of the water from the *water-jackets* (around the cylinders) through the *radiator* (cooling medium in the airstream) and back to the engine relying upon *thermo-cycle* flow. This means that the hot water from the engine is taken to the top of the radiator. As it cools it falls to the bottom, inducing a flow which carries this lower-temperature water back to the engine.

At its best it was not a particularly effective means of cooling, which meant that all of these early in-line engines overheated very easily, and an engine which overheats is both inefficient and unreliable. It meant also that attempts to produce engines with increased output were doomed to failure from the start, for increased output meant that more heat needed to be dissipated, and effective means of cooling engines of low power still had to be devised.

The Wright brothers' achievement of powered, sustained, controlled and manned flight in a heavier-than-air craft, on 17 December 1903, might so easily have been the second flight in that category. On 7 October 1903 the 48ft (14.6m) wingspan *Aerodrome*, designed and built by America's Samuel Pierpont Langley, stood poised on its launching ramp, above a houseboat moored in the Potomac River. Its engine roared, the moment of release came and—anti-climax—as the *Aerodrome* surged forward it fouled the launcher and dived into the water. Exactly the same sequence of events occurred at the second attempt, on 8 December 1903. When news of the Wright brothers' success came only a few days later, Langley abandoned further attempts.

Radial Engine

Of particular interest to us is the engine which powered the *Aerodrome*, a five-cylinder *radial* air-cooled engine designed by Langley's assistant, Charles M Manly, and which developed approximately 52hp. The radial engine was evolved as a means of overcoming the cooling problems associated with in-line engines. It has an odd number of cylinders disposed radially around a circular crankcase, the crankcase facing fore and aft, so that all of the engine's cylinders face the airstream. Such an arrangement offers other advantages in addition to improved cooling: the weight of a water-cooling system is eliminated; the very short crankshaft, with a single *throw* (single offset from the crankshaft with two webs and one crankpin), could be made strong enough to prevent it from whipping or bending – then a serious problem with the crankshafts of in-line engines.

During the four years that followed the success of the Wright brothers, there was little significant change in engine design. The greatest progress came in the creation of new radial engines, since they were intended specifically for use by aircraft. In-line engines tended to remain big and heavy, for the primary demand for in-line engines came from the motor sport enthusiasts and the growing motor car industry.

In France, in 1907, Laurent Seguin and his brother began to investigate the shortcomings of the power plants then being used in aircraft. They discovered, only too quickly, that the fundamental problem with all engines then in use was one of overheating. The in-line engine had the advantage of small frontal area but, in addition to its overheating problem, was still penalised by the weight of the cooling system. The air-cooled radial was of no great power, in fact reliable in-line or radial engines of more than 50hp output were very much the exception. The increased drag caused by the larger frontal area of the radial meant that the forward speed of the aircraft in which it was installed was low, impairing cooling efficiency.

The Rotary Engine

The solution evolved by the Seguin brothers was a third type of piston engine known as a *rotary* engine. In all previous engines the crankcase had been mounted rigidly to the *airframe* (the aircraft's basic structure) and had remained stationary while the crankshaft and propeller rotated. In the Seguins' engine the propeller was attached to the crankcase, and propeller, crankcase and cylinders rotated as one, while the crankshaft was stationary and fixed, being attached, indirectly, to the airframe.

Immediately, the cooling problem was resolved, for the cylinders not only faced the airstream, but also milled around in it. And with the cooling problem out of the way the Seguin brothers were able to prove, quite quickly, that reliable engines of increased power output were a practical proposition. Admittedly, it was a little disconcerting on the first occasion you were confronted with a Gnome engine, as the Seguins named it, for it looked distinctly odd with propeller and cylinders spinning around. In fact, this conferred another advantage, for the rotating mass of the engine acted like a large flywheel, so that it ran smoothly at all speeds. It had, also, two disadvantages. Firstly, because crankcase and cylinders were rotating, no very effective exhaust system was feasible, which meant that they were noisy engines. Secondly, the design of the Gnome required that both fuel and oil be fed into the crankcase, which made it essential to use a lubricant that was immiscible with petrol. This accounts for the vegetable castor oil of nostalgic memory. Because the major proportion of this oil reached the cylinders, due to centrifugal action, it was either consumed during combustion or ejected through the exhaust valves. This meant that the oil consumption of early Gnome engines could be anything between 25 and 50 per cent of the fuel consumption, which was a wasteful and filthy business, and both aircraft and pilot received liberal quantities of oil spray.

Not that this in any way deterred the pilots of that era. At last they had available a reliable power plant with an output in excess of 50hp. In fact, by late 1912 there was a range of six Gnome engines varying in horse power from 50 to 160. The latter weighed 312lb (141.5kg), which meant that it produced one horse power for 1.95lb (0.88kg). Compare this with contemporary engines of what were then the four major aircraft building nations. A.B.C. 115hp (Britain): 3.32lb (1.51kg); Anzani 44hp (France): 3.50lb (1.59kg); Curtiss 60hp (America): 5.26lb (2.39kg); Daimler-Mercedes 100hp (Germany): 5.10lb (2.31kg). Within a period of less than five years, the Seguin brothers had developed a range of aircraft engines that, on average and by comparison with engines of other nations, produced double the power for an equivalent weight.

The year 1912, in which this full range of Gnome engines became available, was notable for another happening. On 5 December, at the Gordon-Bennett banquet of the Aero Club of France, a Frenchman named Jacques Schneider offered a trophy valued at £1,000, plus a £1,000 cash prize annually for three years, for a *hydro-aeroplane* (seaplane) race. The rules stipulated, amongst others, that the race must take place over open sea, that competing aircraft must be seaworthy, and that the race must be over a distance of at least 150 nautical miles (173 miles; 278 km).

Jacques Schneider was a well-known figure in France in motor racing and ballooning circles. He had seen how the spur of competition had developed the motor car into a reliable form of transport, capable of long-distance travel. He believed that similar competition between aircraft would achieve similar results. Why seaplanes? He, like many others connected with early aviation, believed that aircraft able to operate from and to a water surface would prove ideal for long-range air travel. After all, seven-tenths of the Earth's surface was covered with water and, like many other people, Schneider believed mistakenly that water would prove softer than land if a forced landing became inevitable.

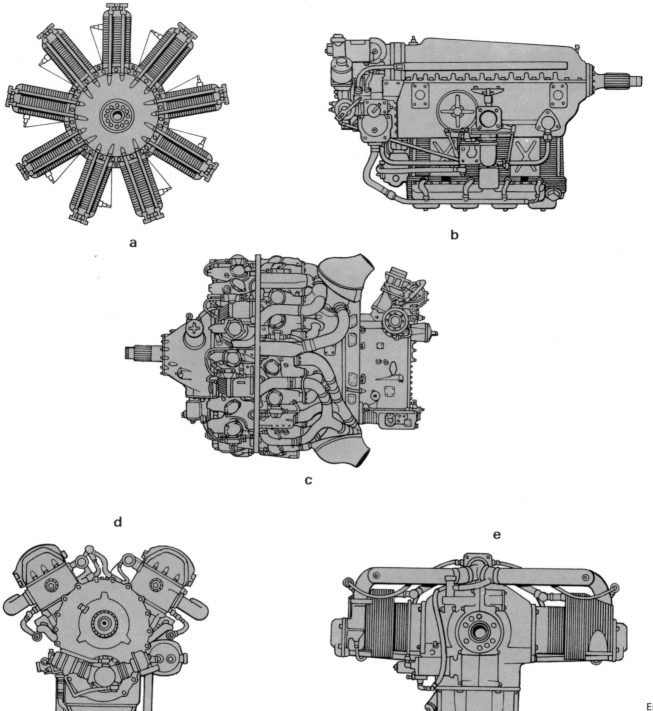

Engine types
(a) Clerget 130hp—rotary
(b) de Havilland Gipsy Major—
in-line four (c) Wright Turbo
Compound—14 cylinder two-row
radial (d) Rolls-Royce Merlin—
Vee 12 (e) Continental IO-360—
flat six

In 1912 it is unlikely that anyone could have forseen the impact that the Schneider Trophy Contests would have, in the nineteen years from their beginning to end, on the development of high-power engines.

Less than two years from the announcement of the Schneider Trophy Contests, World War I began. Not surprisingly, the Gnome power plants assumed a new and even greater importance. Their high power and reliability, by comparison with contemporary engines, meant they were in great demand, not only in France, their country of origin, but by France's allies.

War Developments
It has been stated frequently by aviation writers, some of them historians, that World War I was

responsible for accelerated development of the aeroplane. This is not strictly true. It was responsible, however, for speeding the development of more powerful engines, and their availability brought bigger, but not necessarily better, aircraft.

At the war's outset the Gnome engines dominated the field, but the extensive use demanded by large-scale operational service very quickly pinpointed their shortcomings. The large rotating mass of the engine produced a very pronounced gyroscopic effect, raising considerable complications when installed in a fighter aircraft requiring maximum manoeuvrability. Their fuel and oil consumption was very high, making them totally unsuitable for installation in aircraft intended for long-range roles. When attempts were made to build rotary engines with power outputs in excess of the 160hp of the largest Gnome, it was found that materials then available made the task impracticable.

This meant that the in-line and/or radial engine would have to be developed as rapidly as possible to satisfy the requirements for thousands of engines. On the face of it the radial engine seemed the best bet for military usage: it was easier to maintain, it had no liquid cooling system vulnerable to enemy fire and was also lighter in weight relative to power output, and because of its short, single-throw crankshaft, was not liable to suffer from the crankshaft 'whip' and bearing trouble that was plagueing the early in-line engines.

The in-line enthusiasts were quick to point out that the large frontal area of the radial engines meant excessive drag and that slow speed was inevitable. They forgot, conveniently, that the benefit of the far-smaller frontal area was offset by the weight penalty of a cooling system, its vulnerability to enemy fire, the parasite drag of the cooling radiator/s, and the fact that an in-line engine with its cooling system was more difficult to maintain.

It will be remembered that radial engines had preceded the rotary Gnomes, and that inferior cooling had prevented development of more powerful radials. The upsurge of the Gnome engine had made it imperative for radial engine manufacturers to take a hard look at their cooling problems. Inevitably some water-cooled radial engines appeared, but this was not a solution at all. It merely added together the disadvantages of the radial and in-line types.

The real answer, as was soon discovered, lay in paying far more attention to cylinder design; in particular to the shape, material and disposition of cooling fins so that they could dissipate more heat to the airstream, and also in the development of between-cylinder baffles that ensured the airstream was carried completely around the cylinder.

The Vee-type Engine

The designers and manufacturers of in-line engines had a far more serious problem to resolve. It was not too difficult to improve cooling, by using a water pump to speed circulation of the cooling water and by attention to radiator design. But the mechanical failures resulting from crankshaft whip and the breakdown of bearings needed complete redesign where high-power engines were concerned. This resulted in the evolution of *Vee-type* engines. When viewed from the front there were two banks of cylinders: 8-cylinder engines usually had the two banks of four cylinders separated by an angle of 90 degrees, while a 12-cylinder engine had two banks of six cylinders, separated by an angle of 60 degrees. The result of this design change meant that the length of the crankshaft was almost halved, reducing the tendency to whip, and making for much improved reliability.

It was the in-line engine which benefited most from the demanding development of wartime. In Britain Rolls-Royce produced the Hawk, Falcon and Eagle, the latter a Vee-12 with a maximum power output of 360hp. From Germany came a number of large-capacity six-cylinder water-cooled engines of great reliability. But perhaps the most significant new design was the American Liberty, a water-cooled Vee-12 of simple design intended for mass production. When its teething troubles were overcome it proved to be a reliable engine in the 400hp class.

Many of the successful designs, such as the Hispano-Suiza in-line Vee engines, were built under licence in enormous numbers by Britain, France and the United States, as were many thousands of rotary engines from designers other than the Seguin brothers. By the war's end there were many reliable engines in the 300–400hp class, a significant improvement from the situation at the war's beginning.

Reduction Gears

One feature introduced late in the war was *reduction gears*. Prior to then, the propeller was secured by a hub attached directly to an extension of the crankshaft. This caused inefficiency of both propeller and engine. Of the propeller because it must be small enough and of suitably fine pitch to allow the engine to turn as fast as possible: and the engine would have been more efficient if it could be allowed to turn much faster. A reduction gear between engine and propeller allowed the engine to be run at its optimum speed for maximum output, and reduced the speed of the propeller shaft so that larger diameter, slower turning and more efficient propellers could be developed.

Carburization

It has been mentioned, in connection with the Otto four-stroke cycle, that during the induction stroke a combustible mixture of fuel and air is drawn into the cylinder of an engine. This mixture is supplied by a device known as a *carburettor*, a word derived from carburet, which means to combine an element with carbon. The carburettor combines fuel (a hydrocarbon) and air in the correct proportions to ensure satisfactory combustion. A mixture which is deficient in fuel is known as a *weak* mixture, one which has excess fuel is *rich*.

Air is drawn through the *choke tube* of a carburettor when a piston descends in a cylinder on its induction stroke. The choke tube is, in effect, an annular orifice with a cambered surface. As with an aerofoil section, air is speeded up as it passes through this cambered area, with a localised drop in pressure, this causing fuel to be sucked from a metering jet which is often centrally mounted in the choke tube. Choke tube and jet are matched carefully so that a correct fuel/air mixture reaches the cylinders. A piston engine which gets its combustible mixture in this way is called *normally aspirated* (normal breathing). Clearly, the mixture will be correct only when the air is flowing at a certain speed. Variations of air speed, related to the speed at which the engine is running, are catered for by devices known as slow running, auxiliary and compensating jets, and an accelerator pump supplies extra fuel when sudden increases in engine speed are needed.

Air has density, it will be remembered. If we accept that its relative density at sea level is 1.0, then at 5,000ft (1,525m) it will have fallen to 0.86, at 10,000ft (3,050m) it will be 0.74. At 22,000ft (6,705m) it will be 0.497, which is less than half its density at sea level. What effect has this on an engine as it leaves the ground and begins to climb? Let us imagine that our engine is at 22,000ft (6,705m). The volume of air drawn into the cylinder will be practically the same: the amount of oxygen available to support combustion will be about half. Unless we have done something to reduce the amount of fuel drawn into the cylinders we shall have an excessively rich mixture. If we have reduced the amount of fuel then, quite clearly, with approximately half the fuel and half the oxygen missing, the power output of the engine will suffer drastically.

This means that for every aircraft which is powered there is a height above which it cannot climb, known as its *absolute ceiling*, because that is the height at which the maximum power output of the engine is incapable of taking it any higher. This explains why the under-powered aircraft of the early days could only fly at comparatively low altitudes.

Superchargers

The motor racing fraternity had, quite early in the development of the motor car, discovered they could obtain a greater power output from an engine of any given size if, instead of allowing it to remain normally aspirated, they pumped additional air – plus a balanced amount of fuel – into the cylinders. The pump which they devised for this job they called a *supercharger*: it supercharged the cylinders.

Not surprisingly, supercharging was adopted for aero-engines. It was not required normally to provide additional power at sea level, but to pump more fuel/air mixture into the cylinders as the aircraft climbed, so that its ceiling could be increased very considerably.

Unfortunately, such refinements as reduction gears and superchargers carried penalties. They made the engine bigger and heavier, more complex, and needed power from the engine to drive them. Initially the gains were minimal, but with growing experience and improving technology both of these devices became commonplace and valuable.

Two paragraphs back is the statement that superchargers were 'not required normally to provide additional power at sea level'. One of the obvious exceptions is for racing aircraft, which usually compete against each other at low altitudes, to provide a spectacle for ground-bound enthusiasts. In such applications the supercharger forces fuel/air mixture into the cylinders at low level to allow the engine to develop more power than possible with normal aspiration.

The Schneider Trophy Contests

Between the wars, the pressure of competition did much to bring about aircraft engines of improved reliability and greatly increased power.

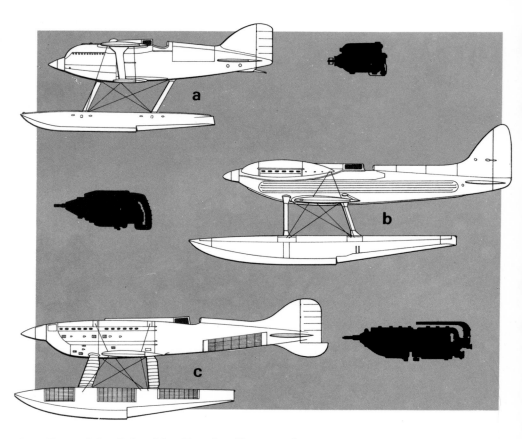

The effect of the Schneider Trophy Contests has been mentioned briefly. In Britain its first impact was on the Napier Lion, a 12-cylinder engine known as a double Vee or 'broad arrow' type, because when viewed from the front its three banks of four cylinders looked like an inverted arrowhead, the two outer banks each being inclined at 60 degrees to the central, vertical bank. Designed by A J Rowledge in 1916, it emphasised the desire to reduce the engine length to a minimum to achieve a high-powered compact unit with a short crankshaft. His success is measured by an engine which produced 450hp in 1919 being developed progressively to give no less than 900hp in the Lion VIIA version of 1927.

In America a very significant piston engine was developed for use in the aircraft known originally as Curtiss Navy Racers. Built first to take part in the Pulitzer races, they were later modified and re-designated to compete in the 1923 Schneider Contest. The engine which powered them was the Curtiss D-12, combined with a special all-metal Curtiss/Reed propeller. Very compact, and of abnormally small frontal area, it developed 480hp. Its Curtiss/Reed propeller, of small diameter, was able to provide very efficient performance without requiring a reduction gear, so that more of the engine's power was available for propulsion.

When Britain's Richard Fairey (later Sir Richard) first saw this engine/propeller combination he realised immediately its great potential and obtained licence rights to build it in Britain. Installed in a new two-seat day bomber for the Royal Air Force it proved almost embarrassingly successful, for the Fairey Fox, as it was called, could outpace any contemporary fighter aircraft in service.

For Italy, too, the Contest spurred development of a number of exceptional engines. The penultimate Contest in which the Italian team competed, in 1927, produced Fiat in-line engines

Engine development through Schneider Trophy racing
(a) Curtiss R3C-4, Curtiss V-1500 engine, 708hp (b) Supermarine S6B, Rolls-Royce 'R' engine, 2350hp (c) Macchi MC72, coupled Fiat AS6 engine, 3300hp

of 1,000hp. At Calshot, in 1929, the Macchi M.67s were powered by Isotta-Fraschini engines of 1,400hp. The ultimate of Italian in-line engine development was the Fiat AS.6, a 24-cylinder Vee-type evolved by combining two AS.5 engines on a common crankcase. In its finalised form, installed in the Macchi MC.72 seaplane, and burning an exotic fuel mixture prescribed by Britain's F Rodwell Banks, it developed 3,100hp. With this aircraft/power plant combination Italy set a world speed record of 440.68mph (709.20 km/h) which remained unbroken until mid-1939.

In Britain, Rolls-Royce began development of an engine known as the Buzzard to power the new Supermarine S.6 seaplane being designed by R J Mitchell to take part in the 1929 Schneider Contest at Cowes. A Vee-12 liquid-cooled engine, it had developed 925hp on bench tests in July 1928. Just over a year later, Rolls-Royce engineers had advanced this engine to produce no less than 1,900hp. Two years later, the basic design remaining the same, the engine known as the 'R' (racing) developed 2,350hp when it powered the Supermarine S.6B to carry off the Trophy for Britain. This aircraft/engine combination had considerable influence on the Spitfire/Merlin configuration which by its wartime exploits won a permanent place in the history of Britain and its Royal Air Force.

World War II did much to advance still further the capability and reliability of high-powered piston engines. By its end power outputs in excess of 2,000hp were commonplace, and in America Pratt & Whitney and Wright had both evolved superb air-cooled radial engines of even higher power. By then, however, the supreme reign of the piston engine was nearing its end.

Sir Frank Whittle
In 1928, while a Cadet at RAF Cranwell, Frank Whittle (later Sir Frank) wrote a thesis in which he proposed a new type of engine to power future generations of aircraft. Far simpler, and potentially lighter in weight than piston engines of equivalent power, this engine of which Whittle wrote was not a completely new idea. Earlier inventors had suggested that it should be possible to propel an aeroplane by a reaction jet: it was Frank Whittle who first detailed the thermodynamic principles upon which such an engine would operate.

Before we can even start to consider the development of the turbojet engine and its derivatives, it is essential that we clear up exactly what is meant by two words in the previous paragraph – reaction jet. The great English mathematician and scientist, Sir Isaac Newton, published in 1687 a work entitled Philosophiae Naturalis Principia Mathematica. One very small item in this publication, his third law of motion, contains the propulsive secret of the turbojet. Newton stated quite simply that 'to every action there is an equal and opposite reaction.' However simply stated, it is not quite so easy for the layman to understand. Let us try to do so by thinking of everyday examples. Our garden hosepipe, when the water is turned on, quite noticeably tries to move towards us, away from the jet of water it is discharging. This is not because the water is pressing against the air, but because of the opposite reaction of the pressure of the water's discharge. If the tap is full on, then slowly turned down, we can feel the difference in the reaction of the hosepipe. If we connect the hose to a garden sprinkler, when the water is turned on the rotating jets will spin, by reaction.

Most readers of this book will, by the medium of television or film, have seen a giant manned or unmanned rocket being launched into space. Earlier in this chapter we spoke of the density of the air to which we give a relative figure of 1.0 at sea level. As mentioned there, this falls to below half at a height of 22,000ft (6,705m). At 40,000ft (12,195m) it is below a quarter: at 300,000ft (91,440m), which is a little more than 56 miles (91km) high, the atmosphere has no significant density. Our relative density of 1.0 has, at that height, fallen to 0.0000015. In other words, if the efflux (gases being discharged) from a rocket needed something against which to push, then space flight above 56 miles (91km) would be impossible. By our own knowledge rockets can travel millions of miles into space, and still be directed onto new courses by the reaction of small rocket motors – which have no air to push against.

Perhaps this is a good point to distinguish between rocket engines and air-breathing engines, whether they be piston engines or turbojets. Conventional engines carry with them a fuel supply: this must be combined with the oxygen in the air to create a combustible mixture. These are the air-breathing engines, which must be operated within Earth's atmosphere where there is sufficient oxygen available for combustion. Rocket engines carry with them fuels which, by chemical decomposition or by combustion with liquid oxygen carried in the rocket, make them independent of atmosphere oxygen and able to operate in the airless conditions of outer space.

The Jet Engine
The engine which Frank Whittle demonstrated for the first time on 12 April 1937, was the world's first turbojet engine designed specifically for aircraft propulsion. Essentially a heat engine, using air as a working fluid to provide thrust, it may be termed more accurately a gas turbine engine. It is interesting to record that working quite independently in Germany, Dr Pabst von Ohain was bench testing a very similar engine in September of the same year. A developed version of this engine powered the world's first jet-powered aircraft, the Heinkel He 178, which made its first real flight at Marienehe airfield on 27 August 1939. It was not until 15 May 1941 that the Gloster/Whittle E.28/39, powered by a single 860lb (390kg) static thrust Whittle W.1 turbojet engine, became Britain's first jet-powered aircraft.

What many people do not appreciate is that a gas turbine has a working cycle that is very similar to that of the Otto cycle. Air is drawn in through the intake, corresponding to the induction stroke; it is compressed in an axial or centrifugal flow compressor; and combustion is followed by exhaust of the propulsive gases via the tail pipe. This is a very simplified description. There is one aspect in which it is very different from a piston engine: the working cycle of the gas turbine is continuous, not intermittent, with the result that it is a much more smoothly running engine. Combustion occurs at moderate pressure, by comparison with the peak pressure of the piston engine, which must serve to power three other strokes of the engine, meaning that the combustion chamber/s can be of quite lightweight construction. One other point should be understood: equivalent thrust can be provided by giving low velocity to a large mass of air (piston-engine/propeller combination), or by giving high velocity to a small mass of air (turbojet).

The turbojet is, as stated earlier, essentially a heat engine, air being the working medium which takes in and gives up heat. The air is at *ambient temperature* (that of the surrounding air) until it is compressed; this increases its pressure and temperature and reduces its volume. When fuel is added to produce combustion there is an increase of temperature and volume, and since there is little resistance to the exit of this air the pressure remains almost constant. In the final stage, when the gas stream has work to do – driving the turbine to turn the compressor – temperature and pressure falls but the volume of the gas increases enormously to produce the high-velocity jet efflux and its equivalent reaction.

In its simplest form a turbojet comprises a shaft mounted on bearings, carrying at its forward end a compressor and at its aft end a turbine. This is mounted within a closely tailored casing. Between the compressor and the turbine is a combustion area. If we assume that the engine is running, air is being taken in at the forward end and is then passed through the compressor. Compression ratios vary quite considerably, governed by the type of compressor; the higher the pressure ratio, the higher the engine efficiency. Air leaves the compressor and enters the combustion chamber, where fuel, usually kerosene, is added to the air by atomiser jets and burns to produce a large volume of hot gas. Of the total airflow something less than about 30 per cent is used for combustion, the remainder being mixed with these high-temperature gases to help cool them before they pass into the turbine. The gas passing through the turbine provides the necessary power to drive the compressor and such essential accessories as fuel and oil pumps. Once the engine has been started it is self-sustaining until all the fuel has been consumed, or the engine has been purposely stopped.

Compressors

There are two basic kinds of compressor: the centrifugal and axial flow. The former was used for most early turbojets, being easier to manufacture and proving far more robust. The axial flow compressor has since been extensively developed, so that by utilising one which consists of several stages it is possible to achieve fairly high rates of compression, with ratios of 30:1 (thirty times atmospheric pressure) being obtainable without difficulty. The axial compressor also has the advantage of consuming far more air than

a centrifugal compressor of similar frontal area: this means that it produces more *thrust* for the same frontal area.

Thrust is the term we use to compare the power outputs of turbojet engines. The maximum thrust it can develop for take-off, the engine being stationary, is expressed in pounds (kilograms) of *static thrust* (st).

If we look at a diagram of a turbojet engine, we can see that as air enters the inlet it comes first to the several stages of the compressor. Their number will vary according to the degree of compression required, for up to a point each additional stage will increase the pressure of the air. Aft of the compressor is the combustion chamber which, in the early turbojets, consisted of a number of individual *burner cans*. The current trend is for an *annular combustion chamber*, capable of passing a greater volume of air, but at least one American manufacturer prefers a combination of the two, known as a *can-annular chamber*.

One of the most critical design and manufacturing areas of the turbojet is that of the compressor, the primary problem being to find ways and means of keeping the air moving smoothly through the compressor under the majority of conditions. If surging develops the compressor blades stall and lose their efficiency. One way of overcoming this is to have an engine which has a two-shaft layout. This comprises a large-diameter outer shaft mounting, say, a four-stage compressor at its forward end and a single turbine stage to drive it at the aft end. Running co-axially within the outer shaft is a smaller-diameter shaft with, perhaps, three more compressor stages forward and a turbine stage aft. The four-stage compressor at the front is termed a low-pressure (LP compressor), the three-stage compressor immediately behind it is known as the high-pressure (HP compressor). This permits the two shafts, or *spools* as they are called frequently, each to be run at the best possible speed to maintain a smooth airflow through the engine, having regard to the operating conditions.

Early turbojets soon demonstrated their advantages by comparison with the highly developed piston engines, being lighter in weight for a given power output, smoother running and able to move aircraft into new, higher speed

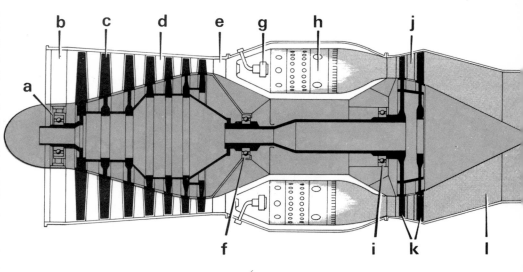

Section through typical jet engine
(a) Front bearing (b) Inlet guide vanes (c) Compressor blades (7 stages) (d) Stator blade (e) Diffuser section (f) Centre bearing (g) Fuel spray manifold (h) Combustion chamber (i) Rear bearing (j) Turbine guide vane (k) Two-stage turbine blade (l) Exhaust duct

ranges. The major disadvantage was their much higher fuel consumption, and this led to development of the *turboprop* (propeller-turbine) engine. This is another of the compromise solutions, a certain amount of speed and cruising altitude being sacrificed to save fuel, and there is a plus: the benefit of the lighter weight, smooth turbine. In this type of engine a reduction gear and propeller is driven from the turbine shaft, and a turbine engine which is used with a geared power take off for helicopter propulsion is called a *turboshaft* engine.

Since the introduction of turbojet engines they, like the piston engines which formerly dominated the scene, have been developed progressively. Today they are able to produce thrust ratings undreamed of at the time that the Gloster/Whittle E.28/39 first took to the air; they are far easier to maintain and have TBOs (time between overhauls) running into thousands of hours; and fuel consumption has been brought down to a far more realistic level.

Turbofan Engines

The most significant contribution to lower fuel consumption has come from the evolution of *turbofan* engines. Engineers developing a new two-spool turbojet discovered that by increasing the diameter of the low-pressure compressor it was possible to channel off the air from the tip of the compressor blades, taking it through a duct surrounding the HP compressor, combustion chamber and turbines, and discharging it to mix with the hot gases in the *tailpipe*, or ducting leading away from the engine. This means that the jet efflux is of low velocity and high propulsive efficiency. However, less thrust is produced as a result of this lower velocity, which means that a

turbofan in any particular power rating is of greater diameter than a turbojet of equivalent thrust so that it can pass a larger total mass airflow. Early turbofan engines had a by-pass ratio of less than 1:1; the American Pratt & Whitney JT3D had a ratio of 1:1, meaning that as much air was by-passed around the engine as was used in the combustion process. Pratt & Whitney's engines which power the Boeing 747 'Jumbo jet' have a by-pass ratio of more than 5:1.

Pulse- and Ramjets

Our review of the development of power plants would be incomplete without a brief mention of *pulse-jets* and *ramjets*, two other types of jet engine. The former was the type of engine which powered the German wartime V1 flying-bomb, and has inlet shutter-valves which are spring-loaded into an open position. Air passing the open valves enters the combustion chamber, mixes with injected fuel and burns. The sudden rise in pressure slams the inlet valves shut and the efflux streams from the tail pipe. When the pressure drops the inlet valves re-open and the intermittent cycle of operations continues.

A ramjet, unlike any of the engines discussed in this section, is purely and simply a heat engine with no major rotating components. It is known technically as an aero-thermodynamic-duct, or athodyd for short, and this is an accurate description of the engine. It has another unique distinction, it must be moving through the air before it can operate, and cannot be used by an aircraft which has to take off conventionally. When it is moving, air is forced into its intake and, because of the aerodynamic profile of the continuous intake, combustion and propulsion duct, immediately loses speed and gains pressure. This is increased by the combustion of fuel, and the expanding gases accelerate to atmosphere through the propulsion nozzle.

It appeared at one time that the ramjet had no application as a power plant for aircraft, it being considered suitable only for missiles which had already been accelerated to high speed by other means. This is no longer strictly true, for as designers look into the future to find ways and means of travelling even faster, this type of power plant becomes of considerable interest. Engines like those used in Lockheed's SR-71A reconnaissance aircraft are such that only about 18 per cent of the propulsive thrust comes from the turbojet when the aircraft is travelling at speeds in excess of Mach 3 (three times the speed of sound). The remaining thrust is developed by aerodynamic formation of the inlet and exhaust nozzles, meaning that, in effect, the major portion of the thrust comes from the ramjet principle.

It will be interesting to see whether, as further evolution of the turbojet takes place, future generations of very high-speed aircraft are powered by engines which are classed as turbo-ramjets, working as turbojets for take-off and acceleration to a speed where the ramjet is able to produce the total thrust. Only time, and the unending process of power plant development, will provide an answer to this question.

Types of gas turbines
(a) Turboprop (b) Turbofan
(c) Turboshaft

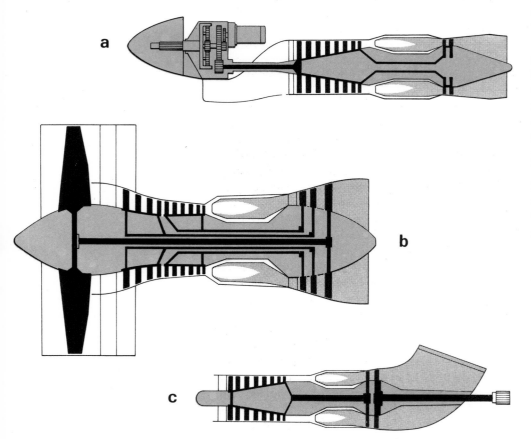

Design Revolution II Airframes

Towards the end of the 18th century Britain's Sir George Cayley was busy with design and construction of a model heavier-than-air craft. When this flew in 1804 it became the world's first successful model glider, comprising a kite-form monoplane wing and movable cruciform tail surfaces, mounted on a fuselage pole which might well have originated from a domestic broom.

In less than one and three-quarter centuries this simple basic idea has been developed to provide giant transports able to speed passengers safely and comfortably across oceans and continents, military aircraft of great deterrent power, and a host of specialised aeroplanes which help the peoples of the world to cope with the changing environment in which they live. But before any of this astonishing progress could take place, men had to find the means of accomplishing heavier-than-air flight.

The first really successful individual was the German. Otto Lilienthal, who achieved more than 2,000 flights in his beautifully built hang gliders. He was their power plant, using his muscles to launch the aircraft into the air and a combination of muscle and weight to control them in flight. Such aircraft demanded very lightweight construction, and Lilienthal achieved this by making the framework of peeled willow wands which he covered with waxed linen cloth. There was no landing gear, power plant or controls. Lilienthal controlled the aircraft in flight by body movements, a factor which caused him to crash to his death in 1896.

By the time that the Wright brothers first flew, just over seven years later, there had been quite a few changes. The *Flyer*'s airframe was constructed from wood, the wings and control surfaces covered with muslin, and it was powered by a piston engine driving contra-rotating pusher propellers. It was of biplane configuration, resulting from the necessity of having a lightweight but reasonably rigid structure with the maximum lifting surface. The forward-mounted biplane elevators were controlled by a lever in front of the pilot; wing-warping and movement of the dual rudders were achieved by cables attached to a hip-cradle moved by the pilot's body. The aircraft's landing gear consisted of two wooden skids. Innumerable bracing wires laced together wings, elevator mounting and rudder mounting.

This sort of construction, in varying configurations, was to become reasonably standard for some time. Lack of engine power dictated the lightest possible structure and large wing area.

Gross wing area of the *Flyer* was 510sq ft (47.38m²), more than double that of a Spitfire: these two aircraft – separated by only 33 years – had maximum gross weights of 750lb (340kg) and 8,160lb (3,700kg) respectively.

Blériot's Feat

A significant event occurred on 25 July 1909, when the Frenchman Louis Blériot succeeded in winning a prize of £1,000 offered by the *Daily Mail* newspaper for the first crossing of the English Channel by a heavier-than-air craft. Significant, because it emphasised for the first time that natural barriers, such as the Channel, no longer offered to a nation isolation and security.

The aircraft which Blériot flew on that day was of his own design and construction, and represented at a very early date what was to become a standard configuration. Monoplane wings, forward-mounted engine with tractor propeller, pilot's cockpit aft of the wings, rudder and tailplane at the aft end of the fuselage, and a tailwheel type landing gear. Its wing area was only 150sq ft (13.93m²), and with a gross weight of 661lb (300kg) it had a wing loading almost three times that of the *Flyer*. An engine of double the power and airframe of far 'cleaner' configuration showed, even at this early date, that development of airframe and power plant would soon make the aeroplane a vehicle of importance.

A little over 8 months later, on 28 March 1910, Frenchman Henri Fabre achieved the world's first take-off from water by a powered heavier-than-air craft. This was another dead-end design of odd configuration, the fuselage comprising two beams that supported biplane surfaces at their forward end, and an immense vertical fin and a monoplane wing aft. Its most important feature was the design of the floats, three of which supported the aircraft on the water, and Fabre floats were to be used to equip many of the early water-borne aircraft. Power plant of this machine was an aft-mounted Gnome of 50hp, driving a two-blade pusher propeller.

Less than a year later, on 26 January 1911, Glenn Curtiss in America flew a *hydro-aeroplane* (seaplane) version of his *June Bug*. Like the Blériot monoplane, it took enormous strides forward. The Curtiss water-cooled engine was mounted between the biplane wings, the pilot seated forward of the wings, with a forward-mounted elevator and aft-mounted tailplane and rudder.

These four aircraft, mentioned briefly, show how quickly came initial development of the aeroplane's structure. Though we read and hear much of the stick-and-string construction of the pioneers, none of these aircraft can really be said to fall into such a category. In any event, the term 'stick-and-string' gives a very wrong impression, because most of the early aircraft benefited from the high skill of woodworkers able to fashion components of functional beauty.

It is important to remember that many of the pioneers were attempting to produce an aeroplane with little, if any, financial backing. Typical was Britain's A V Roe (later Sir Alliott), who practically starved himself to save enough money to continue with his experiments. This meant that his Roe I triplane was constructed of wood instead of steel tubing as intended, covered with brown paper instead of fabric, and powered by a totally unsuitable 9hp J.A.P. engine. With it he achieved the first flight in Britain in an all-British aeroplane, on 13 July 1909.

One of the vital factors in the accelerating development of the airframe was the evolution of the Gnome rotary engine. For the first time there was available a reliable engine with a margin of power. This meant that designers could concentrate on improving the airframe, instead of being compelled to build the very lightest aircraft possible, cutting out new ideas in case they proved aerodynamically detrimental.

When they began to look around, the pioneers soon realised they could do much to improve the performance of their aircraft by concentrating their efforts to lessen drag. They started by using streamline sections, found ways and means of improving construction so that a reduction could be made in the mass of struts and wires that were used to give rigidity, and began to appreciate that a robust-looking, heavy component was not necessarily the strongest.

Reconnaissance Craft

Competitive involvement of aircraft in Europe and Britain did much to improve performance as did their use for military purposes. But as they were a noisy and expensive means of getting from A to B, high-ranking officers of the Army could see little employment prospects for them. They admitted, a little grudgingly, that because they could fly over a battlefield they might prove useful for reconnaissance.

Such attitudes help explain that despite the fact a British Royal Flying Corps (RFC) was founded in 1912, with Military and Naval wings, the RFC went to France in the late summer of 1914 with only 63 aircraft. France had rather more aircraft, generally of better performance, plus the best aircraft industry in the world. This was to prove invaluable to the Allies, for France was able not only to meet her own needs during the four years of World War I, but to supply hundreds of excellent aircraft to those countries helping to fight the battle for French survival. German military leaders had been sufficiently farsighted to visualise the aeroplane as a useful adjunct to the Army, and entered the war with the largest air force in the world, comprising approximately 260 aircraft.

Most advanced of the aircraft flown by the RFC at the war's beginning was the BE2a, originating from the Royal Aircraft Factory at Farnborough, where it had been designed by an up and coming young man called Geoffrey de Havilland. Of biplane construction, with conventional tailplane, elevators and rudder, wheeled main landing gear with twin skids forward of the axle to prevent 'nosing over' and a tail skid, the BE2a was powered by a 70hp Renault engine, driving a four-blade tractor propeller. There was an aft cockpit for the pilot and a forward cockpit for the observer. It carried no armament.

It did not take long for these reconnaissance aircraft to prove their worth. So much so, indeed, that they were soon equipped with cameras so that visual evidence could support a written report. The provision of simple wireless made it possible to spot and range for artillery batteries, making the ground-based units more effective than ever before. Within a short space of time it was appreciated by both sides that the reconnaissance aircraft had become a confounded nuisance, and something must be done to prevent enemy aircraft from having free access to your airspace.

The Birth of Fighters

From this need the fighter aircraft evolved, more accurately fighter-escorts, their duties including the destruction of enemy reconnaissance aircraft and the escort and protection of their own 'recce' counterparts over enemy territory. There was little doubt that the most suitable vehicle for such a task would be a small, highly manoeuvrable aircraft with a forward-mounted engine, tractor propeller and forward-firing machine-gun. Unfortunately, the ideal position for the gun meant that it would have to fire through the propeller disc, which was quite impossible without shooting off one's own propeller blades.

France's Roland Garros overcame this problem by fitting metal deflectors to the blades of his propeller so that, when a gun was mounted in the ideal position to be sighted by the pilot, the occasional bullet which hit the blades glanced off the deflectors without causing damage. His new

Wing sections
(a) Wright Flyer—all wood
(b) Sopwith Camel—all wood with wire trailing edge (c) Armstrong Whitworth interwar type—light alloy, fabric covered (d) Hawker Hunter—all metal, pressed ribs (e) B70—all metal, honeycomb panels and steel spars (f) A300B—machined ribs and skins (g) Modern sailplane section (typical)—bonded glass-fibre

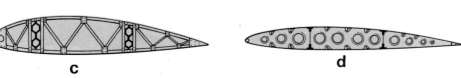

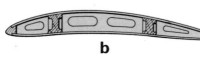

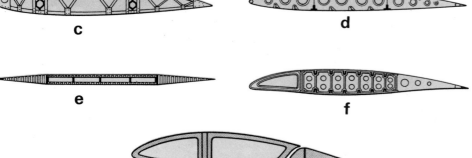

tactics brought immediate success, and he destroyed three German aircraft before having to force-land in German territory, where the significance of his forward-firing gun was soon appreciated. It did not take very long for Anthony Fokker to design an interrupter gear that 'timed' the firing of the machine-gun so that bullets could pass between the blades of a revolving propeller. When fitted to Fokker Type E monoplanes the resulting combination was so effective that, during the latter half of 1915 and early 1916, the German air force almost shot the Allied air forces from the sky. It was this period of German ascendancy which gave rise to the legendary 'Fokker scourge'.

You will have noticed the comment that the Fokker Type E was of monoplane configuration. Germany and France had both discovered the benefits of the monoplane wing, which was free of so many struts and bracing wires. The biplane wing not only suffered from the parasite drag of these struts and wires, but it was discovered there was a phenomenon called *biplane interference*. Simply put, the low-pressure area above the lower aerofoil surface tended to be destroyed by the high pressure beneath the upper aerofoil, both becoming less efficient in the process. One solution was to increase the gap between them, but obviously one must effect a compromise between aerodynamic gain and the increased structural weight and drag. Another remedy was to stagger the wings in relation to each other, most often the upper wing being mounted forward of the lower, and the optimum gap and stagger were usually combined. A third method of easing the problem was to adopt a sesquiplane configuration, in effect a compromise between monoplane and biplane construction. Generally a small-span lower wing was retained to assist structural integrity, allowing a major proportion of the larger-span upper wing to function as a monoplane wing, more or less free from biplane interference.

Not that British designers were blind to the benefits of a monoplane wing – in fact, many had favoured such a configuration before the beginning of World War I. Unfortunately, a number of accidents involving monoplanes had caused the War Office to impose a temporary ban on the construction of such aircraft. By the time it was lifted the war had started, and manufacturers were kept too busy to alter designs.

As the war progressed it became clear that it was inadequate to rely upon anti-aircraft guns, fighters, fighter-escorts and reconnaissance aircraft alone. Such a course meant that the side with the best fighters held the trump cards, which made it desirable to attack the airfields from which they operated or the factories where they were built.

Bombers

Thus evolved the bomber aircraft, large machines with two or more engines, their size being necessary to give sufficient payload capability for weapons to attack the enemy targets, plus adequate fuel to confer medium or long-range capability. In Britain Handley Page developed the 0/100 and 0/400 to this requirement, the latter being powered by, among other engines, two 360hp Rolls-Royce Eagles or 350hp Liberty 12s. Tests showed the latter configuration could carry a bomb load of 3,000lb (1,360kg).

Germany, faced with a similar requirement, developed first the Gotha G IV and G V, used in daylight raids on Britain. Subsequently they evolved the Zeppelin Staaken 'R' series of giant aircraft, powered by four 245hp Maybach or 260hp Mercedes 6-cylinder water-cooled engines. Over short ranges these could carry some 4,400lb (2,000kg) of bombs, and one of them dropped the first 2,200lb (1,000kg) bomb on Britain on the night of 16/17 February 1918.

As the war neared its end Vickers Ltd., in Britain, produced a large twin-engined night bomber known as the Vimy. The most significant version was the Mk IV, powered by two 360hp Rolls-Royce Eagle engines, but no Vimys were completed in time to see operational service in World War I. It was, as we shall see a little later, to become an important aeroplane.

The pressure of war had done much to develop new, more powerful and reliable engines. Because these power plants were so much better than those at the war's beginning, bigger aeroplanes had become reality.

It was certainly not a case of aerodynamic refinement making possible bigger and better aircraft on very much the same sort of horsepower. In fact, the eternal cry of the designer to the engine maker was 'give us more power'. And when they got it, it was used to its full potential without any real improvement in the airframe.

The All-Metal Monoplane

The war had seen the beginning of some improvements in airframe construction, especially from Fokker and Junkers in Germany. The Dutch-born designer, Anthony Fokker, had decided early in the war to forget about conventional wooden construction and concentrate on the use of a welded steel-tube fuselage structure which was fabric covered. Dr Hugo Junkers had pioneered the construction of all-metal monoplanes early in the war, but though performance was then somewhat indifferent, due to the combination of heavy weight and low power, aircraft of all-metal construction and the Fokker type of steel-tube construction were one day to become normal, instead of exceptional.

With a return to peace it was expected that there would be a boom in civil aviation. This failed to materialise, largely because air travel was very expensive, but also because the general public believed that it needed rather more than average courage to become involved in such a risky form of transport. But if aircraft were to be developed to new standards of speed and reliability, to make them suitable as mass carriers, then a thriving travel and aircraft industry was necessary to generate the money to finance development. Many advances in later years were to come as a result of the evolution of new military aircraft when, in effect, a manufacturer was subsidised by the government. In the years immediately following World War I few governments

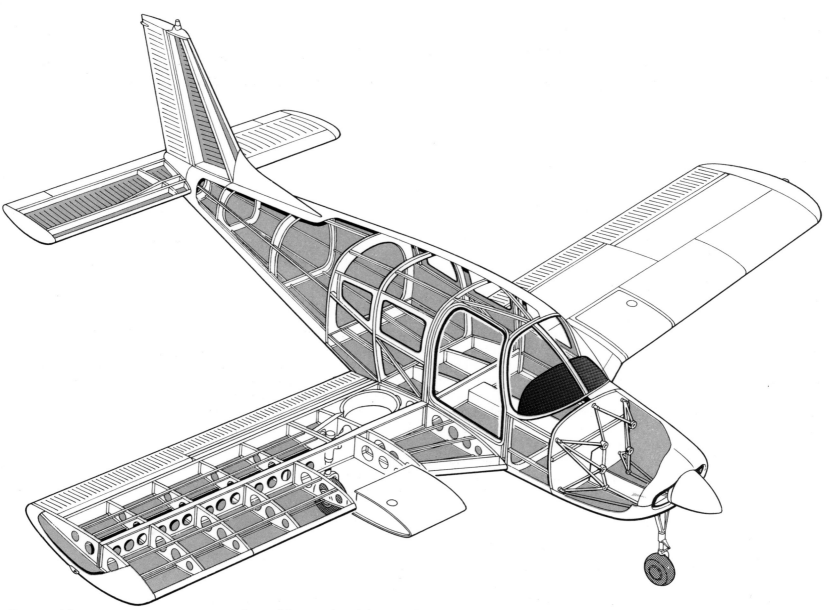

Cutaway of the structure of a typical light aircraft, the Piper Cherokee

wanted anything to do with aeroplanes, unless it was to dispose of as profitably as possible the large numbers of surplus aircraft, engines and accessories with which they had ended the war.

More advanced thought, around the world, could see that the solution was to make the general public conscious of the fact that air travel was safe and, comparatively speaking, fast. When sufficient people wanted to travel by air, designers of aircraft, engines and all related equipment would soon discover ways and means of providing suitable aircraft. The first real hurdle was for the potential customer to realise that air travel could be both safe and fast.

Two flights across the North Atlantic and the design of a revolutionary aircraft in Britain did much to make the man-in-the-street, wherever he lived, aware that the aeroplane had become more than a toy of the wealthy sportsman, or a weapon of war.

The first of the two flights, made in June 1919, was that of Captain John Alcock and Lieutenant Arthur Whitten Brown, from St John's, Newfoundland, to Clifden, Eire, a distance of 1,890 miles (3,042km) non-stop, in a time of 16hr 27min. The aircraft used on this historical flight was a Vickers Vimy, which explains the comment earlier that it was to prove an important aircraft. In fact, the Vimy was used also for Ross and Keith Smith's first England to Australia flight in December 1919, when a distance of 11,130 miles

(17,912km) was covered in an elapsed flying time of 135hr 55min. Vimys too, were used also for the first – but not completely successful – attempt to fly from England to Cape Town.

The next event, chronologically, was the design and construction of a small biplane aircraft by the de Havilland company in Britain. Known as the D H Moth, it first flew on 22 February 1925 and was an immediate success. It is an important aeroplane because, more than any other aircraft, it was responsible for development of the flying club movement around the world. In a D H Moth an unknown girl from Hull, Yorkshire, called Amy Johnson flew solo from England to Australia in May 1930, to record her name in aviation history.

Charles Lindbergh

The real clincher came in 1927, the flight that electrified the world and convinced men and women that the aeroplane had really come of age. Taking off from New York on 20 May 1927, in an aircraft named *Spirit of St Louis*, a little-known American airmail pilot called Charles Lindbergh headed out over the Atlantic and into history. Just $33\frac{1}{2}$ hours later he landed his single-engine aircraft safely at Le Bourget airport, Paris, after a 3,600-mile (5,794km) non-stop flight. Brave people like Alcock and Brown, Amy Johnson, Charles Lindbergh, Charles Kingsford Smith (who achieved the first crossing of the Pacific

Ocean) and Floyd Bennett, who piloted Admiral Byrd on the first crossing of the North Pole, showed that the time had come to accept the aeroplane as a transport vehicle of real importance. Unfortunately, it was still an expensive form of travel.

By this time there had been some important developments with many new and significant aeroplanes entering service. Junkers in Germany had evolved the Ju 52/3M, a three-engine transport used widely on European routes in the 1930s. Ford in America and Fokker in Holland had developed similar types, the Ford Trimotor proving so enduring that isolated examples remain in service to this day. All three had more than monoplane configuration as a common factor: all were of light alloy (aluminium alloy) construction.

The Schneider Trophy Contests, mentioned briefly in the previous chapter, had contributed to the evolution of new, clean monoplane designs. Some really beautiful streamlined seaplanes had emerged as designers sought to gain the Trophy for their country, notably from Britain and Italy. And although the machines designed to compete in the Contests had not directly supported the development of long-range transport by air – the dream of Jacques Schneider – one class of water-borne transport aircraft, in the shape of the long-range flying-boat, dominated the overseas intercontinental routes until the advent of World War II.

Flying-Boats

Flying-boats such as Britain's 'Empire Boats' built by Short Brothers for Imperial Airways, Germany's Dornier Wals for the infant Lufthansa, and Martin M.130 and Sikorsky S.42 Clippers for America's rapidly growing air routes are remembered nostalgically to this day. And it was the American-built Boeing 314 flying-boat with which Pan American inaugurated the first scheduled passenger services across the North Atlantic on 8 July 1939. The future of the flying-boat might then have seemed reasonably secure. In fact, its life span had been limited some nine years earlier.

In May 1930 the Boeing Company, in America, had flown one of the most revolutionary aircraft in the history of commercial aviation. Known as the Monomail and powered by a Pratt & Whitney Hornet radial engine of only 575hp, it achieved completely new standards of performance as a result of aerodynamic refinements. Of all-metal construction, it had a smooth monoplane wing free from struts and bracing wires, main landing gear that retracted into the wing after take-off, and the drag of its single radial engine was reduced enormously by a newly developed cowling.

The success of the Monomail inspired Boeing to evolve a multi-engine transport designated Model 247. First flown in 1933, it featured such advanced ideas as variable-pitch propellers, de-icing equipment for the leading-edges of aerofoil surfaces, and control-surface trim tabs. Like the Monomail which had preceded it, it had re-tractable landing gear and its two 550hp Pratt &

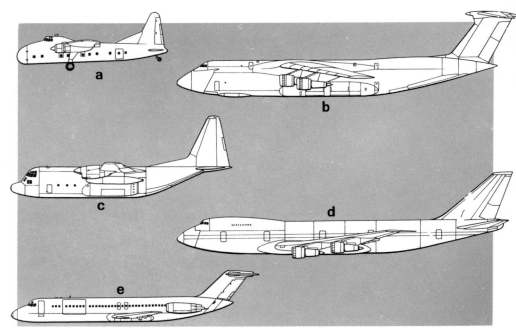

Freight aircraft types
(a) Bristol Freighter (b) Lockheed Galaxy (c) Lockheed Hercules (d) Boeing 747F (e) McDonnell Douglas DC9

Whitney radial engines were housed in improved cowlings. The Boeing 247 provided completely new standards of air travel, and its ten passengers were assured of equally new standards of safety for it was the world's first twin-engined monoplane airliner able to climb on only one engine with a full load.

The Douglas DC-3

In its wake came first the Douglas DC-1 and DC-2, followed by one of the most famous airliners in the entire history of aviation, the Douglas DC-3. First flown in December 1935, this superb twin-engined passenger aircraft dominated the American air transport scene in the late 1930s and more than 10,000 were built for military use in World War II. Many remain in airline service around the world to this day, more than 40 years after its first flight.

In retrospect it seems surprising that, when Britain and France became involved in war with Hitler's Germany in the autumn of 1939 they, and many other nations, should still have considerable numbers of biplane aircraft. Isolated examples served and survived with distinction, primarily because they had special characteristics that more than made up for lack of performance. A typical example is the Fairey Swordfish flown by pilots of Britain's Fleet Air Arm. Slow, rugged and dependable, its magnificent handling qualities were to ensure that it survived its intended replacement and remained in operational service until the war's end.

But, in the main, all-metal monoplane aircraft emerged as the dominant configuration during the six years of the war. And once again the spur of combat accelerated the rate of development. This time airframe, power plants, equipment and armament all advanced rapidly.

War in Europe tended to give emphasis to performance improvements in the areas of speed, altitude, payload capability and medium to long range. Some of the solutions discovered then were signposts into the future. Multi-engined aircraft enabled heavy loads to be carried, in the form of troops, weapons and supplies, and improved technology increased wing lift by the addition of leading- and trailing-edge flaps. And because such aircraft needed to land and take off with heavy loads all aspects of landing gear equipment, their shock-absorbers, tyres and brakes, received close attention from designers.

Fighter and reconnaissance aircraft needed to retain their manoeuvrability and to gain new capabilities in respect of speed, range, altitude and weapon load. This brought development of improved and more powerful engines, propellers of new efficiency, a better appreciation of aerodynamic requirements, the beginnings of such advanced concepts as swept wings, delta wings and, of course, new power plants that included the turbojet, ramjet, pulse-jet and rocket engine. With the capability to reach high altitudes came early applications of new fuselage construction for pressurisation, so that pilots could live and breath in a new and hostile airspace.

In America, concerned more directly in fighting a war across the vast reaches of the Pacific Ocean, designers and manufacturers were forced to concentrate on the development of aircraft able to lift heavy payloads and carry them across very long ranges. Boeing and Douglas, the companies which had created the outstanding civil transports in the pre-war era, were in the forefront of this development. From Douglas came the C-54, evolved from the DC-4 which the company was building for its national airlines in 1940, and from Boeing the B-29 which brought the war against Japan to an end when atomic bombs were dropped over Hiroshima and Nagasaki.

At the war's end America had gained valuable experience in the design, construction and operation of long-range transports. This knowledge was to ensure for that nation a lead in civil transport aircraft which it retains to this day. In the vanguard were the Boeing 377 Stratocruiser, sired by the B-29 Superfortress, the Douglas DC-6 and Lockheed Constellation.

Britain could not compete against such superb aircraft, being compelled by economic reasons and lack of suitable equipment to make do with converted versions of wartime bombers. During the war, by agreement with America, British manufacturers had concentrated on the production of combat machines, relying upon US manufacturers to supply Britain's requirements for transport aircraft. It was clear to designers and manufacturers in Britain that America held such an enormous lead in the design and construction of superb piston-engine transports that there was no possibility of catching up.

Comet 1

Instead, they decided to utilize their own area of specialised knowledge, for by that time Britain was leading the world in the development of turbojet and turboprop engines. Unfortunately, it was not quite simply a case of installing such power plants in the airframe of conventional aircraft. Turbojets are so fuel-thirsty at low levels that they would be uneconomic to operate: they must cruise at high altitudes where conditions enhance their efficiency. But at such heights it would be impossible for passengers and aircrew to breathe without special oxygen equipment, a feature unlikely to attract the cash customers.

This meant that, instead, the cabin and flight deck of the aircraft needed to be *pressurized* (have air pumped in under pressure) so that the new aircraft could be flown at heights of 35,000ft (10,670m) to 40,000ft (12,195m) without causing discomfort to anyone on board.

This combination of turbojets and a completely new, advanced-technology airframe came from the de Havilland company and was known as the Comet 1. When it entered service on British Overseas Airways Corporation's London-Johannesburg route, on 2 May 1952, it seemed that Britain's bold bid had succeeded. Unfortunately, the technology was too advanced, and when three Comet 1s had been lost in inexplicable circumstances some brilliant scientific detective work discovered that cycles of pressurization had caused metal fatigue. As a result the aircraft's cabin had disintegrated as the internal pressure had ruptured its structure.

This information was given to aircraft manufacturers around the world, and by the time that de Havilland had developed the Comet 4 to overcome this weakness, the Boeing Company in America was ready to introduce a turbojet-powered airliner of its own design, designated Model 707. When it entered service on Pan American's transatlantic route on 26 October 1958 it became very quickly one of the most successful commercial jet transports in the world, and very large numbers are in use to this day.

The second string to Britain's bow in this post-war period had been the turboprop engine, and the Vickers Viscount and Bristol Britannia were the first two highly successful aircraft in this category. The turbine engine gives the smooth power of a turbojet, but with far better fuel economy, and this type of power plant has been produced in a wide range to power fixed-wing aircraft of all sizes as well as rotary-wing aircraft.

As had been anticipated there was a tremendous increase in air travel in the post-war years. During the war years hundreds of thousands of men and women, both in the services and as civilians, had travelled by air on innumerable occasions. They had soon discovered that it was far from being a hazardous form of transport and had come to accept it as just another routine means of travel. If airlines could provide services at realistic prices which would speed them on business or holiday, and make it possible to visit areas of the world which, because surface travel took too long, had previously been out of their range, then the public would quickly adopt this new, far-ranging fast-flying vehicle.

Air Cargo

In parallel with this expansion of passenger travel by air came an increasing demand for air cargo capacity. The first goods to be sent by air had been in the precious, perishable or panic categories. Bullion and precious stones were safer by air because thieves could not gain access to them; speed put exotic fruits on the world's tables in the pink of condition; and urgently needed medicines could reach their destination in time to save lives or bring relief from suffering. But shippers were soon to discover that there were many other advantages to be gained by sending goods by air, and the growing demand for air cargo capacity has caused aircraft manufacturers to find ways and means of adapting passenger transports to carry cargo only, or in convertible passenger/cargo layouts, and to build specialised aircraft of large dimensions and detailed configurations. One of the early successful and unusual applications for cargo aircraft in the post-war years was the provision of an air bridge across the English Channel to speed cars and their passengers between Britain and France.

Military requirements in this category have produced aircraft such as the Lockheed Model 82 Hercules, powered by four 4,508hp Allison turboprop engines and able to carry a maximum payload of almost 20 tons (43,811lb; 19,872kg). It can accommodate 92 troops with full kit, or such weapons as a 155mm howitzer with its high-speed tractor. On an even larger scale is the specially developed C-5 Galaxy, which has an upward-hinged nose and loading ramp which permit direct straight-in loading of such cargo as 16 three-quarter-ton lorries; or two Bell Iroquois helicopters, an M-60 tank and five military trucks. Its four 41,000lb (18,642kg) st turbofan engines enable the Galaxy to take off at a maximum weight of more than 343 tons (769,000lb; 348,810kg), with a maximum payload of close on 100 tons. A very different cargo indeed from the carton of Osram electric lamps which comprised the world's first air cargo, carried in a Valkyrie monoplane from Shoreham to Hove, Sussex, on 4 July 1911. Russia, too, has developed a large cargo transport, the An-22 Anteus, and while this has a gross weight of little more than 246 tons (551,160lb; 250,000kg), the aircraft holds a number of world payload-to-height and speed-with-payload records.

High-Speed Craft
The availability of so much power has made it possible to develop aircraft able to travel faster than the speed of sound, as mentioned in Section 3. For reconnaissance purposes the Lockheed-California Company developed a remarkable aircraft designed by a team led by C L ('Kelly') Johnson. Designated SR-71, 93 per cent by weight of its structure is constructed from a specially developed titanium alloy which has a tensile strength of up to 200,000lb/sq in (14,060kg/cm^2). This metal is able to retain its structural integrity at the high temperatures to which the aircraft is subjected by *kinetic heating* (the heat generated as the aircraft passes through the air), these being as high as 1,131°F (593°C) on certain parts of the engine nacelle structure, and some sections of the wing can attain temperatures up to 833°F (427°C). Flying at heights up to 80,000ft (24,380 m), these aircraft have a maximum speed of more than 2,000mph (3,220km/h) in level flight.

Modern high-speed military aircraft have benefited from advanced technology. The French Mirage 5 is an example of a high-performance aircraft which evolved over a period of more than ten years. It has a delta wing, one which not only has the sweepback to allow an easy transition from subsonic to supersonic speed, but which is a

shape and structure of great strength and rigidity. This very potent ground attack aircraft is powered by one Snecma Atar turbojet engine which provides sufficient thrust to give the Mirage 5 a speed of 1,460mph (2,350km/h) at 39,375ft (12,000m).

Supersonic transport aircraft have also been evolved, the Soviet Union being the first nation to put such an aircraft, the Tu-144, into service in 1975, albeit on a cargo basis. The Concorde supersonic transport, designed and built by industrial collaboration between Britain and France, entered service with Air France and British Airways simultaneously on 21 January 1976, and from the outset has proved the long-held belief that passengers would find this high-speed transport a pleasant aircraft in which to fly.

It is not just cargo aircraft which have become very big and able to carry immense loads. Following upon the success of the Model 707, Boeing developed from it a three-engined 727 and twin-engined 737 and then, in April 1966, announced that the company intended to produce a new

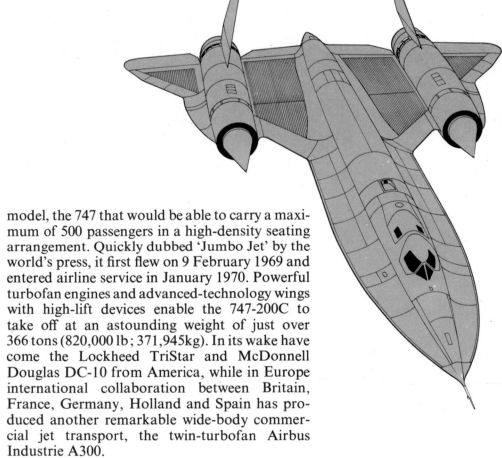

State of the art—high performance aircraft Lockheed SR71 (YF-12) Blackbird

model, the 747 that would be able to carry a maximum of 500 passengers in a high-density seating arrangement. Quickly dubbed 'Jumbo Jet' by the world's press, it first flew on 9 February 1969 and entered airline service in January 1970. Powerful turbofan engines and advanced-technology wings with high-lift devices enable the 747-200C to take off at an astounding weight of just over 366 tons (820,000 lb; 371,945kg). In its wake have come the Lockheed TriStar and McDonnell Douglas DC-10 from America, while in Europe international collaboration between Britain, France, Germany, Holland and Spain has produced another remarkable wide-body commercial jet transport, the twin-turbofan Airbus Industrie A300.

We have come a long way from the Wright *Flyer*, which in 1903 showed the world that powered flight was reality. If we had a big enough balance scale to hold a fully laden Boeing 747-200C in one pan, then we would need to put no fewer than 1,093 Wright *Flyers* in the other pan to be anywhere near balancing. But despite the fact that it is nearly 1,100 times heavier than the Flyer, the Boeing 747 has a wing area only 10.78 times greater. Which, in layman's terms, is a better indication than most of the process of development which has brought into being these exciting aircraft of today.

Post-War Airliners

By the time that the jet-fighters had become established in service, the war in Europe was in its closing stages. In the Far East the Americans had been fighting their way towards Japan. When the giant B-29s became available in quantity they began to destroy Japanese industry by devastating incendiary attacks. And it was the B-29s that were to drop the only two atomic bombs used operationally. The first, carried by the B-40 **Enola Gay**, was dropped over Hiroshima on 6 August 1945. Three days later the B-29 **Bock's Car** dropped the second weapon over Nagasaki. On 14 August 1945 the Japanese surrendered, and World War II had ended.

It was realized that there would be a tremendous upsurge in civil aviation, for during the war thousands of men had learned to fly, and millions of men and women had come to accept air travel as routine.

The circumstances of war had put America in a position to make the most of the situation, for her aircraft industry had been forced to specialize in the construction of long-range bomber and transport aircraft.

Boeing, for example, had designed in 1942 a military transport which became designated C-97 Stratofreighter. Its introduction was delayed by the need to concentrate on Boeing B-29 production, but between 1947 and 1949 56 civil airliner versions of the C-97 were built. Designated as the Model 377 Strato-cruiser **(77)**, these introduced post-war inter-continental travellers to undreamed of standards of comfort and service.

The UK had not been in the same league as the Americans when it came to post-war civil airliners. Instead of the comparatively smooth transition of purpose-built transport from military austerity to civil luxury, Britain had to make do with hasty conversions of wartime bombers. Not surprisingly, they could not compare with such aircraft as the Boeing Stratocruiser, Douglas DC-4 and Lockheed Constellation. Furthermore, prior to the war BOAC had operated her long-range Commonwealth routes with flying-boats that offered superb standards of comfort. Six years later these aircraft could not compete economically with the long-range landplanes developed to satisfy military requirements. Very soon BOAC was losing traffic to the US airlines, and had to buy Constellations and Stratocruisers to stay in business.

But Britain had one ace up her sleeve: a distinct lead in turbine engine technology, and the de Havilland Company set about building a civil airliner around four of these power plants. The resulting Comet 1 began the world's first jet-airliner service on 2 May 1952, to Johannesburg, and it seemed the British aircraft industry had a world-beater on its hands. Then came the tragic loss of three Comet 1s. Painstaking detective work by scientists and engineers was to prove that metal fatigue had brought about disintegration of the pressurized cabin.

It was not until 4 October 1958 that BOAC was able to renew transatlantic services with the Comet 4 **(78)**, developed by de Havilland to overcome the structural failure of the Comet 1: but by then, Britain had already lost her design lead.

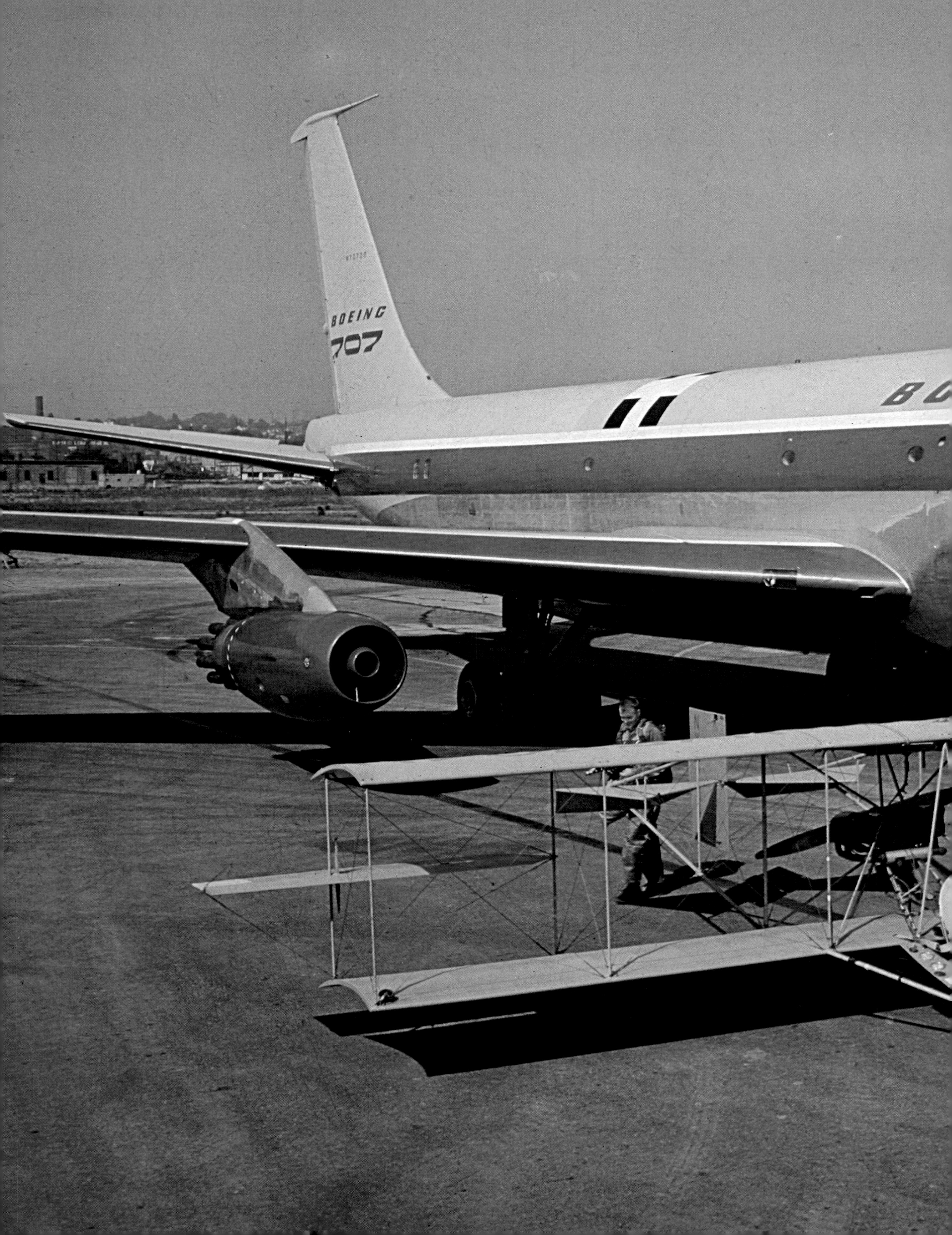
BOEING
707

Preceding page:

The American industry, very busy supplying piston-engined airliners to satisfy a huge world market, had not so much incentive to speed the development of turbine-engined transports. So it was not until 15 July 1954 that the Boeing Company flew the prototype of their Model 367-80, a remarkable four-engined transport, which has since become known the world over under the designation of Boeing 707.

But this aircraft had been developed initially as a flight refuelling tanker for the United States Air Force (USAF), and it was not until two years after the first flight of the 'Dash Eighty'—as the prototype is known affectionately to all Boeing employees—that the USAF gave permission for commercial development.

Pan American were to record the first transatlantic flight with the 707 on 26 October 1958, and when the longer-range 707-320 Inter-continental became available in 1959, it very soon found employment in the service of the major airlines of the world. A lighter-weight shorter-range version designated Boeing 720 entered service with United Air Lines (UAL) on 5 July 1960, and as a measure of success it can be recorded that no fewer than 895 Boeing 707/720s had been delivered by 1 June 1975.

Our picture **(79)** shows the 'Dash-Eighty' prototype with Peter Bowers' Curtiss replica in the foreground.

This page:

It should not be thought, of course, that introduction of turbine power plants had eliminated the piston-engine from the aviation scene. Years of development have ensured that modern engines of this type are both reliable and efficient: the turbojet scores for power and speed, but is by comparison a fuel-thirsty engine.

It must be remembered also that there are far less glamorous roles for civil aircraft than prestige inter-continental services: there is also the bread-and-butter job of carrying air cargo, an ever-expanding market in the post-war years.

The Bristol Aeroplane Company were to build a far from beautiful but successful aircraft for this role, the prototype of their Type 170 Freighter and Wayfarer (G-AGPV) making its first flight on 2 December 1945, powered by two Bristol Hercules engines. These aircraft were to provide valuable and reliable

80

81

service to their users, employed on a wide variety of tasks, and will be remembered especially for their cross-Channel car ferry role with Silver City Airways. Illustrated is the final version, the Super Freighter **(80)**, developed at the instigation of Silver City.

There were also many military require-ments that could be satisfied effec-tively by piston-engined aircraft, particularly for primary trainers and lightweight communications aircraft.

Typical of this latter category is the Hunting Percival Pembroke **(81)**, which replaced the veteran Avro Anson in some RAF Communication Flights in 1953. Its two 540/560 hp Alvis Leonides piston-engines made it economical to operate, and mounting of the engines on the high wing, coupled with tricycle landing gear, made the type very suitable for operation from unimproved airstrips.

With rearward-facing seating for eight passengers, it has proved valuable not only for the communications role but, like the Anson before it, was readily convertible to a 'flying classroom' for the training of air signallers and navigators.

For the British aircraft industry the failure of the Comet 1 had come as a serious and crippling blow in the attempt to gain world markets for civil aircraft.

It was fortunate that they had a second string to their bow, evolving from another pioneering project aimed at achieving greater economy from turbine power plants. Known as a turboprop engine, this retains a turbine as its heart, but drives a conventional propeller through the medium of reduction gearing. The result is economical operation—by comparison with a pure turbojet—while retaining the unique smoothness of an engine devoid of reciprocating parts.

The first combination of this type of engine and a civil airliner came with the Vickers Viscount, and the supply of 60 of these aircraft to Capitol Airlines of America represented the first major sale of a British civil transport into the American market. Typical of many excellent turbo-prop airliners is the Dutch medium-sized short/medium-range Fokker-VFW F.27 Friendship **(82)**. Still in production, over 21 years after the first flight of the prototype, the F.27 has been 'stretched' progressively from a 28-seater to a 48-seater.

82

Britain's Viscount was a distinct success, and was followed by the larger Bristol Britannia which entered service on BOAC's London–Johannesburg route on 1 February 1957. The Britannia, which must surely rank as one of the most graceful post-war aircraft, was to prove another success for British industry.

Vickers, meanwhile, were busy on the development of an aircraft of Britannia size, a demand spurred by both BEA and Trans-Canada Air Lines, resulting in the Vanguard (83) with Rolls-Royce Tyne turboprop engines. The prototype flew for the first time on 20 January 1959, but it was not until just over two years later that the first Type 951 Vanguards went into service with BEA.

The majority of the Vanguards remaining in service have since been converted to serve as cargo aircraft, those which were in Air Canada (successor to TCA) service being known as Cargo-liners, while those of BEA are known as Merchantmen.

83

Very much in the same size category as the highly successful Viscount was the product of another well-known British company. This was the Handley Page Herald (84), which was, however, powered by only two Rolls-Royce Dart turboprop engines.

But the prototype of the Dart-engined Herald flew for the first time on 11 March 1958, almost ten years after the first flight of the Viscount. What, then, were the market hopes for such an aircraft? Was it not ten years too late?

Indeed no. The Herald is used to illustrate that two aircraft of a similar size can be built to satisfy quite different requirements. The Viscount was for conventional airline service, its low-wing configuration providing easier refuelling and servicing, a better chance of survival if the aircraft had to be ditched, and allowed also the use of a lighter weight landing gear structure.

The Herald was intended for civil or military service, operating from all types of airfields. Thus the high-wing setting gave greater clearance between ground and propeller, reducing the likelihood of damage; the high landing gear allowed the use of long shock-struts, giving a smoother ride on undeveloped strips; and the underslung fuselage made loading and unloading easy without a need for sophisticated ground equipment.

In Russia a requirement to transport large volumes of both civil and military cargo over long distances has speeded the development of large transport aircraft.

The An-22 Antheus (85) represents the solution offered by Oleg Antonov's bureau, design studies originating in 1962 and the prototype making its first flight on 27 February 1965.

When displayed at the Paris Air Show, on 15 June 1965, it came as something of a surprise to the Western World. Certainly everything is on a large scale, for the wings span 211 ft 4 in (64·40 m), its contra-rotating propellers are 20 ft 4 in (6·20 m) in diameter, and each main landing gear unit comprises three pairs of levered suspension units.

Four 15,000 shp Kuznetsov turboprop engines allow the giant to lift-off at a gross weight of 551,160 lb (250,000 kg) — about 245 tons — and carry a payload of 176,350 lb (80,000 kg) — almost 80 tons — over a range of 3,100 miles (5,000 km).

85

88

Following the initial success of the Comet 1, the resurgent French industry joined battle by designing a short/medium-range airliner which was to acquire the name Caravelle.

It differed from the ideas or hardware of other countries in one important respect, it introduced rear-mounted turbojet engines, with a Rolls-Royce Avon on each side of the aft fuselage.

What advantage did this arrangement offer? At the stage of the art it permitted a cleaner and more efficient wing, improved take-off performance and last, but by far from least, a quieter cabin environment.

Designed by the French company Sud-Ouest (subsequently Sud-Aviation, and now Aérospatiale as a result of industry mergers), a prototype flew for the first time on 27 May 1955, and Caravelle Is entered service with Air France and SAS in mid-1959. Illustrated are Caravelle IIIs **(86, 87)** of Air Charter International and Air France.

Other nations soon followed the French lead bringing into service the Hawker Siddeley Trident **(88)** and the Russian Tu-134 **(89)**.

Unlike the Caravelle and the Tu-134 the Trident was supplied with three rear-mounted engines, Rolls-Royce Spey 505 turbojets providing 9,850 lb (4,477 kg) of thrust.

The first Trident flew in 1962 followed two years later by the flight of the first production model.

The Trident introduced the 'T' tailplane design which was copied in the Tu-134.

The Tu-134 is a modified Tu-124 in which the engines were moved to the rear. Powered by two 14,990 lb (6,814 kg) thrust Soloviev D-30 turbofans it first flew in 1964. It entered regular service in 1967 and can carry between 64 and 72 passengers.

86

87

89

One of the outstanding successes of BAC is the twin engined One-Eleven (90). Like the Caravelle it was designed as a short/medium-range transport jet. Design changes stretched the aircraft, first to make it suitable for American operators (Series 400) and subsequently to BEA specifications (Series 500). The 500 is powered by two Rolls-Royce Spey-25 Mk 5 turbofans, each providing 12,550 lb (5,992 kg) of thrust. It has a range of anywhere from 100 miles (160 km) to 1,700 miles (2,735 km). It has accommodation for 90 to 119 passengers.

The One-Eleven 475 is the newest member of the family and is designed specifically to operate under difficult conditions and is certified for operation from unpaved and gravel surface runways. With the same power plants as the 500 it can carry 74 to 89 passengers. Over 220 One-Elevens had been sold by the mid-70's.

At about the same time that the Caravelle first entered airline service, Boeing in America began design studies of a short/medium-range airliner. Similar in appearance to the highly successful 707—and with a commonality of many parts—it had been decided that to achieve the most economic operation factors it was necessary to reduce from four to three engines. As an asymmetric layout was quite impractical, it was decided to rear-mount the three engines: one on each side of the rear fuselage, the third at the base of the T-tail assembly. Thus, a second rear-engined aircraft came into service, but for different reasons.

Flown for the first time on 9 February 1963, 727-100s entered scheduled service with Eastern Air Lines on 1 February 1964. Just over 11 years later, on 1 June 1975, the amazing total of 1,132 Boeing 727s (91) had been delivered to the world's airlines.

91

This delightful view, from the other side of the world, shows the fleet of light aircraft operated by New Zealand's Southern Scenic Airways (92).

They are employed primarily to convey tourists to out of the way beauty spots, so that even if it is their one and only visit to that delightful country they will remember, forever, not only the beauty and peace, but these wonderfully safe lightweight aircraft which carry out such pleasant duties all over the world.

Strangely, pilots of aircraft often have an affinity for water. Perhaps this is because the systems of navigation evolved by our seagoing forebears have proved invaluable to the airborne fraternity. Despite the development of sophisticated navigational systems, it is good to be able to use the basic methods of 'finding your way', for even the most advanced electronics can go on strike.

Be that as it may, many light aircraft, such as this Rollason-built Druine D.31 Turbulent (93) which was designed as landplane, have been converted to operate on floats. There is a fascination in landing and taking off from water, heightened especially when its venue is some remote stretch of lake that can be reached only by such craft as these.

Another aspect of aviation is covered also by lightweight aircraft, for many aeroplanes in this category provide much of the fun and excitement still to be enjoyed by participating in, or merely being a spectator at, one of the many air shows. In Britain, which is not renowned for the reliability and duration of its summer, the calendar still seems to be crowded with aviation events.

So popular, indeed, have air shows become that aerobatic teams, like that once sponsored by the Rothman Tobacco Company, were often booked a good year ahead, for the precision and skill of their display was a real crowd-puller.

The illustration **(94)** shows the team flying its Stampe SV-4Cs, used with distinction before the acquisition of their squad of Pitts S-2A Specials.

95

The Pitts aircraft flown by the Rothman team originate from the drawing-board of Mr Curtis Pitts, one of the best-known US designers of high-performance sporting aircraft. His original single-seat Pitts Special was designed in 1943–44, and many examples have been constructed by devotees of the homebuilding movement which is very active in America.

Such factors as good weather and, in the past, cheap and plentiful petrol, have contributed to the growth of this movement, aided considerably by the Experimental Aircraft Association (EAA) which gives help and advice to amateur constructors.

Typical of the very basic craft designed for and built by these enthusiasts is the RLU Breezy **(95)**, which was designed by three professional pilots. More than 350 sets of construction plans had been sold by early 1976, with examples being built in Australia, Canada and South Africa, as well as in its homeland.

More professional in appearance, and of course more difficult to build, is the Bede BD-4 **(96)**.

Designed especially for the home-builder by Mr James R. Bede, that illustrated shows the extremely high standard of product quality achieved by enthusiastic amateurs. It is for these real enthusiasts that men like Jim Bede have devoted untold hours of work. Their aim has been to simplify methods of construction so that builders of quite moderate skill can create aircraft of which they can be proud, and which they can fly easily and safely.

Even more advanced in the US home-built category are those aircraft which are built to participate in the very popular National Air Races.

Illustrated is a Knight Twister Imperial **(97)**, intended for air racing in the Sports Biplane class, and which was built by Mr Don Fairbanks of Cincinnati, Ohio. The plans for this little aeroplane, which has a wingspan of only 17 ft 6 in (5·33 m), were specially modified from the standard Knight Twister. Designed by Mr Vernon Payne, kits of parts are also available to help simplify the task for the 'do-it-yourself' plane builder.

And when completed, even the standard Knight Twister can provide a maximum 160 mph (257 km/h) from a 90 hp engine.

Still in the lightplane class there is, of course, a wide variety of one to six-seat aircraft of superb quality manufactured by companies all over the world who cater for the private pilot who wishes to buy his aircraft ready-made.

In America there are a host of manufacturers, headed by the 'big three' of Beech, Cessna and Piper, whose aircraft are not only a pleasure to see, but a delight to fly, or be flown in.

The illustration **(98)** shows production lines at the Beech factory in Wichita, Kansas. The foreground is dominated by a line of Barons, many of which have entered USAF service, serving to remind us that even light aircraft have military potential.

For example, the Beech T-34 Mentor **(101)**, which derived from the basic Beech Model 35 Bonanza, was selected first by the USAF as a primary trainer.

Both the US Army and Navy were to buy substantial quantities of these aircraft, and they were built in Canada for the USAF and RCAF, in Japan for the JASDF and Philippine Air Force, and at Cordoba in the Argentine.

The aircraft illustrated carries a Mexican registration, and these trainers have been supplied also to Chile, Colombia, El Salvador, Saudi Arabia, Spain, Turkey and Venezuela.

100

A fairly recent entrant into the American lightplane market is Grumman, who in late 1972 merged with American Aviation Corporation, thereby gaining a product line of lightplanes, which are marketed under the name Grumman American Aviation Corporation. And in West Germany the company of Rhein-Flugzeugbau (RFB) also became interested in the same market, acquiring a 50 per cent holding in the German lightplane company Sportavia-Pützer.

In April 1974 these American and German companies announced they had jointly developed an unusual lightplane powered by a Wankel-type engine driving a ducted-fan system evolved by RFB. Known as the Fanliner **(102)**, it utilizes the adhesive-bonding technique of airframe construction, as well as many components of the Grumman American Trainer and Traveler. It demonstrates, very well, that new ideas still abound in the aviation world.

99

New applications are evolving constantly, and these have given rise to specialized aircraft which provide an important contribution to modern life. Typical are the agricultural aircraft in widespread use throughout the world, spreading fertilizers and crop spraying or crop dusting.

These are, indeed, specialized aircraft, such as the Quail Commander (101) built in Mexico. This was designed originally by the Rockwell Standard Corporation, with careful attention to safety features,

101

102

Special Aircraft

for it is no easy and safe task following the contours of hilly terrain at low level. Hence there are provided wire cutters, in case of collision with hard-to-see telephone cables, rugged seats and safety harness, well padded cockpit interiors and tough tubular steel structures to maintain the integrity of the cockpit area in a crash.

And, of course, they need also hoppers for chemicals or liquid, fan or engine-driven spray booms, medium and high volume spreader systems, and even floodlights for night operations: specialized indeed.

An unusual category of special aircraft is the water-bomber, the Canadair CL-215 **(102)** being designed and developed in Canada to deal with the problem of controlling large-scale forest fires.

There is, of course, nothing like water for damping the enthusiasm of even the most spirited fire, and the CL-215 is designed to uplift 1,200 Imp gallons (5,455 litres) of water which can be dropped in one vast all-enveloping mass. Water plus chemical retardants can be loaded before take-off, or the water bomber can scoop up its own supply in 16–20 seconds while skimming the surface of a lake, river or the sea. One CL-215 operated in France by the Protection Civile dropped a total of 98,397 Imp gallons (447,309 litres) of water in a single day during the summer of 1970, representing a weight of almost 432 tons!

103

But perhaps the most strange aircraft of today are the remotely piloted vehicles (RPVs), pilotless high-performance aircraft which are designed for a specific role. They have already proved themselves in the violence of war, for reconnaissance RPVs not only brought back superb pictures of enemy positions and defences in Vietnam, but achieved this without putting a human pilot at risk.

The Lockheed Hercules has already been mentioned as an RPV carrier, and here we see the scene beneath the wing of one of these big transports (103), which shows a Teledyne Ryan Model 234 RPV (BGM-34A) mounted on its launch pylon. It is a case very similar to that posed by the well known verse: 'Big fleas have little fleas upon their backs to bite 'em; little fleas have lesser fleas, and so **ad infinitum**,' for you will see that the RPV is itself being given a payload beneath its wing.

In fact, the load carried by the RPV is a HOBOS (HOming BOmb System) developed by Rockwell International. This is, in effect, a modular kit which is used to convert a conventional general-purpose bomb into a homing bomb.

When launched from the RPV by remote command, the guidance section of the nose of HOBOS seeks the target, locks on to it, and is guided by its own autopilot to the point of impact.

The illustration (104) shows the Hercules climbing away on a mission, an RPV beneath the starboard wing, and the RPV itself carrying two weapons beneath its wings.

When it is still many miles from the target the Hercules is able to launch and control the RPV, which is in itself a complex mini-aircraft, although one must not be confused by that word mini.

The Ryan Model 234, for example, has a wing span of 14 ft 6 in (4·42 m), length overall of 23 ft 7¼ in (7·19 m) and a launch weight of 2,800 lb (1,270 kg). Its power plant consists of a 1,700 lb (771 kg) thrust turbojet engine, and while its maximum speed is secret information, it is known that many RPVs are capable of performance in the Mach 1 to Mach 1·8 range.

Not surprisingly, it is a difficult target to intercept by any means, their weapons scoring an even higher percentage of direct hits (105).

104

105

We must not overlook the other main category of aircraft, once considered to be little more than inventors' follies—the helicopter.

Wood and metal propeller toys had given convincing proof that a rotary wing could climb straight up into the air. It even worked to some extent for experimental aircraft, but as soon as there was any forward motion of the vehicle it would overturn and crash.

It took many years to appreciate why this happened. Once understood it was ridiculously simple. The blade advancing into the airstream caused by the aircraft's forward motion, developed more lift than the opposite retreating blade. It was not until 1923 that the Spaniard, Juan de la Cierva, invented an ingenious flapping hinge for each blade which made the rotary wing a practical proposition. Roughly twenty years later Igor Sikorsky flew the world's first practical single-rotor helicopter, and a whole new category of heavier-than-air craft became reality.

One of the earliest helicopters in British military service was the two-seat Saro Skeeter (106) which, powered by a 200 hp engine, was able to record a maximum speed of about 100 mph (160 km/h).

First British-designed helicopter to enter service with the RAF was the Sycamore, developed by the Bristol Aeroplane Company. Very similar in appearance to the Saro Skeeter it was, however, considerably bigger and could accommodate a crew of two or three passengers. Powered by a 550 hp Alvis Leonides engine, the Sycamore had a maximum speed of 127 mph (204 km/h) at sea level but, like most early helicopters, had a somewhat restricted range.

Nevertheless, it was to prove an important aircraft for the RAF, for with it they discovered and developed new techniques that were to become inseparable from the role of the helicopter: rescue and pick-up by power-driven hoist; and the ability to put down or pick up troops in areas inaccessible to any other form of transport.

The Royal Navy were also to use a small number of Sycamores (107) for experimental purposes.

As a result of their experiments the Royal Navy was convinced, very quickly, that the helicopter could prove to be an important naval auxiliary.

Its ability to hover or match its speed to that of a surface vessel was particularly exciting, not only for tasks such as rescue patrol alongside aircraft carriers, but because it suggested the possibility of even very small ships being able to carry an aircraft. If this was feasible, then ship-to-shore and ship-to-ship communications would be greatly improved, and a ship's commander would have his eyes extended far beyond the normal limit of the horizon.

Time was not only to prove these premises to be true, but to show that much more could be achieved by a vessel with its own attendant helicopter.

The Westland Wasp (108) was the Navy's first helicopter to operate extensively from platforms on frigates and smaller vessels. It was soon discovered that they could not only fulfil such tasks as those mentioned above but that, small though they were, they could deploy torpedoes and air-to-surface missiles.

106

107

Far more sophisticated is the turbine-powered Westland Wessex, serving both the Royal Navy and Royal Air Force.

A development of the piston-engined Sikorsky S-58, this British-built helicopter has been given the benefits of turbine power, the first production version having the designation H.A.S.Mk 1, and entering service with the Navy in 1960. The RAF's version is the H.C.Mk 2, which differs in its power plant, comprising two coupled-shaft turbines, replacing the single larger turbine in the Naval version.
The RAF Wessex illustrated **(109)** can carry up to 16 troops, be used as an air ambulance with seven litters, transport up to 4,000 lb (1,814 kg) of cargo, and has provision for the fitment of machine-guns and rocket-launchers.

Westland Helicopters at Yeovil, Somerset, has a close technical association with Sikorsky Aircraft in America. The link stretches back for more than a quarter of a century, for the company's first helicopter was built in 1947 after acquisition of a licence to build the Sikorsky S-51, which it produced as the Westland Dragonfly.

A more recent and closer tie has been developed with Aérospatiale in France for, under the Anglo-French helicopter agreement of 1967, the two companies have worked together to design and develop some important new helicopters.

One of these is the Aérospatiale/Westland SA341 Gazelle which is in production in France for the French Army, military export and civil use, and by Westland for the British Army, Navy and Air Force. Illustrated **(110)** is the civil version, which offers luxurious high-speed transport for a pilot and up to four passengers.

Igor Sikorsky was the pioneer of the helicopter in the US, and the company which he founded in 1923 was to lead the world in helicopter production for some time.

Since then other manufacturers have come along with new ideas and designs to challenge that lead, including Bell, Boeing-Vertol, Kaman and Lockheed.

Bell's Model 47 achieved the distinction of receiving from the US Civil Aviation Authority the first helicopter Approved Type Certificate in 1946, and was to remain in production for 25 years. This remarkable, but very basic, three-seat helicopter is a far cry from Bell's Long Ranger **(111)** first announced in late 1973. A general-purpose civil helicopter, it has standard accommodation for a crew of two and four passengers. First production aircraft were delivered in late 1975.

It introduces a remarkable breakthrough in the long-term search for a means to eliminate the vibration associated with all rotary-winged aircraft. Named the 'Noda-Matic' system, it utilizes the long-known scientific fact that a beam subjected to vertical vibration develops flexing in a wave form. In such a beam nodal points, equidistant from the centre, have no relative motion, and Bell have used the nodal points of a beam to connect fuselage and rotor system so providing an exceedingly smooth helicopter ride.

110

111

Helicopters introduced into the Korean War showed immediately that rotary-winged aircraft were to be a most valuable addition to the equipment of the fighting services. Not only were they able to put down and pick up troops in areas where no other vehicle could go, but their speedy evacuation of front-line casualties was to reduce the incidence of death from wounds to the lowest recorded in military history.

It was discovered very soon, however, that at the moment when a 'chopper' was dropping or picking up men or cargo, it was extremely vulnerable to enemy attack. Weapons were required to provide a hail of fire and force the enemy to 'keep their heads down' until the no-movement period of maximum vulnerability had passed. Highly effective gunship helicopters have evolved from this small beginning, and their deployment in Vietnam showed them to be a valuable close-support weapon.

Bell developed the Model 209 Huey-Cobra (112), a turbine-powered armed helicopter with various armament installations, which include Miniguns and/or grenade-launchers in a chin turret, and folding-fin rockets, cannon or Minigun pods carried beneath stub-wings. Progressive development of the type has meant that Bell is one of two manufacturers who in 1975 were building prototypes of a potent Advanced Attack Helicopter (AAH) for the US Army.

The prototype of Bell's AAH has the designation YAH-63, and its family likeness to the HueyCobra can be seen in the accompanying illustration (113). It is, however, a very different aircraft, with two 1,500 shp advanced technology turboshaft engines replacing the single 1,800 shp turboshaft of the Huey, a large ventral fin with a horizontal surface mounted at the tip of the upper fin, and a very advanced dynamic system which includes rotor blades with dual stainless steel spars to improve combat survivability.

Primary task of the AAH is the destruction of enemy armour, which means they will be equipped with 'tank-busting' weapons. Those of the Bell AAH include a three-barrel 30 mm gun in an under-nose turret, 2·75 in folding-fin rockets or TOW anti-tank missiles beneath the stub wings, with a stabilized telescopic sight to guide the missiles by day and an infra-red vision system for use by night.

113

115

116

In a much heavier class is the Boeing Vertol CH-47 Chinook **(114)**, a twin-engine twin-rotor medium transport helicopter that entered service with the US Army in late 1962.

The illustration shows typical battle-field usage of the type, lifting a field gun and its ammunition to a forward position, the gun crew with additional ammunition and supplies accommodated within the helicopter's cabin.

Cabin accommodation will cater for a maximum of 44 troops, or 24 litters and two medical attendants for casualty evacuation from front-line positions. Alternatively, the Chinook can be used for all-cargo missions, when the latest CH-47C has a maximum internal payload of 18,600 lb (8,437 kg) or an external cargo capability of 23,212 lb (10, 528 kg).

These aircraft proved especially valuable in Vietnam for the retrieval of crashed aircraft, and during their use in this theatre of operations they were responsible for recovering at least 11,500 aircraft that were worth well over $3·0 billion.

In the Soviet Union the development of rotary-winged aircraft has gone ahead for the same reasons as in the West, but it would appear that large passenger-carrying helicopters have been produced in far greater quantities. The Mil Mi-6, when first announced in 1957, was then the largest helicopter flying anywhere in the world. Powered by two large turbo-shaft engines to drive its single 114 ft 10 in (35·00 m) main rotor, it has accommodation for 65 passengers.

Somewhat smaller is the Mil Mi-8 **(115)**, that illustrated being in Aeroflot service and equipped to carry up to 32 passengers. Following large-scale use of gunships by US forces involved in Vietnam, Russia has become interested in this class of helicopter. The Mi-8 has been used for picking up and putting down troops during army exercises, and it is believed that outriggers on the landing gear have been used to mount a variety of weapons.

In a totally different class to the Mi-8 however, is Mil's Mi-12 **(116)** four-engined twin-rotor heavy duty helicopter which holds a string of records for pay-loads lifted to various height levels.

The four Soloviev turboshaft engines that power this Soviet giant have a combined output of 26,000 shp for take-off, enabling the Mi-12 to become airborne at a maximum gross weight of 231,500 lb (105,000 kg), and to carry a payload of 78,000 lb (35,400 kg) for a distance of 310 miles (500 km).

The unusual layout for the twin rotors, namely side by side above the tips of fixed-wings, was chosen because it is believed to offer better stability and longer life than the more conventional tandem layout as used for the Chinook.

In the course of time very large helicopters were developed for both civil and military requirements.

In America, Sikorsky Aircraft produced the prototype of its S-64 *Skycrane* and this flew for the first time on 9 May 1962. A military version, designated CH-54A, gained three international height records in 1965 including a 2,000 kg payload to a height of 28,743 ft (8,761 m) and a 1,000 kg payload to a height of 29,340 ft (8,943 m).

Typical of civil applications is the on-site delivery of a pre-fabricated house, as shown in the illustration **(117)**.

The Navigational Miracle

On 25 August 1919 a small group gathered around a somewhat functional de Havilland DH.4A 'airliner', belonging to a new Company called Air Transport & Travel Ltd., to wish its pilot 'God speed' as he set out on the first regular scheduled international air service between London and Paris. They would not then have believed in their wildest imagination that 56 years later one of the world's busiest international airports, Heathrow, London, would be established within sight of where they were standing at Hounslow, Middlesex.

They would probably have viewed the solitary passenger with a mixture of envy and awe, for a flight from London to Paris was not without hazard in those days. There were no meteorological services to warn the pilot of what weather he might expect to find on his route. He had no radio with which to seek even elementary assistance – or psychological comfort – in dealing with the problems that might beset him. He had no navigational equipment beyond a very simple compass, the accuracy of which might be suspect. His 'airliner' was a converted day bomber, his own position being in the forward cockpit. The passenger 'cabin' had been created by eliminating the aft cockpit which had once housed the observer and his machine gun. A closure was provided for the open top, windows inserted in the fuselage sides and two wicker chairs were crammed into the limited space available. Perhaps it would have been better to say that the solitary passenger on that first flight was regarded with awe and envy. And he had paid £21 in 1919 currency for the privilege.

If the aircraft with which these pioneer air services began were a little on the austere side, at least no expense had been spared in providing ground support equipment and ensuring that the customer should suffer no discomfort in the unheated cabin. A stout pair of household steps was always available so that passengers, clad in layers of voluminous clothing to keep out the cold, could climb easily to a position where they had to do their best to stow themselves into the limited accommodation. If it happened to be a chilly day the airport manager could be relied upon to provide a hot water bottle. And, of course, if the passenger was accommodated in an open cockpit, flying helmet, goggles and gloves were provided without extra charge.

Just over a week after that inaugural flight by Air Transport & Travel, Handley Page Transport Ltd. began a competitive service to Paris, operating from a grass field which lay between Cricklewood Broadway and Golders Green. Their fleet included a number of Handley Page 0/400 bombers which had been modified to accommodate ten passengers and, not surprisingly, a fully laden aircraft was something of a handful to get into the air from the confines of the Cricklewood airfield.

Wing Commander R H McIntosh, one of the pilots who flew for Handley Page Transport in its early days, describes a take-off in his fascinating autobiography *All-Weather Mac*. He tells how: 'Down the Edgware Road we flew struggling to keep 50mph (80km/h) on the airspeed indicator. At the optimum angle of climb we couldn't do more. With a prevailing headwind of say 25mph (40km/h) our actual ground speed was 25mph or thereabouts. When I came to fly this route regularly it seemed to me that I could overtake the old open-topped L.G.O.C. (*London General Omnibus Company*) No. 16 buses going towards London – but only when they stopped to pick up passengers! All too often it appeared to me that the buses were overtaking us.'

In a nutshell, the early days of civil aviation were very much a matter of experimentation and making do. In the forefront of development of the embryo air services was the pilot himself, learning the hard way how to maintain some kind of regular service between points A and B. Apart from the fact that the aircraft he flew was, usually, quite unsuitable for the job and inadequately powered, he was accommodated in an open cockpit. This meant that he was exposed to the slipstream and, except on rare occasions, chilled to the marrow. In rain or sleet it became a cruel form of punishment, especially when it was necessary to remove protective goggles because it was impossible to see through them.

One of the hazards of these early days was the unreliability of power plants. This may seem an odd comment, for you will have read earlier that World War I had developed more powerful and reliable engines. The problems came from the fact that in order to make these early services pay the aircraft needed a full complement of passengers, and this meant that it was heavily laden having regard to the engine power available. Engines overheated when they ran for long periods at maximum power, and overheated engines are unreliable. Fortunately, the aircraft of those days could be put down safely in most fields of average size, and many early pilots have commented how it was normal to search constantly for a suitable emergency field en route. Having passed it by, they immediately looked for another some distance ahead, and continued this precautionary measure along their route.

Flying by Bradshaw

Almost certainly the greatest problem was navigation, the difficulty of finding one's way from A to B. It was not possible to stop and consider whether the route was left or right of track, and a lone pilot in an open cockpit was not in the ideal situation to open and examine a sheet map. From these days evolved the technique known as 'flying by Bradshaw', the name being associated with a comprehensive guide to Britain's railways. It meant that the pilot travelling from London to Paris would look over the side to follow the steel track heading towards the coast. On one ill-fated occasion two aircraft, travelling in opposite directions on a day of poor visibility, collided head on. Their pilots had been concentrating on the railway line below them.

Over a period of time the pilots operating these pioneer air services became very knowledgeable of the landmarks on their particular routes. Houses of unusual colour, village ponds, church towers and other distinctive markers were pigeon-holed in their memory to provide turning points and route corrections. In conditions of poor visibility or failing light rivers and ponds were of enormous assistance. Compasses were of help only to give a general heading on those occasions when the sky was a uniform grey, giving no hint of the sun's position. When the sun was visible, or its position reasonably certain, it was a far better guide than most compasses then installed in aircraft.

One of the most vital pieces of information for a pilot of those days was 'how high am I flying?' It was not easy to determine and, when visibility was bad, meant that pilots would do their utmost to maintain visual contact with the terrain over which they were passing. Prior to the evolution of electronic instruments, the principle upon which all *altimeters* (height-recording instruments) worked was exactly the same as that of an aneroid barometer. In such an instrument a sealed capsule is compressed by rising atmospheric pressure, or expands when the pressure falls. Instead of being calibrated to record atmospheric pressure, the altimeter has height readings on its scale, these deriving from atmospheric pressure at varying heights. Of necessity it has to be calibrated for average conditions.

Before take-off a pilot would set his altimeter to record the known height of the airfield from which he was operating. Unfortunately, variations in atmospheric pressure and temperature en route and at the ultimate destination meant that it gave only an approximation of true height. In an aircraft able to operate at an altitude sufficiently high to give ample clearance above any en route hazards, the altimeter was really vital only under emergency conditions or when the time came to make a landing. But most of the early 'airliners' operated at fairly low altitudes and, consequently, information from the altimeter was of some importance all the time. The situation improved only when aircraft became equipped with radio communications, enabling the pilot to readjust the setting of the altimeter for the atmospheric conditions which applied at his destination.

With some indication of direction (compass) and height (altimeter) the pilot needed also some guidance on airspeed to be able to navigate in even an elementary way. The very earliest airspeed indicators consisted of a spring-mounted flat plate deflected by the airstream so that it moved over a makeshift scale. It sounds as if it might be very hit and miss. It was.

Airspeed (a) Vector of forces (b) Pitot static system (c) Airspeed indicator

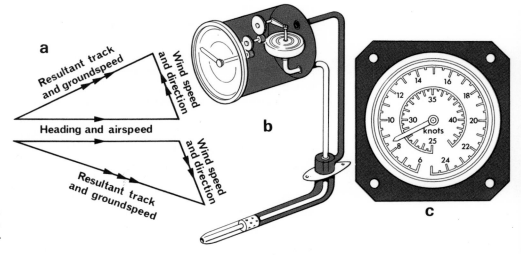

Airspeed Indicator

A far more accurate form of measurement was needed and developed, consisting of a calibrated instrument connected by two pipe lines to a *pitot head*. This is mounted so that the two tubes which form the pitot head are in a forward position on the aircraft, in an area such that the airflow on to the head is not influenced by any adjacent structure. One tube, the pitot tube, has its open end facing into the airstream. The other, the static tube, is closed at its forward end but has a number of small holes at a short distance along the tube. The instrument comprises a sealed case and the pitot tube is connected to a diaphragm box so that the diaphragm can move a needle across a calibrated scale. The static tube ensures that conditions of atmospheric pressure are maintained in the case. This instrument measures the difference of pressure between the static and pitot tube, the difference varying as the square of the speed, and calculation enables the scale to be calibrated to read in kilometres or miles per hour. Like all aircraft instruments depending on pressure reading it requires correction for altitude and temperature if an accurate figure is required. We shall see in due course how these basic flight instruments have changed in the ensuing years.

So far as the engine is concerned, only two pieces of information could be regarded as vital: oil pressure and engine temperature. Both engine instruments were in regular use for motor cars and were modified easily for use in aircraft. The information they gave was essentially of the good news/bad news variety. With both instruments giving a favourable reading it was to be assumed that all was well. If either or both suggested that the engine was on the verge of some form of breakdown, it was imperative for the pilot to cast around for a suitable field in which to make an emergency landing.

Some indication of fuel content was needed, too, but not all aircraft had such a luxury. When gauges were provided they were often far from accurate: most favoured was a sight tube of one kind or another, but this was a hazardous sort of device and was soon to disappear altogether.

The Airlines

Air travel in the early days was only for those with plenty of money to spend. Which meant that it did not take very long in Britain before too many airline operators were trying to attract a very limited market. This resulted, on 31 March 1924, in the formation of Imperial Airways Ltd. to develop the nation's commercial air transport on an economic basis. Formed from four existing airlines, Imperial Airways took over their 'fleets' of aircraft, dispensing with those which were considered to be obsolete.

By the time that this national airline came into being, London had been in possession of its own airport, at Croydon, Surrey, for almost four years. The terminal area was at Plough Lane, with arrivals and departures on the east side of the lane. The majority of the hangars and maintenance areas were on the west side, which meant that aircraft had to taxi across Plough Lane to get from one side to the other. It must have been most exciting in those days to be held up at the crossing while one of Imperial Airways' 'Queens of the air' roared in exultation as it made its way to the take-off area.

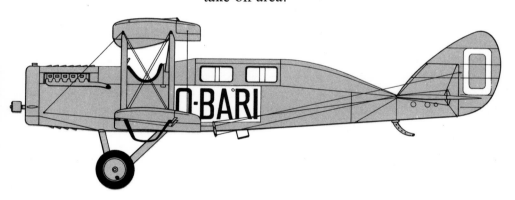

Early transport aircraft
The de Havilland DH-4a of the Belgian line SNETA ran the Brussels to Croydon route in 1921

While Britain had been making some progress in the establishment of an air travel industry, other nations had also begun to initiate the beginning of what, one day, would become important airlines. Australia's Qantas (Queensland and Northern Territory Aerial Services Ltd.) was registered in Brisbane on 16 November 1920. The inaugural flight of a subsidised service, between Charleville and Cloncurry, was made with an Armstrong Whitworth FK.8 aircraft on 2/3 November 1922.

Canada was slower off the mark, its approach to the problem of establishing air services over what were then enormously long ranges being conditioned to some extent by what was happening in America. Thus it was not until 1927 that the Canadian Government allocated a sum of money for experimental air mail services,

leading to the beginning of regular mail flights by Canadian Transcontinental Airways and Western Canada Airways on 11 and 25 January 1928 respectively.

In America the beginning of air transport had been very different from anywhere else, originating in an air mail service between Washington and New York, via Philadelphia, flown by pilots of the United States Army Air Service. The first flight was made on 15 May 1918 and was continued until 12 August 1918, by which time the Army pilots had shown that with reasonable equipment and trained personnel a regular scheduled air mail service could be maintained. As a result the Post Office Department of the US administration acquired its own aircraft and pilots and set about the task of pioneering mail routes across the length and breadth of America.

Air Mail Service

This phase lasted until 1926. A bill, known as the Kelly Act, was passed by Congress in 1925 'to encourage commercial aviation and to authorise the Postmaster General to contract for air mail service.' This was the true beginning of commercial air transport in the United States, but it was not until January 1926 that prospective contractors were able to put in bids for the available routes.

It was in the spring and summer that these contractors first began to operate over the established routes. One of the successful contractors was a wholly owned subsidiary of the Boeing Company, known as Boeing Air Transport, and one day to be far better known as United Air Lines (UAL).

Another of the contractors was known as Robertson Aircraft Corporation, its three pilots responsible for maintaining five round trips each week – come what may – between St Louis and Chicago. One of those three pilots was Charles Lindbergh, to become forever famous a year later. In his classic book *The Spirit of St. Louis* he wrote of those early days: '. . . now winter is creeping up on us. Nights are lengthening; skies are thickening with haze and storm. We're already landing by floodlight at Chicago. In a few more weeks it will be dark when we glide down onto that narrow strip of cow-pasture called the Peoria air-mail field. Before the winter is past even the meadow at Springfield will need lights.'

It was this operation by the original air mail contractors that established the airline routes which today criss-cross the whole of America. As time and money would allow, landing lights and light beacons were set up to guide those who, like Charles Lindbergh, helped to create the routes which one day would allow safe and fast travel throughout the United States.

European Air Services

At much the same period as in Australia, Britain, Canada and the United States, the first air services were established in France, and in Holland on 7 October 1919 KLM Royal Dutch Airlines was founded. In Germany had come the very first regular scheduled air mail services in the world when, on 6 April 1919, Deutsche Luft-Reederei

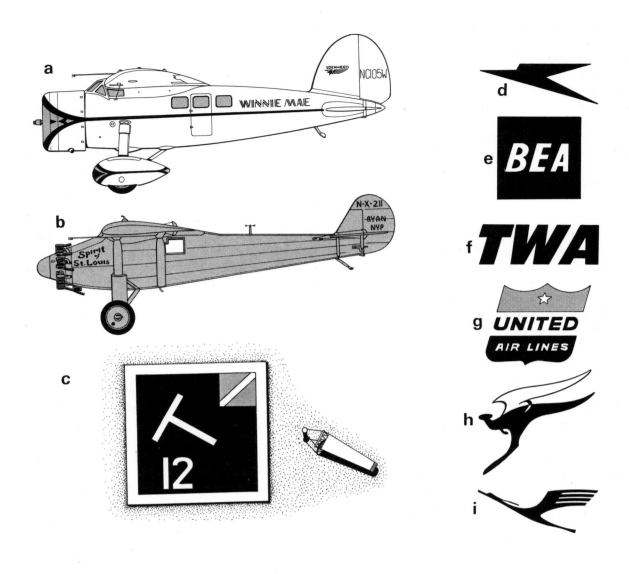

Pioneer long distance aircraft
(a) Lockheed Vega (b) Ryan Monoplane (c) Airfield signal square and windsock

Airline symbols
(d) British Overseas Airways Corporation (e) British European Airways (f) Trans World Airways (g) United Air Lines (h) Qantas (i) Lufthansa

began a service from Berlin to Weimar, later extended to Leipzig, Hamburg, an area along the Lower Rhine and to the shores of the Baltic Sea.

In Germany, as in Britain, a number of small airlines began competing for a very limited revenue and in 1925 the moment came for a merger to establish a national airline. Thus was established Lufthansa, on 6 January 1926, to link Germany with other European centres and to those countries outside Europe with which close trade ties existed: notably North and South America and the Far East.

This period, from the mid-1920s to the outbreak of World War II, was one in which everything seemed to be happening at the same time. Airports were being established in all the major countries; new, faster aeroplanes of greater capacity were entering service; the beginnings of air traffic control were apparent; and more sophisticated equipment became available to speed airliners safely from one point to another.

This latter factor was one of the very important points, for the predominant aim of everyone connected with civil aviation has been to ensure that safety was the primary consideration at all times. From the first days of flying the pioneers had had to learn by trial and error the best way of controlling their machine in the air. There had been no instructors for such men as Lilienthal, Pilcher, Chanute and the Wrights. All, however, had started by flying simple gliders which gave them a 'feel' of what it was all about.

When it came to flying a powered aircraft which could lift only one man into the air the situation became a little more difficult. It was fortunate that most early aircraft had easily frangible structures which disintegrated on impact. The greenhorn pilot, doubtless somewhat shaken, would find as the dust settled that he was sitting virtually unharmed amongst a heap of bits and pieces that had once been an aeroplane.

'Seat of the Pants' Flying

Having learned to fly in this manner the pilot acquired an instinctive understanding of the movement of his aircraft in the air and how to control a turn that was in the wrong direction. 'Seat of the pants' flying, they called it, implying that the pilot could feel, or sense, the movements of the aircraft.

This was all very well if the pilot had visual references by which to fly. There inevitably came the moment when, even at low altitudes, mist or low cloud blanketed the land from view, and pilots soon discovered that their 'seat of the pants' references were not quite good enough. Very often aircraft flew into dense clouds and, in far too many cases, their aircraft went into a spin and crashed.

It was not until 1930 that the mysterious behaviour of aircraft in clouds was resolved by an instructor of the British Royal Air Force's Central Flying School. One of the School's aircraft was fitted with a hood which could be pulled over the rear cockpit so that its occupant was compelled to fly without any visual reference. In his history of the Central Flying School, John W R Taylor explains what happened:

'On average it was found that a good pilot could fly more or less straight and level in "blind" conditions for a maximum of eight minutes, after which he lost all sense of equilibrium and usually began to spin without realising he was doing so. If he did recognise that he was spinning, he usually managed to make a satisfactory recovery in the normal manner, only to go back into the same spin. The reason was that, when he pulled out of a left-hand spin, the forces on his body produced the same sensations as if he were spinning to the right. With no datum to help, he felt so certain that he was in a right-hand spin that he inevitably tried to correct it and resumed his left-hand spin.'

It seems odd, in retrospect, that this factor had not been established far earlier. The explanation, of course, is that those who were killed in such accidents could communicate nothing. Those who survived usually commented that the compass was spinning wildly, but that the aircraft was otherwise flying normally. This explains why so many strange stories abounded of electro-magnetic forces within large clouds. These, it was claimed, had disturbed the compass and sent so many men to their deaths. Only those flying at sufficient height to arrest the spin after their aircraft came out of the cloudbase lived to tell the tale of the spinning compass.

From the foregoing you might assume that at the time aircraft were not equipped with instruments which would give the pilot some sort of reference if, for any reason, he was compelled to fly – even for very short periods – in 'blind' conditions. This is not true, for most aircraft of any size had been equipped with a turn-and-bank indicator since the closing days of the war; even light aircraft had been fitted with a cross level by which, with a fair degree of skill, an aircraft could be maintained on a level keel.

The problem was not that suitable instruments did not exist, but that the 'seat of the pants' pilots believed that their skill and instinctive 'feel' were superior to any man-made instruments.

In America, a highly respected and skilled pilot of the United States Army Air Corps (USAAC) had been giving considerable thought to tne problems associated with flight in conditions of poor to bad visibility. They interested him in particular because he had realised that wide-scale, dependable military and civil flying services would never become firmly established until it was possible for a pilot to fly safely in 'blind' conditions. The alternative form of long-distance transcontinental travel in those days was the railway. Only freak weather would stop a train: almost any kind of weather but fine and sunny was likely to upset the schedule of an air-line, or prevent a military aircraft from reaching its target.

Already well known in America for a record-breaking trans-continental flight from Pablo Beach, Florida, to San Diego, California, in 21 hrs 19min; and known world-wide for flying the winning aircraft in the Schneider Trophy Contest of 1925, as well as by creating a new world speed record for seaplanes shortly after, this man was the legendary James Doolittle.

The Guggenheim Fund

The Guggenheim Fund for the Promotion of Aeronautics, under the presidency of Harry Guggenheim, formed a world-wide group to study the problems associated with flight in poor visibility. Requiring an analytical pilot to head a flight-test set-up, Guggenheim succeeded in interesting Doolittle in the job. Furthermore, because it was a matter of such importance to aviation in general, the USAAC gave Doolittle indefinite leave of absence to enable him to give whatever time was necessary to this task.

It was far more complex than he had at first appreciated. Not only was it considered desirable

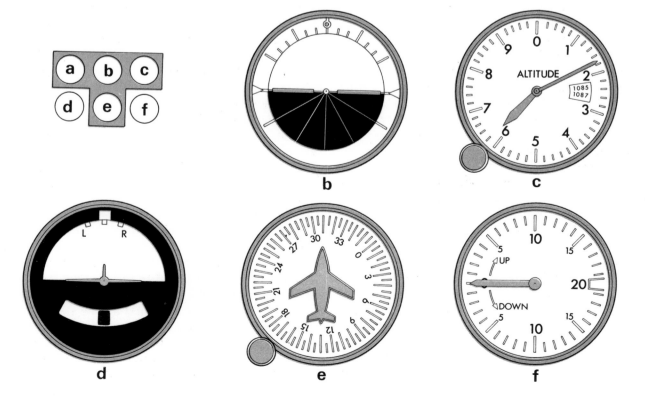

Layout of basic instrument panel
(a) Airspeed indicator–see p130
(b) Artificial horizon **(c)** Altimeter
(d) Turn co-ordinator **(e)** Gyro
compass **(f)** Rate of climb indicator

133

to investigate the problems of flight in poor visibility, but to explore also the possibility of making blind landings. To achieve these goals a number of things were needed: a radio beam to direct the aircraft on the right line in its approach to the airfield; a vertical marker beacon that would tell the pilot the instant that his aircraft crossed the airfield boundary; a superbly accurate altimeter; and some form of guidance that would give an accurate direction of flight. This last-mentioned instrument was essential. Despite the fact that there had been some development of the magnetic compass for use in an aircraft, it was suitable only for navigational cross-checks. As an accurate instrument for blind flight it was quite useless.

The provision of the guiding radio beam and the vertical marker beacon was comparatively easy. It was the requirement for two extremely accurate flight instruments which caused the greatest problems.

As with most projects of this kind, the word soon spread among aviation circles regarding the nature of the research work that was being undertaken at Mitchel Field, Long Island. Information came to Doolittle of a man named Paul Kollsman who had been working on the development of an extremely accurate barometric altimeter. The new standard of accuracy had been achieved by the use of a very sensitive barometric capsule, and by the provision of drive gears for the instrument's pointer that were so accurately cut and responsive that it was possible to mount another pointer recording in feet as well as the original pointers recording in units of ten and one hundred feet.

As regards the line of flight instruments, the Sperry Company in America had been manufacturing gyro-stabilised compasses for marine navigation for many years. Doolittle believed that some form of lightweight gyro compass was needed for this particular application. When Dr. Sperry was approached he showed immediate interest because, apparently, the company had developed something similar in the early days of World War I.

The result of these two initial contacts was that Paul Kollsman added to his altimeter a device which allowed the instruments to be adjusted in flight to compensate for changes in barometric pressure. This enabled the altimeter to record as accurately as possible the height of the aircraft above the landing field for which the instrument had been readjusted. This updating came from information over the radio of any change of barometric pressure at the destination airfield.

Dr. Sperry's son was responsible for rigging up two gyros in the aircraft which was to be used for the flight-tests. One had a compass dial that maintained an unchanging relationship with the electrically driven high-speed gyro. As the aircraft turned, the gimbal-mounted gyro maintained its original heading and the changed position of the compass scale in relation to the aircraft could be read through an aperture. A milled adjustment screw was provided so that the gyro could be set before take-off. Thereafter it held a constant heading so that, despite how many times the aircraft was turned in flight, if it was brought back onto the original pre-set heading, then it would be on exactly the same course. Doolittle was able to prove, time and time again, that this was so, for he would fly precisely and at low-level over a length of railway track and adjust the compass to zero. After flying around for some time he could again align the aircraft over exactly the same section of railway track and check the compass reading.

Artificial Horizon

He had gained an unexpected bonus from the second gyro installed by Elmer Sperry, for this was set so that the gyro's axis was vertical and it was possible by looking at the flat disc of the spinning gyro to gauge whether the aircraft was flying on a level keel, both fore and aft and laterally. Doolittle suggested that a reference bar could be added to represent the plane of the gyro, and that it could be called an artificial horizon. By viewing this reference bar it would be possible to see whether the aircraft was in a bank, as well as whether it was climbing or diving.

With these instruments, and with Lt. Ben Kelsey as check pilot in the rear cockpit, Doolittle disappeared beneath the hood of the front cockpit on the morning of 24 September 1929, one of dense fog. Taking off and concentrating on his instruments, Doolittle completed a 15-mile (24km) flight before landing back at Mitchel Field, gently and accurately. *The New York Times* for 30 September used banner headlines to declare FOG PERIL OVERCOME.

It was great, but of course very premature, for only in comparatively recent years have landing systems been developed that can be said to have defeated fog. This story has, however, been given at some length because the directional gyro and artificial horizon, plus a gyro-stabilised turn-and-bank indicator and rate-of-climb indicator, forms the standard blind-flying instrumentation panel with which aircraft are equipped to this day.

It was exactly the right moment for such equipment to be developed, for aircraft were then coming into service with the pilot accommodated inside the cabin. There were many protests at such outrageous behaviour, for there were people who seemed to believe that, deprived of the discomforts of an open cockpit, the pilot might just drop off to sleep.

In America, in 1930, Boeing Air Transport was using Boeing Model 80 tri-motor biplane airliners on its San Francisco–Chicago route. Seating twelve passengers in its large cabin, it featured such modern ideas as forced air ventilation, leather upholstered seats, individual reading lamps and hot and cold running water in the toilet facility. As if that wasn't sufficient innovation for one aircraft, the company had decided that a full-time cabin attendant was necessary to look after the comfort of the passengers. Such cabin crew was provided when the company took into its employment a number of registered nurses. These were the very first airline stewardesses in the world, a category of aircrew now employed universally by the majority of airlines.

In the following year Britain's Imperial Airways introduced its famous Handley Page H.P.

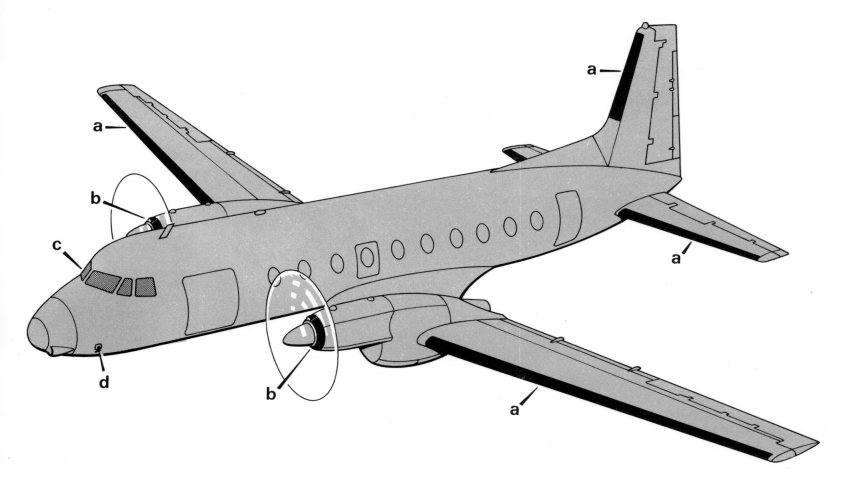

De-icing
(a) Leading edge pneumatic boots
(b) Engine and oil cooler intake
de-icing (c) Electrically heated
windscreen panels (d) Electrically
heated instrument pitot head

42s on the London–Paris route, G-AAGX *Hannibal* operating the first service on 11 June. These towering aircraft with massive fixed landing gear were dignity personified. Their huge biplane wings enabled them to more or less float away from Croydon airport, their stately pace allowing ample time for a full-course meal to be served en route to Paris. It was the almost regal progress of the H.P.42 which prompted Dutch designer Anthony Fokker to describe them as 'having built-in headwinds'.

Their cruising speed was, in fact, less than 100mph (160km/h) but they offered standards of comfort and safety that no other aircraft of the day could equal. As a result, they skimmed off the cream of the European traffic, carrying more passengers between London and the Continent in the 1930s than all other airliners combined. Together, the fleet of eight aircraft flew approximately ten million miles without harming a single passenger until, in 1940, one of them just disappeared on a wartime flight.

But aircraft like the Boeing Model 80 and the Handley Page H.P.42 represented the end of an era. They were excellent examples of the biplane developed to a high standard of comfort and safety for passenger service, but were about to be replaced by aircraft like the Boeing Model 247 and Douglas DC-2 and DC-3. These new monoplane all-metal aircraft brought a completely different standard of performance to airline operations.

In the section dealing with the development of airframes some details of the Boeing Model 247 were given. This is a good point to expand upon one or two features of this important aeroplane. Important because it emphasises the extent to which the Boeing Company studied carefully the

needs of airline operators. And because of experience in operating its own Boeing Air Transport System, later to become United Air Lines, the company had first-hand knowledge of requirements and the economies that could be achieved by the operation of such aircraft.

The Model 247s had accommodation for a crew of three, including a stewardess, and ten passengers. There was room in the nose for additional radio equipment and 400lb (181kg) of mail. The late version 247D had two 550hp Pratt & Whitney Wasp radial engines which gave it a cruising speed of 189mph (302km/h) and service ceiling of 25,400ft (7,740m).

De-Icing

As mentioned earlier, the 247 introduced pneumatic de-icing boots for the leading-edges of aerofoil surfaces for the first time on any airliner. This was an important safety feature for the maximum low-pressure area above the wing is adjacent to an aerofoil's leading-edge. Therefore, not only does the airstream which accelerates over the maximum camber area lose pressure, its temperature falls also, so that if icing conditions are prevalent this is one of the areas where ice will build up. The pneumatic de-icing boots are fed with pulses of air so that they expand and contract; any ice which forms is loosened by this action and blown clear in the slipstream.

This was an important safety feature because ice changes the aerofoil section and adds weight, and if the ice surface is rough it creates turbulence and drag, all of which help to destroy lift.

There are three other areas where aircraft of this kind often suffer from ice accretion. One is the pilot's windscreen, usually de-iced by hot air or alcohol spray, although more modern aircraft

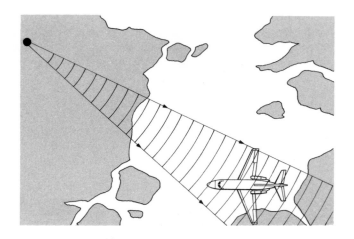

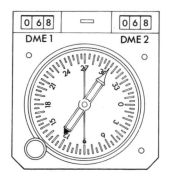

Left
Radio beacon for bearing and distance measuring equipment

Right
Very high frequency–
Omnidirectional–Rangefinding
equipment (VOR)
(a) Transmission pattern of
beacon (b) Aircraft flying on
course 270, bearing of VOR 1,204 .
bearing of VOR 2,314 (c) VOR
compass display

Below
Avionics in cockpit of modern
fighter aircraft, F-15 Eagle
(a) Head-up display (HUD)
(b) IFF remote controller
(c) Vertical situation display
(Radar) (d) HUD controller
(e) Nav-aids selector (f) Radar
controller (g) TEWS (Tactical
Electronic Warfare System)
controller (h) IFF controller/
selector (i) Communications panel
(j) UHF selector (k) Mode
selector (l) TEWS display
(m) Horizontal situation indicator
(n) Central warning panel
(o) Navigation control panel

sometimes have a gold film element which can be heated electrically. Propeller blades, because they are aerofoil surfaces, suffer for the same reason as the wing, and are usually de-iced by alcohol or electrical heating. Engine carburettors and their intakes are also prone to ice build up, and hot air is used normally to eradicate this. The pitot head, which supplies pressure to the airspeed indicator and a static reference for all pressure-operated instruments, is so important that it is vital that snow or ice should not prevent it from working. To ensure that this does not arise they are usually electrically heated and, for double safety, an alternative static source is often provided.

Other important features of the Model 247

included *oleo-pneumatic* (air/oil) shock-absorbers on the main and tail landing-gear units; electrical retraction of the main gear; hydraulic brakes; controllable-pitch propellers for optimum performance; engine-driven generator and storage battery to provide electric power for landing-gear retraction; cabin dome lights and individual reading lights; and a thermostatically controlled cabin heating and cooling system.

It is not surprising that a company which could produce such an advanced aircraft in 1933 is responsible for the design and production of the Model 707/727/737/747 series of jet airliners of which more than 2,500 examples have been sold to serve the world's airlines.

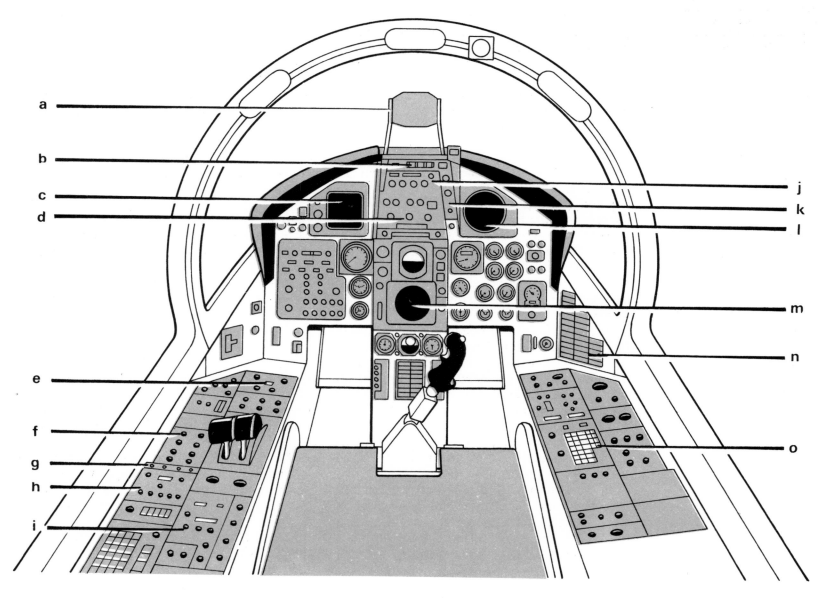

Douglas DC-3

When the Boeing 247 went into service its impact was such that United Air Lines began to acquire passengers from their principal rival, Transcontinental and Western Air (TWA). Because Boeing would not, understandably, supply 247s to TWA, this latter company asked Douglas Aircraft to produce a superior aircraft to their specification, this leading to the prototype DC-1, production DC-2 and a wider-fuselage sleeper version of this designated DST (Douglas Sleeper Transport). The wider fuselage of the DST could obviously accommodate more standard seating,

beginning of the war to determine range, altitude and heading of unidentified aircraft, it became refined and adapted for carriage in a fighter aircraft so that contact could be made with attacking enemy aircraft under conditions of darkness or poor visibility. That type of equipment was called *AI* (air interception).

As research continued it was discovered that a radar transmitter could be used to scan the terrain beneath an aircraft so that what was, in effect, a map of the land and its features was built up on the radar display in the aircraft. This had immediate applications in operations against an

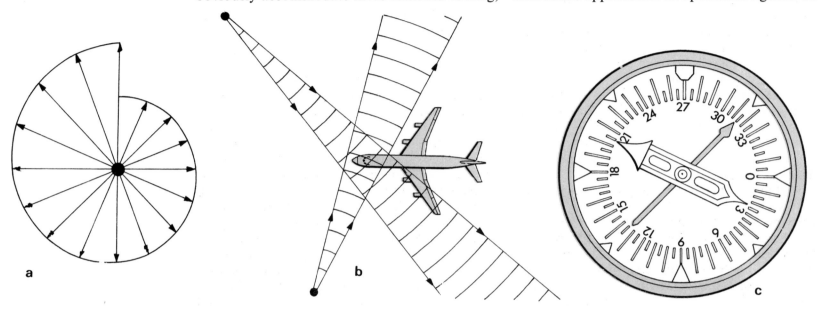

leading to production of the 21-seat Douglas DC-3. This remarkable aeroplane revolutionised air travel in the United States, to the extent that by the time the country became a combatant in World War II, some 80 per cent of all her scheduled airliners were DC-3s.

When America took up arms against Japan, on 8 December 1941, the day following the surprise attack on Pearl Harbour, the war in Europe had already lasted for $2\frac{1}{4}$ years: the Soviet Union had been involved for almost six months. Whereas World War I had speeded the development of aircraft engines, the pressures of this new major conflict were to accelerate not only the development of conventional airframes and power plants, but to introduce a whole range of completely new concepts in aircraft, engines, accessories, equipment and weapons, as well as to transform long-established ideas on navigation.

Radar

When the war clouds were forming on the European horizon scientists in Britain were working to perfect a system of radio location that would make it possible to give ample warning of enemy air attack. It had been known for some time that a radio wave was reflected by a metal object. It was suggested that if it were possible to transmit a signal that would hit a target, and be reflected back to its source, calculation based on the time for the signal to travel out and back would give the target's range.

Known originally as radio detection and ranging, this became condensed subsequently to the now universally known *radar*. Used at the

enemy, for the radar system enabled bombs to be dropped on a target despite cloud cover, allowed leaders of pathfinder squadrons to locate a target with accuracy before illuminating it for the following bomber stream, and was found to be a useful navigational check at any time.

For wartime use this latter system, known as H_2S, was of great importance. It was unlikely that it would have peacetime applications, but the really vital factor was that equipment such as AI carried by night fighters to locate their quarry, and the H_2S that equipped the bombers, had evolved from desk-size modules to small black boxes that could be carried in aeroplanes. It was clear that when peace returned, new generations of civil aircraft would find that radar would be able to add its quota to new safety standards.

In much the same way, the demands of war improved beyond measure the old *DF* (direction finding) systems which had been in use during the between-war years. The traditional system was for the navigator of an aircraft to obtain a positional fix from two ground-based radio stations. Requesting and receiving a broadcast signal from one station, the radio operator would rotate a loop aerial until he was receiving a signal at maximum strength. A scale then enabled him to read off the aircraft's bearing in relation to that station, and on receipt of this information the navigator could put a line on his chart extending from the transmitting station on the perceived bearing. A second fix from another station would give a different bearing, and the intersection of the second plotted line would indicate the aircraft's position.

Radio DF fixes of this nature are reasonably accurate over short ranges. Over greater distances, or if he had reason to doubt the information presented to him, the navigator had recourse to the traditional instrument of the mariner – the sextant – and could confirm his position by observation of the sun by day or stars at night.

On long transoceanic crossings the navigator had a difficult and responsible job, especially if the aircraft's range capability was at all marginal on the route flown. To him it was vital to be fed with a deal of accurate information and he, in turn, expected a pretty high degree of accuracy from the pilot.

But flying an aircraft to such a high standard on, say, an Atlantic crossing, was most demanding. The navigator's task was fundamentally that of navigating from one point to another. The pilot – or captain – of the aircraft, was flying it and also trying to monitor its performance, as well as being responsible for the activities of the crew and the well-being of his passengers.

Automatic Pilot

One of the most valuable aids given to him to ease the work load was the *automatic pilot*, this deriving from the gyro-stabilised instruments which had been developed for blind flying. The basic principle of an elementary autopilot depends upon the use of three gyros which are related to the surfaces which control the aircraft about its three axes of motion. If, for example, the aircraft's nose drops a few degrees, then the

Autopilots of modern design can not only hold preselected altitudes and headings, but can be linked also to radio navigational systems so that they fly the aircraft to a predetermined point.

The radio aids available to the pilot of almost any type of modern aircraft can provide him with clear voice communications over long ranges, accurate position checks, distance to destination and course to steer. If his aircraft is suitably equipped he can use *ILS* (instrument landing system) at many airports. The radar systems developed during the war now provide him with an eye that can look ahead of the aircraft's track and determine if there are adverse weather conditions that need to be avoided.

Radio Aids

Let us take just a brief look at the radio aids because they are important due to their great accuracy. The sky around us is filled with all kinds of radio waves, transmitted in every direction and in a host of frequencies. Aircraft communication systems make use of many of them, according to the particular requirement. Aircraft transmissions do not pose so difficult a problem as that of a nuclear submarine, passing information via an aircraft, for onward transmission to a fixed or mobile base; but all can be catered for.

The airline or private pilot can receive invaluable navigational aid from a device known as VHF (very high frequency) Omni-Range, *VOR* for short. It is based on a network of ground beacons, each of which transmits a continuous

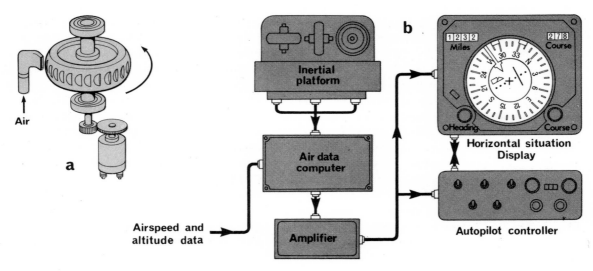

Inertial system
(a) Air driven gyroscope (b) Inertial system, autopilot controller and Horizontal Situation Indicator (Flight Director)

gimbal mounting of the gyro controlling pitch moves with the aircraft, the gyro maintaining its horizontal position. The resulting movement between gyro and gimbal mounting allows for switching to control electric or electro-pneumatic actuators that take appropriate remedial action on the elevators to restore the aircraft to level flight.

Modern autopilots have high degrees of accuracy and sophistication, even those of comparatively modest cost and proportions which are installed in many private aircraft. Whereas the elementary autopilot discussed briefly above can maintain the aircraft in level flight it cannot, if the aircraft has lost several hundred feet of altitude, regain the lost height.

signal radiating the full 360 degrees around the beacon. The signal, however, varies slightly throughout the full circle of rotation, beginning again with the original signal when the beacon starts its next rotation. This slight change in signal allows an indicator in the aircraft to show its position in relation to that station. A fix can be obtained by taking a reference from another VOR beacon, or by using *DME* (distance measuring equipment) in conjunction with VOR.

DME is based upon a transmitter in the aircraft which sends out a radio pulse to a selected ground station. When the signal is received it triggers a pulse to the aircraft, allowing a very accurate measurement of distance. DME is combined with VOR to give bearing as well as distance.

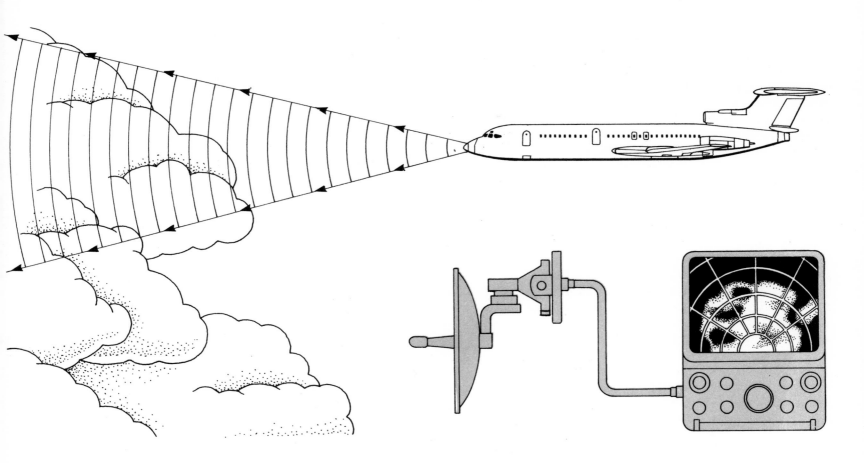

Loran (long-range navigation) is based on the use of constant transmissions from a series of linked radio stations. Sited and separated in a specific way, they produce a pattern of distinctive lines over the oceans, and correspond to a reference chart. Equipment in the aircraft receives these complex signals and interprets them as distinctive lines of reference on the chart, enabling the aircraft's position to be fixed with reasonable accuracy.

Doppler consists of an airborne transmitter and receiver. The transmitter sends a radio wave to the terrain below the aircraft; the receiver picks up its echo. Special equipment analyses the difference between transmitted and received signal and can compute the aircraft's ground-speed and drift. If linked to an autopilot it enables this device to follow closely the intended flight track.

As World War II was nearing its end, Britain found itself on the receiving end of the V2, the German ballistic weapon which, launched from sites on the continent of Europe, climbed some 60 miles (96km) into the air before falling on to its target. From this comparatively small beginning has evolved the entire range of military missiles, and the spacecraft which have taken men to the Moon and unmanned spacecraft out far into space.

Inertial Navigation Systems

To guide a rocket over such enormous distances needed a navigational controller of great accuracy. One factor which makes this so important in space flight is that course corrections consume irreplaceable fuel. This resulted in the development of *INS* (inertial navigation systems), later adopted for use in aircraft. They comprise in their most elementary form an inertial platform so mounted within the aircraft that it is free to pivot about any axis. On this platform are mounted three highly accurate gyroscopes perpendicular to each other. One of these is parallel to each of the aircraft's three axes, and between them they maintain the platform in a constant alignment and relationship to the fixed stars. This platform is thus a perfect reference base for three highly sensitive accelerometers which record, via a computer, their acceleration, and therefore that of the platform and aircraft in the three axes.

This provides the computer with the necessary information to integrate the linear displacement from the beginning of the flight, and since the starting point is known the INS can at any time provide the exact position of the aircraft, and this can be achieved without any reference to an outside source. To ensure that no error can arise there are usually duplicated, occasionally triplicated installations, each of the computers being self-monitoring and each continuously checking the other. To gild the lily, some INS have an optical star tracking unit providing reference figures that enable the computer to monitor and check the accuracy of the gyros and accelerometers.

Electronics evolved as spin-offs of the American space programme have brought a new sophistication and accuracy to many other aspects of aviation. And the fact that miniaturisation has been essential, to allow much of this equipment to be packed into the very limited confines of space probes, satellites and spacecraft, has resulted in compact lightweight units that can be housed in a modern fighter aircraft. This not only reduces the pilot's work load, but means that these new-generation fighters have capabilities undreamed of during World War II.

Take, as an example, a brief look at the electronics that equip the McDonnell Douglas F-15A Eagle air superiority fighter of the United

States Air Force. It has a pulse-Doppler radar system for long-range detection and tracking of high-speed targets at all altitudes, this information being processed by an on-board computer which programmes the launch of the aircraft's missiles or the firing of its internally mounted 20mm six-barrel cannon. In a dogfight situation the radar automatically acquires the target and projects all essential information on *HUD* (head-up display), enabling the pilot to intercept and destroy an enemy aircraft without having to take his eyes off the target. The HUD also presents navigation and steering information to the pilot under all flight conditions, as well as reporting faults in the aircraft's systems. It carries an automatic system to alert allied ground stations that it is a friendly aircraft; to supply positional data and identification to air traffic controllers; and to inform the pilot whether an aircraft spotted visually or by radar is friend or enemy. An air data computer integrates information from many on-board sources, and an altitude and heading reference unit feeds information on the aircraft's pitch, roll and heading to cockpit displays and serves as back-up to the INS, which can navigate the aircraft accurately to any point in the world. Electronic countermeasures equipment is carried to confuse an enemy's defensive system; there are devices to warn of enemy radar activity and of electronic warfare operations; and its *UHF* (ultra-high-frequency) communications have cryptographic capability. There are also other navigational systems, automatic direction finder

In recent years multiple redundant systems of high reliability have been evolved to bring improved standards of safety into what is still one of the most hazardous areas of the entire flight parameter. The first completely automatic landing on a scheduled passenger flight was made as long ago as 16 May 1969, when a BOAC Super VC10 landed at Heathrow after a transatlantic flight from Montreal. There is little doubt that in the not too distant future little 'black boxes', that can 'see' in any weather conditions, will have the responsibility of maintaining the very high standards set by the pilots of today, but extending that capability into the area where human vision can no longer cope.

The basic ground equipment of the ILS comprises radio transmitters that emit a narrow beam of signals, to left and right of the centre of the runway, and pointing upward from near the desired touchdown point along an ideal glide-slope of between 3 and 6 degrees. The signal transmitted laterally from each side of centre is quite distinctive, with a third continuous signal identifying the runway's centreline. A similar vertical arrangement of transmitters permits identification of positions above and below the glideslope, and this information is received on board the aircraft and presented visually on an instrument. To effect an automatic blind landing this information is fed to an advanced autopilot which can not only fly the aircraft in level flight, but can handle also the control of power plant and other variables.

Instrument landing system (ILS) **(a)** Runway threshold markings **(b)** Runway lighting **(c)** Threshold lighting **(d)** Visual Approach Slope Indicators **(e)** Glide slope transmitter **(f)** VOR localizer transmitter **(g)** Inner marker lights **(h)** Outer marker lights **(i)** Airliner on final approach

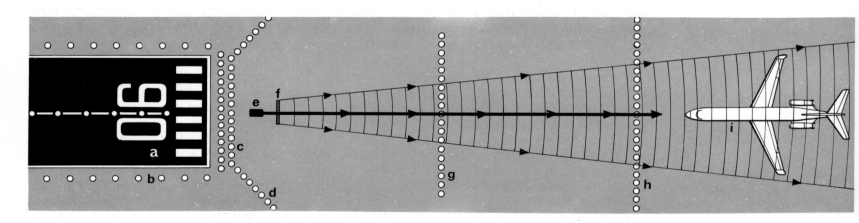

and receivers for ILS. Certainly a little more professional than the weapon systems of the earliest World War I reconnaissance aircraft, which at first comprised only the pilot's personal revolver.

Instrument Landing Systems

Instrument landing systems (ILS), have been developed over a very long period of time for both military and civil aircraft. The advantage of a highly sophisticated, safe and reliable ILS has been apparent for years, its aim being to bring an aircraft in to a safe, controlled landing in conditions when a pilot would not have a sufficiently safe margin of vision. Research and development to evolve a satisfactory system has been more or less continuous since the fog-landing experiments subsidised by the Guggenheim Fund in America almost forty years ago.

Airports

The airport at which the landing is made will almost certainly have seen just as much progress since the 1919 era as have the aircraft which operate from and to them. A pioneer pilot seeing one from overhead for the first time would be amazed, possibly puzzled, by the long concrete runways, with lengths usually in the 10,000ft (3,050m) to 13,000ft (3,960m) range. The main runway at New York's John F Kennedy airport is getting on for 3 miles (4.8km) in length.

The apron at the terminal area, where a single biplane once stood to load a total of passengers that could be counted on a single hand, has been enormously expanded to handle, as smoothly as possible, the thousands of passengers that depart or arrive every day of the year.

Refuelling, at one time carried out by hand from cans of petrol, now requires super-tankers or underground hydrant systems that can dispense to a Boeing 747 anything up to 45,000 US gallons (170,300 litres) of fuel, weighing approximately 134 tons, in the shortest possible time. In fact, the arrival of a wide-body transport from a long-range flight involves a large team of people and vehicles to fuel, check, clean and provision before it can begin to load another group of passengers for a new destination. The aim is to reduce to a minimum the turn-around time, that is the period from when the aircraft's wheels stopped moving to the moment when they turn again as the aircraft is taxied away to its take-off point. This is terribly important when it is appreciated that these huge aircraft cost astronomically large sums to purchase and operate. It is only when they are airborne with a worthwhile complement of passengers and/or freight that they can earn any revenue to offset the airline's capital investment.

A modern airport is so complex and comprehensive that it is almost a little world of its own. One expects there to be provision for the efficient handling of baggage, easy supply of tickets and information, comfortable waiting rooms and easy access to one's aircraft. But so much more is necessary to ensure the smooth operation of the airport, and the aircraft that use it. Rest rooms, restaurants, shops, book stalls, banks are all part of the scene. So is baggage handling, air mail, customs, quarantine, medical services and the now essential screening to eliminate the terrorist from the skies. Around the airport are offices,

Modern airport

stores, buildings and hangars concerned with such factors as maintenance, cargo, emergency services, fuel, animals in transit, communications, air traffic control and meteorology.

If, at this moment, you were a passenger in one of the lounges, awaiting to hear a loudspeaker announcement advising you to board your aircraft for a flight from London to New York, it would be interesting if you could walk around with the captain of the aircraft as he, and his crew, prepare to make your journey as safe, incident-free, comfortable and enjoyable as possible.

A Typical Flight

All of them will probably have been at the airport for some time, as they have a fair amount of preparation despite the fact that it is everyday routine. The captain will have checked on the meteorological conditions applicable at the take-off point and the weather forecast for his route and destination. Most important, he will have studied carefully the computer flight plan, covering the period of the flight, which is compiled from the published tracks from oceanic centres. This gives such information as wind velocity, track, air temperature and true airspeed. It gives also a computed figure for fuel load and flight time, and the captain must check to affirm that these figures are accurate. Having satisfied himself of weather conditions at diversionary airports near the route, and the serviceability of radio facilities, he will approve the aircraft flight plan.

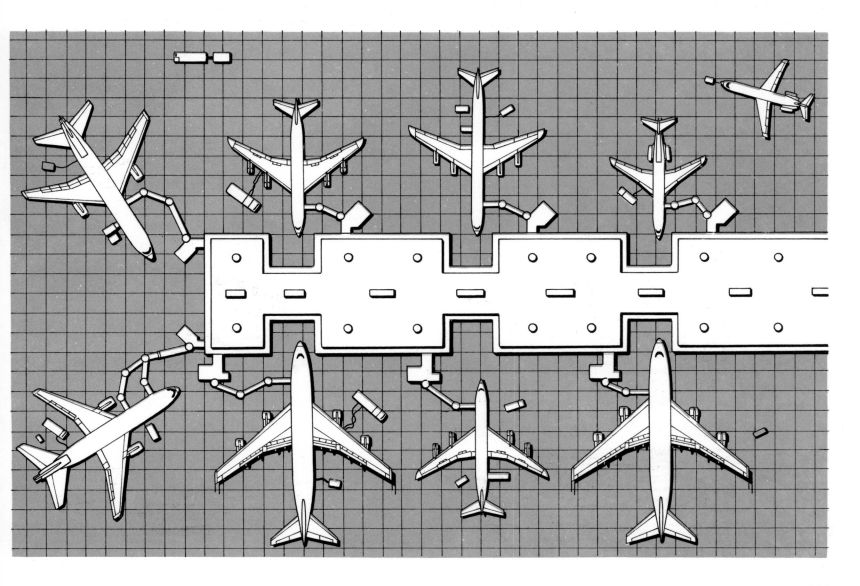

On arrival at the aircraft the captain will brief the crew in respect of special information and conditions before proceeding with certain vital checks. He must satisfy himself that exactly the correct weight of fuel is on board, that the engineers are completely satisfied as to the serviceability of the aircraft, and will examine and sign his approval of the load form that confirms the correct distribution and balance of the total payload about the aircraft's centre of gravity.

As the stewards and stewardesses ensure that they, too, are prepared and ready with ample supplies of food and other refreshments, and that safety equipment in their care is as it should be, the captain and his flight crew will have begun the time-consuming process of working through the pre-start check list.

At about this time you will be approaching the aircraft, to be welcomed aboard by a stewardess, one of several whose duty is to make you feel at home, to look after your comforts and ensure that you have essential information on procedures designed for your safety and the action to be taken in event of emergency. This latter part of their duties is probably one of the most boring, for the majority of cabin staff will fly year after year without the slightest hint of alarm. How will they react in an emergency? Past experience has shown how passengers have been full of admiration for the calm and confident behaviour of cabin staff in a crisis, an expertise perfected by regular routine drills to ensure that each of them knows exactly what to do in an emergency and when to do it.

As you and your fellow passengers settle in your seats there will come a whine of sound as engines are started up, dropping in pitch as the revolutions steady. By the time that security of seat belts has been checked, the aircraft will already be taxying towards the take-off point. On the flight deck eyes, hands and voices are still busy with the seemingly endless check list: as the last vital items are being cleared an instruction is received from airport control for the aircraft to make its take-off.

On receipt of this directive the captain manoeuvres the aircraft on to the runway, aligning it in the centre before applying the parking brake. With the pre-take-off checks completed the captain releases the brakes, advances the engine thrust controls smoothly and immediately the enormous power of the jet engines becomes apparent to you as the aircraft surges forward, accelerating rapidly down the runway. This manoeuvre, and that of landing, requires the full concentration of the flight crew.

As the speed of the aircraft increases, confirmation is given to the captain that the engines are developing full power, and the co-pilot will call out readings to him as progressively higher speeds are attained. Should an engine failure occur before a certain speed has been reached, then the take-off must be abandoned. At a higher speed there will be insufficient runway for the take-off to be aborted without some risk: but at that higher speed an engine-out take-off is perfectly safe, and the aircraft will orbit the airport until it is able to come in for a landing.

Such an event is most unlikely, and as the aircraft gains flying speed its nose will lift and, in most cases, it will climb steeply away from the runway. As this occurs, the captain will give orders for landing-gear retraction, and as speed

Aviation today is a many-headed creature with wide-ranging uses. Here a Sikorsky helicopter (S61) serves a North Sea oil platform.

and height increase the wing flaps will be raised, in stages, until they are fully retracted. As the captain concentrates on flying the aircraft to comply with noise-abatement procedures, the post-take-off checks proceed; systems which are coming into operation at this stage need to be monitored and, in fact, this is invariably one of the busiest stages of any flight. Clearance for the oceanic stage of the flight has to be requested, approved and read back for confirmation, and is followed by an instruction from *ATC* (air traffic control) to climb to a new flight level.

With receipt of this order the climb is initiated, and the aircraft put on to a course that will bring it to a turning point where altitude and route will be set for the transatlantic crossing. High above a blanket of cloud which obscures the ground nearly six miles below, a needle on the dial of the VOR indicator gives the only physical sign that they have left the land mass of Britain and are heading out across the Atlantic towards the northern tip of Newfoundland.

Like most modern transports your aircraft has an INS, and as the track across the ocean is confirmed this is brought into operation and coupled to the autopilot so that, in effect, the aircraft can now navigate itself accurately to a landfall at Newfoundland. The routine of the flight is now established and in the cabin the crew will be taking orders for cocktails and other refreshments prior to serving lunch or dinner, according to the time of day.

As the bustle of preparation for the meal is taking place, a change in the aircraft's attitude and the note of its engines indicates that an ATC instruction has been received for a climb to its cruising flight level. This flight level is one which will be recognisable accurately by all aircraft flying over the ocean, for although the setting of their barometric altimeters may differ according to their point of take-off, a uniform standard setting is imposed so that vertical separation of aircraft in differing air lanes can be maintained with accuracy to minimise the risk of collision. When the flight level is attained the tone of the engines will fall as they are brought back on to an economic cruise setting and, at this point, the autopilot will be switched to 'altitude lock' so that it will maintain both course and height.

The maintenance of an accurate cruising speed is as essential as the height factor, and will have been established in the details of the oceanic clearance for that particular flight. It is important for two reasons, one being to keep the necessary lateral separation between aircraft in the same air lane, the other to achieve the best possible fuel economy. A conventional airspeed indicator is not sufficiently accurate for such a purpose at the altitude at which these aircraft fly. Instead, an instrument called a *Machmeter* is used, which records in Mach numbers the aircraft's speed as a percentage of the speed of sound. Because sonic speed varies according to altitude, falling as height increases (pressure decreases) and also rises and falls as temperature rises and falls, it is a far more complex instrument than an airspeed indicator. Because it measures temperature and pressure and automatically corrects the speed reading as

required by these variables, great accuracy is attained. This means that throughout the entire flight the Machmeter, and other instruments, are monitored continuously. If the Mach number is found to vary – most usually through temperature changes – it is corrected immediately by an adjustment of the engine thrust settings.

While the passengers are enjoying their meal in the cabin, listening via headsets to a variety of stereophonic music, or perhaps watching a film show, the vigilance of the flight crew is undiminished. There is always something to demand their attention: for example, winds which can attain as much as 170mph (275km/h), and which come from any direction, mean that despite such advanced features as the INS it is desirable to double-check the aircraft's position from time to time by alternate means, Loran being the most usual. And as the aircraft passes certain positions on its course, progress is reported to ATC. From take-off to longitude 20W and from 40W to the North American Continent, this is done automatically by the aircraft's transponder, as well as being supplemented by verbal reports from the captain or co-pilot. In the mid-ocean gap between those two points, voice communication between the crew and air traffic controllers is maintained by HF radio.

A muted alarm bell on the flight deck may give warning that a ground station wishes to pass a message and the pilot who is monitoring an emergency guard frequency throughout the ocean crossing will select his receiver to take the incoming call. Perhaps it is a *Sigmet* (meteorological communication) giving warning of thunderstorms or clear-air turbulence reported by other aircraft. The aircraft's weather radar cannot detect turbulence and a slight change in flight level or track may be desirable if bad turbulence has been reported. However desirable, this is rarely given, except in an emergency, for any lateral or vertical displacement from track can cause infringement of adjacent air lanes or flight levels. Clear-air turbulence is caused usually on the periphery of jet-streams or other high-velocity winds, the shear between these and the main mass of slow-moving air creating invisible and sometimes violent whirlpools of air. If the warning is one of thunderclouds, the weather radar will confirm at long range whether a diversion is necessary or if the aircraft can pass safely through their imposing mass.

The aircraft's flight level may now be 350, that is 35,000ft (10,670m). Way down below, on the tumbled waters of the Atlantic, an ocean weather ship is stationed. Their numbers have reduced steadily until now, in 1976, only three remain, the task of their crews very much the same: to observe, measure and report to land-based meteorological stations weather data at the surface and at high levels. Their small numbers emphasise the changing times, for with something approaching 200 aircraft per day travelling above and reporting weather conditions over the North Atlantic, as well as a mass of meteorological information received from geo-stationary satellites and other, more conventional sources, even their days must be numbered.

By now our aircraft has almost completed the oceanic stage of its crossing to North America, and the VOR is picking up the beacon at St. Anthony, which is at the northern tip of New-foundland. From there a string of VOR beacons can lead off to a variety of destinations, but our course is over the Gulf of St. Lawrence and following a well marked corridor across the border which separates Canada and America.

By this time the flight crew will be preparing for their landing at New York's John F Kennedy airport (JFK). There is much to do in the period remaining and over the mainland, clear from the comparatively traffic-free reaches of the Atlantic, the air lanes are crowded with aircraft. One of the first tasks is to establish the New York weather conditions. If satisfactory, all well and good; if at all doubtful the captain will seek information on alternatives in case deteriorating weather will force a diversion.

Another task is to establish with reasonable accuracy the quantity of fuel remaining in the aircraft's tanks. This is necessary for two reasons: firstly, to establish the margin of fuel available in the event of a protracted *hold* (orbiting a point until clearance for landing is given) or diversion; secondly, to ascertain as near as possible the aircraft's landing weight, for this affects its approach speed as it nears the airport.

Dusk is creeping over the land as we pass close to Boston, lights twinkling below when the ground can be seen between low banks of cloud. The passengers with window seats, however many times they have flown, experience a strange feeling of return as the sight below reminds them that time and distance have been strangely condensed and that, already, another totally different world is awaiting them down below.

On the flight deck the captain will be viewing the clouds with a far more jaundiced eye, concerned only whether they presage rain squalls on his approach to JFK. He is, however, far too busy to linger on the prospects and tucks the information away in a corner of his mind as ATC gives instructions for the aircraft to begin a descent, at some 2,500ft (760m) per minute to a height of 11,000ft (3,350m) above Deer Park VOR, around which it must orbit until instructed to begin the landing approach.

Immediately, the first section of the approach check begins, during which barometric altimeters are reset to the local pressure. Circling the Deer Park VOR in the hold pattern, the captain receives radio information confirming that the weather is not deteriorating, and the ceaseless chatter of the air tells him that the aircraft ahead has just landed. Almost immediately comes the instruction to begin the landing approach.

By now it is almost dark, and the crew on the flight deck concentrate their gaze on vital instruments. In the cabin the stewardesses check that 'no smoking' instructions have been obeyed and that the passengers have their seat belts fastened. Still descending, the captain has turned on the ILS and is waiting for the moment when the air-craft is aligned with the localiser beam in level flight. As soon as the needle of the ILS indicator tells him that the aircraft has intercepted the glideslope beam he gives instructions for the landing check to be completed.

Confirmation is given that the landing gear is down and locked, flaps at the optimum settings for the particular approach speed and landing lights on, and power settings are reduced as the run down the glideslope begins. Suddenly the aircraft is free of the low cloud and ahead can be seen clearly the maze of lights which mark the runway, taxi tracks and airport environs. Other lights mark the runway's centreline and edges, brilliantly illuminated Visual Approach Slope Indicators confirm the accuracy of the ILS approach down the glideslope. Unless the air-craft is equipped for automatic landing the pilot now flicks the switch that tells the autopilot its job is completed. This is the supreme moment of the flight for the captain, his charge racing towards the runway at something in excess of 200ft (61m) a second.

Experienced hands feel the living aircraft moving around in its three dimensions, and it is experience which firmly and gently takes com-plete control, aligns the machine with the centre of the runway and, as it crosses the threshold, gives a gentle pull on the control column to lift the nose marginally as thrust is cut off and the main wheels gently but firmly meet the concrete. Immediately, the lift dumpers, or spoilers, are extended to kill aerodynamic lift, the nosewheel touches the ground and the thunder of reverse thrust announces another arrival at JFK.

This is day-to-day routine, mostly completely uneventful because so much has been done since the end of World War II to enhance safety. It is an unending process, because the steady increase of air traffic – until the alarm bells of galloping fuel prices brought a temporary halt in the growth pattern – has made it essential for international bodies concerned with civil aviation to work together in the interests of safe air travel.

Nevertheless, international concern regarding the speed at which world reserves of hydrocarbon fuels are being depleted has brought changes in the usage of aircraft at all levels. The large-body jet-liners have gained new importance because of the economies offered by the combination of their passenger and freight capacity with the effi-ciency of their advanced-technology turbofan engines. Fuel cost has also reduced considerably the volume of private flight in powered aircraft.

The result is a reawakening of enthusiasm in sailplanes and soaring flight – one of the most rewarding forms of private flying. The movement back to the beginning of aviation history con-tinues with a new-found interest in the construc-tion and flight of hang-gliders, and in the growing number of projects that seek to reintroduce the airship for both passenger and cargo transport. These latter vessels would undoubtedly benefit from new materials and modern engines.

With the hot air balloon the wheel has turned full circle. It is now possible for groups of young people to own and fly a balloon. In so doing they can not only come to an appreciation of the realization of flight, but can experience for them-selves the magic which urged the pioneers on to achieve success.

Military Aircraft of Today

With our emphasis being on military aircraft, it is worth taking a final look around at some of the advanced aircraft in use with the world's air forces, or which are being developed as new-generation aircraft.

It will be recalled that Northrop in the US had developed a lightweight tactical fighter designated F-5, which was supplied to Allied nations under MAP When the US Government initiated a design competition to acquire a new International Fighter Aircraft (IFA) to succeed the F-5, Northrop proposed an advanced version of the same aircraft, and in November 1970 it was announced that this company had won the competition.

Their resulting F-5E Tiger II **(118)** has more powerful turbojet engines, advanced electronics and equipment, and is able to deploy an amazingly wide variety of weapons from underfuselage and under-wing hard points, which can accommodate a total of 7,000 lb (3,157 kg). Maximum level speed is Mach 1·6, slightly faster than the F-5, but manoeuvrability rather than speed is considered the most important feature of this new aircraft, which has leading-edge manoeuvring flaps similar to those developed for the Royal Netherlands Air Force's NF-5A/Bs.

Towards the end of 1969, McDonnell Douglas Corporation was announced the winner of a design competition to provide the USAF with a new air superiority fighter.

There is a distinct overall similarity between this aircraft, designated as the F-15A Eagle (119), and Grumman's F-14 Tomcat. The major difference is predictable without even seeing these aircraft, for since the Eagle does not need to have the very wide speed range of the deck-landing Tomcat, it need not be involved in the complexities inseparable from a variable-geometry wing, and this is, indeed, the case.

Eagle will carry up to 12,000 lb (5,433 kg) of mixed weapons on external stations, but the really complex aspect of the weapons system is the advanced electronics, which will not only seek and acquire small high-speed targets, but will ensure that the aircraft's missiles or internal gun is fired at the right moment to ensure the target's destruction. The first aircraft to become operational was delivered to the USAF on 14 November 1974.

Visitors to Farnborough International '74 will have seen the F-15A in flight, performing its routine in appalling weather, and it is this kind of capability which must be the stock-in-trade of a successful combat fighter.

119

Five companies submitted design proposals to meet the USAF's requirement for a Lightweight Fighter Prototype, and in April 1972 General Dynamics and Northrop were selected to build competing prototypes.

This method of acquiring the most effective aeroplane for a particular role dates back to the early days of the US Army Air Service. Then it was essential to get the best machine for the job: today, when computers can predict performance

with surprising accuracy, it is not essential but desirable. Desirable because the old-fashioned rapport between man and machine—called seat-of-the-pants flying—is not so predictable. Both the contenders will almost certainly be flyable to the predicted performance. Just as certainly, one of them will be more pleasant to fly.

General Dynamics' YF-16 prototype **(120)** flew officially for the first time on 2 February 1974, competing subsequently against the Northrop YF-17 which first flew on 9 June 1974. By then the USAF had decided to evaluate these two aircraft in the role of an Air Combat Fighter (ACF), and in January 1975 the YF-16 was declared the winner. With the USAF having a requirement for up to 650 production F-16s, and with 306 more ordered by Belgium, Denmark, the Netherlands and Norway, this aircraft has become a most important weapon in the West's defence.

Though defeated in the USAF's ACF evaluation by the General Dynamics YF-16, Northrop's YF-17 remains a significant aircraft, and the 001 and 002 prototypes are seen in flight in the accompanying picture (121). The US Navy has also a requirement for an air combat fighter and initially showed considerable interest in Northrop's YF-17. However, further evaluation by the Navy showed the desirability of having a slightly-enlarged and strengthened version for service on board Fleet aircraft carriers, and a joint contract for the development of such an aircraft, under the designation F-18, was awarded to McDonnell Douglas and Northrop in May 1975. Some 8,000 lb (3,629 kg) heavier than the YF-17, and to be powered by two General Electric F404-GE-400 turbofan engines rated at about 16,000 lb (7,257 kg) static thrust,

121

122

eleven development aircraft are to be built initially.

In an age when military aircraft can travel at speeds between 1,500 and 2,000 mph (2,414 and 3,219 km/h) as routine, and when one of the major threats is that imposed by missiles, the defences need as much warning as possible of impending attack or the approach of hostile aircraft/weapons. Even when the information is received, a complex control centre is necessary to evaluate the input and initiate suitable action to contain the enemy's attack.

Obviously, the most vulnerable point of such a defence system is the control centre, for once it is put out of action it is unlikely that defensive weapons of the right kind will be launched sufficiently early.

One of the solutions to this problem lies in the provision of Airborne Warning and Control System (AWACS) aircraft. Because of their mobility in three dimensions, they are seen to offer a survivable early warning, command and control system.

Boeing have supplied the USAF with testbed aircraft, based on the 707, designated Boeing EC-137D AWACS (**122**). The large radome, pylon-mounted from the aft fuselage, carries a 24 ft (7·32 m) diameter antenna which scans 360° around the aircraft, and from ground level up into the stratosphere. These aircraft are currently being evaluated and could prove to be an important type of aircraft for the future, with both civil and military applications.

One of the most important aircraft being procured for the USAF at the present time is the B-1 strategic bomber which has been designed and built by Rockwell International. The first of these supersonic bomber prototypes was rolled out on 26 October 1974 (**123**).

A 'swing-wing' design, with the blended wing/body concept used for the company's submission for the F-15 fighter competition, the B-1 is designed to have a maximum speed of Mach 2·2 (approximately 1,450 mph: 2,333 km/h at 50,000 ft: 15,000 m), range of 6,100 miles (9,800 km) at its cruising speed, and the capability to uplift a maximum weapon load of 115,000 lb (52,160 kg). When it is realised that this weapon load equals the weight of nearly twenty Spitfires, one gains some appreciation of the technological advances made in military aircraft in the past 36 years.

124

One of the most important categories of military aircraft must always be the basic trainer. The quality and capability of an air force stems from its standard of training and the Royal Air Force has long understood this first principle. Latest trainer to be built for the RAF is the Hawker Siddeley Hawk (124), a small single-turbofan-powered tandem two-seat aircraft which is to replace the Gnat and Hunter and, ultimately, the Jet Provost.

A moderately swept wing and special trailing-edge flaps give the all-important speed range necessary, providing the essential low control speed required for a basic trainer, coupled with a maximum speed of Mach 1·13 at 48,000 ft (14,630 m), for sparkling performance as an advanced trainer. It is intended also to develop the Hawk for a close-support role, in which configuration it is designed to deploy a maximum external load of up to 5,000 lb (2,270 kg) of mixed ordnance.

The first of these aircraft to be completed flew for the first time on 21 August 1974. This was a production aircraft, which means that the Hawk will probably be unique by becoming the first military aircraft to enter service without a prototype being built and flown.

The Saab 35 Draken, which is in service with the Danish and Swedish Air Forces, is an example of specialized design to meet a specific requirement.

Swedish policy insists that in the event of a crisis her air force must not be tied slavishly to air stations, the exact position of which would be known to an enemy. Instead, they are to be dispersed throughout the country, and aircraft have to be capable of take-off from short sections of the country's main roads. This accounts for selection of the double-delta wing for the Draken, its large area allowing short take-off and landing runs.

The Saab J 35F Draken is illustrated (125), an all-weather fighter or attack aircraft, which can carry missiles, rockets and other weapons totalling 9,000 lb (4,082 kg) on external attachment points. Take-off run with nine 1,000 lb bombs is only 4,030 ft (1,210 m).

Designed to replace eventually the J 35 Drakens at present in use by the Swedish Air Force, the first of the more advanced Saab 37 Viggen prototypes flew for the first time on 8 February 1967.

There was a change of wing configuration with this aircraft in an attempt to enhance short take-off and landing (STOL) capability. The delta wing has been retained, but there is also a foreplane fitted with trailing-edge flaps. This combination has proved most effective and the AJ 37 Viggen (126) is able to take off from and land on hard paved surfaces only 1,600 ft (500 m) in length.

125

126

One of the most technically complicated aircraft to appear on the aviation scene, with the first flight of a prototype on 14 August 1974, is the Panavia MRCA (Multi-Role Combat Aircraft, **127)**. Perhaps one of the really remarkable achievements relating to this aircraft was the creation of a design capable of adaptation to meet the requirements of the British RAF, German Air Force and Navy and the Italian Air Force. This was followed by the formation in 1969 of an international company—Panavia—com-

bining the talents of the British Aircraft Corporation, Germany's Messerschmitt-Bölkow-Blohm and Italy's Aeritalia to build this very important 'swing-wing' aircraft.

The technical complication comes from the need to produce an aeroplane with multi-role capability, and much of the structural complexity is associated with the very advanced wing. Conventional flying controls are replaced by a 'fly-by-wire' system, in which triple redundant circuits and electric actuators move the

aircraft's control surfaces. Most complex of all is the highly sophisticated avionics system which features terrain-following and attack radar together with a laser rangefinder. It is estimated that more than 800 MRCAs will be built to meet the needs of Germany, Italy and the UK, with the first deliveries going to the Luftwaffe in 1978.

The British defence system has available no early warning and control aircraft such as the Boeing AWACS being

developed for the USAF.

Instead, this country relies upon the NATO radar system, covering the whole of Europe and its approaches, to give RAF interceptors time in which to scramble and investigate any potentially hostile aircraft.

Russian reconnaissance aircraft are frequently busy far above the North Sea, and the illustration (128) shows a Soviet Tu-95, known to NATO as 'Bear-D', being shepherded by a Royal Air Force Phantom.

128

127

D-9591

MRCA

Hawker Siddeley Aviation in Britain has developed the only operational fixed-wing vertical/short take-off and landing (V/STOL) strike fighter in the Western world.

Originating from the company's P.1127/Kestrel series of aircraft, the Harrier is in service with the Royal Air Force, the illustration (129) showing typical terrain into which and out of which these aircraft can operate, right up alongside front-line positions.

This capability comes from the remarkable Rolls-Royce Bristol Pegasus vectored-thrust turbofan engine used in the Harrier. With its nozzles rotated vertically downward the aircraft lifts off the ground supported by jet reaction. As height is gained the nozzles are rotated progressively rearward until the aircraft is moving forward fast enough for the wings to generate adequate lift.

Potentially the most important version of the Harrier is that designated AV-8A, a single-seat close-support and tactical reconnaissance aircraft for the United States Marine Corps (USMC).

The first of these was delivered on 26 January 1971, and the total number of firm orders received by early 1974 amounted to 102 aircraft, including 8 TAV-8A two-seat trainers.

Illustrated are five AV-8As (130) of one of the USMCs squadrons which are already operational.

130

129

155

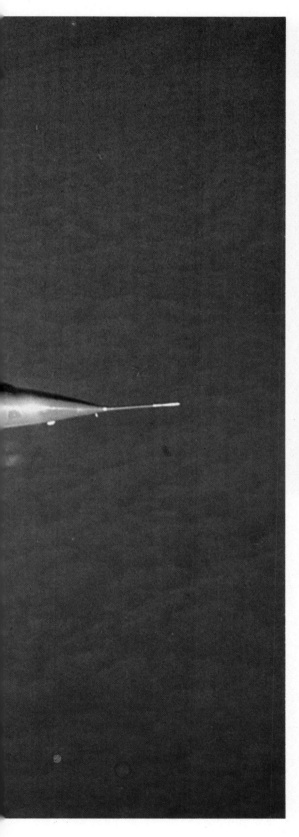

The cost of developing complex new aircraft is fast becoming beyond the means of any private company. This has resulted in international collaboration on many projects, both civil and military.

Typical is the Société Européenne de Production de l'Avion (SEPECAT), the Anglo-French company formed by Breguet Aviation and British Aircraft Corporation in 1966 to produce the Jaguar supersonic strike fighter/trainer for the air forces of France and Britain.

To date, four versions are in production: the Jaguar A single-seat strike version and Jaguar E (131) two-seat advanced trainer for the French Armée de l'Air. Corresponding versions for the RAF have the designation Jaguar S and B respectively. The British S differs from its French counterpart by having an advanced inertial navigation and weapon aiming system, which is integrated with an on-board digital computer.

Another international collaboration has produced a new two-seat basic trainer, advanced light strike and battlefield reconnaissance aircraft, the Franco-German Alpha Jet (132) designed and produced jointly by Dassault-Breguet in France and Dornier in Germany.

First flight of a prototype was made on 26 October 1973 and the first production aircraft are scheduled for delivery in 1976.

Manufacture of the outer wing panels, tail unit, rear fuselage and cold-flow exhaust is carried out by Dornier, who are responsible also for final assembly of the close-support version. France builds the rest of the airframe, and assembles the trainer versions. Power plant, common to both, consists of two SNECMA/ Turboméca Larzac turbofan engines, each of 2,976 lb static thrust.

133

134

135

136

In the scramble for military superiority which has been taking place between East and West since the end of World War II, there have been many changes of ideas as new weapons and counter-weapons evolved. The ICBM was once considered the ultimate weapon, but it was realized that once their fixed launch sites had been identified, they became primary and vulnerable targets for a well-informed enemy. Hence the American B-52 and British Vulcan, both able to deploy nuclear stand-off bombs, providing a mobile rather than static launch site for these weapons. Unfortunately, aircraft need aerodromes, which can be put out of commission

So has developed the nuclear submarine which, invisible beneath the sea, can launch ballistic missiles without surfacing. Their detection and destruction poses a very different problem.

Among the anti-submarine patrol bombers developed to meet this threat is the Lockheed P-3 Orion (135). Carrying magnetic anomaly detection (MAD) equipment and sono-buoys to locate underwater craft, it can be armed with nuclear depth bombs, torpedoes, mines and rockets to deal with the enemy vessel when its position has been ascertained.

France has also developed an effective maritime patrol aircraft to fulfil the same task as the P-3 Orion. This is the

Breguet Br.1150 Atlantic (136), selected from 25 submissions in response to a NATO design competition.

Built by a consortium of European manufacturers, under the overall leadership of Breguet, it is in production for use by the navies of France, Germany, Italy and the Netherlands. Like the Orion it has MAD equipment, but has also a tail-fin pod containing electronic counter-measures (ECM) and a retractable radar 'dustbin' beneath the forward fuselage.

The internal weapons bay of the Atlantic can accommodate all standard NATO bombs, depth charges and homing torpedoes. The illustration shows clearly the radar 'dustbin', and gives some idea of the capacity of the bomb bay.

Marine patrol craft were not neglected in the United States. It came as no great surprise when Grumman Corporation were announced the winner of a design competition to provide a new carrier-based multi-role fighter for the US Navy, for this company has a long tradition of building naval and maritime aircraft.

Required to be fast—it has a maximum design speed of Mach 2·34—the F-14 Tomcat (133) has variable-geometry wings to allow the slow approach speeds required for all-weather deck landings.

Armament will consist initially of four Sparrow air-to-air missiles, carried

partially buried in the fuselage, plus various combinations of other weapons to a maximum external load of 14,500 lb (6,577 kg). The second illustration (134) gives an excellent view of the all-important air intakes, which are so critical for high-performance aircraft, and of the small ventral fins mounted at the rear of each engine nacelle.

Following page:

Britain, too, has an important long-range maritime patrol aircraft, the first turbofan-powered anti-submarine aircraft to be built anywhere in the world.

This is the Hawker Siddeley Nimrod, which has been developed from the Comet 4C airliner, and the first of these was delivered to Strike Command's No. 201 Squadron at Kinloss on 2 October 1969.

Like the Atlantic it has MAD and ECM, plus sono-buoys and an Autolycus ionization detector to 'sniff out' any shipping below. It carries also a search-light for night attack and advanced air-to-surface radar. It can use depth charges, mines, bombs and torpedoes to attack the enemy, as well as Aérospatiale's AS.12 air-to-surface wire-guided missiles, which are carried beneath the wing.

The illustration (137) shows an RAF Nimrod which has located and is circling to inspect a Russian submarine.

137

Significant Aircraft of the World

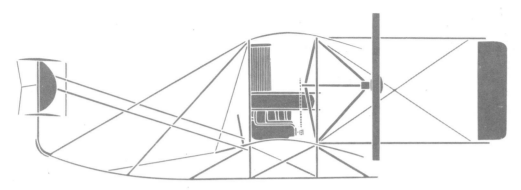

Wright Flyer A

US Wright Flyer A (1908)

Type	two-seat reconnaissance aircraft
Engine	30hp Wright 4-cylinder in-line water-cooled
Armament	none
Maximum Speed	44mph (70km/h)
Ceiling	approx 400ft (122m)
Wing Area	approx 237sq ft (22.00m²)
Weight Empty	740lb (336kg)
Take-off Weight	1,200lb (544kg)
Span	36ft 4in (11.07m)
Length	28ft 0in (8.53m)
Height	8ft 1in (2.46m)

The Military Flyer, first tested in 1908, crashed in September, injuring Orville Wright and killing his passenger, Lt. Thomas B Selfridge. It was rebuilt and taken back into service in 1909.

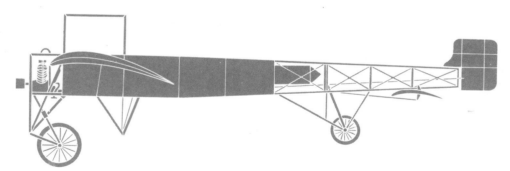

Blériot XI

France Blériot XI (1909)

Type	single-seat monoplane
Engine	22/25hp Anzani 3-cylinder 'semi-radial' air-cooled
Armament	none
Maximum Speed	36mph (58km/h)
Wing Area	150sq ft (13.93m²)
Weight Empty	463lb (210kg)
Take-off Weight	661lb (300kg)
Span	25ft 7in (7.81m)
Length	26ft 3in (8.00m)

The Blériot XI (*Type Onze*), flown by Louis Blériot, was the first heavier-than-air craft to achieve a successful crossing of the English Channel. The flight from Les Baraques, near Calais, to Northfall Meadow, near Dover Castle, was completed in 36½min.

France Fabre Hydro-Aeroplane (1910)

Type	single-seat experimental float-plane
Engine	50hp Gnome rotary air-cooled
Armament	none
Take-off Weight	1,047lb (475kg)

Fabre's Hydro-Aeroplane was the first powered aircraft in the world to take off from water, on 28 March 1910, near Marseilles. It was an odd-looking aeroplane of even stranger construction, two plank-like beams forming the fuselage and supporting biplane surfaces at the forward end and a large monoplane wing aft. The engine was mounted at the aft end of the upper beam and drove a two-blade wooden pusher propeller. The aircraft was supported on the water by three floats of Fabre's own design, and his name is remembered best for the manufacture and supply of floats of this type for a variety of early float-planes; they were so mounted and wire-braced to have positive incidence, enabling the aircraft to plane on the water, as well as providing a certain amount of lift in flight.

France Deperdussin Racer (1912/1913)

Type	single-seat sporting aircraft
Engine	160hp Gnome rotary air-cooled
Armament	none
Maximum Speed	127mph (203km/h)
Wing Area	104sq ft (9.66m²)
Take-off Weight	1,350lb (612kg)
Span	21ft 10in (6.65m)
Length	20ft 0in (6.09m)

The Deperdussin Racer of 1913 is of particular interest because it emphasises the capability of the French aircraft industry at this very early date. Following the general design configuration of the Blériot monoplanes, Armand Deperdussin jumped several stages ahead of all competitors by concentrating his undisputed genius on the achievement of a clean design. The monoplane wing was minimally wire-braced and the fuselage was a true monocoque built up as a three-ply shell of tulip wood, covered subsequently both internally and externally by fabric. Landing gear struts were carefully faired to a streamline section, and even the rotary power plant was enclosed in a neat cowling and 'faired' by an enormous spinner. In this type of aircraft Maurice Prévost captured the world speed record on three different occasions at Reims in 1913, the final and fastest speed being 126.67mph (203km/h).

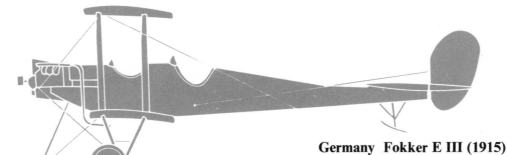

BE2b

Britain Royal Aircraft Factory BE2b (1913)

Type	two-seat reconnaissance air-craft
Engine	70hp Renault 8-cylinder in-line water-cooled
Armament	one 100lb bomb or equivalent in smaller bombs and a variety of small arms for defence
Maximum Speed	70mph (112km/h) at sea level
Rate of Climb	333ft (101m)/min
Ceiling	10,000ft (3,050m)
Wing Area	352sq ft (32.70m²)
Weight Empty	1,274lb (578kg)
Take-off Weight	1,600lb (726kg)
Span	35ft 0½in (10.68m)
Length	29ft 6½in (9.00m)
Height	10ft 2in (3.10m)

The BE2b version of the BE2 series had improved top-decking to provide better protection for the crew, changes in rudder and elevator controls, and some of the later models had ailerons instead of wing-warping for lateral control. BE2s were used for much pioneering work on landing-gear improvements and early wireless experiments.

France Voisin Bomber (1914)

Type	single-engine day/night bomber
Engine	130hp Canton-Unné 9-cylin-der radial water-cooled
Armament	a variety of machine-guns and bombs
Maximum Speed	74mph (119km/h)
Wing Area	484sq ft (45.0m²)
Weight Empty	2,140lb (971kg)
Take-off Weight	3,025lb (1,372kg)
Span	48ft 4in (14.73m)
Length	31ft 2in (9.50m)
Height	12ft 6in (3.81m)

A somewhat functional four-wheel landing gear, the leading pair appearing to be oversize bicycle wheels, gave a first impression of homebuilt frailty to the Voisin bomber. Nothing could have been further from the truth, for its metal frame structure was to assure it of exceptional longevity for a World War I aircraft, and it remained in operational service throughout the war. Distinctive features of the design included the four-wheel landing gear, permitting operation from rough surfaces, the provision of band-type wheel brakes on the aft pair of wheels, and the unusual 130hp Canton-Unné water-cooled radial engine. Its crew of two, accommodated in a 'bath-tub' nacelle, had a variety of armament according to date and role, and included in this variety was a Hotchkiss gun of 37mm or 47mm calibre or a maximum bomb load of 600lb (270kg).

Germany Fokker E III (1915)

Type	single-seat escort fighter
Engine	100hp Oberursel UI 9-cylin-der rotary air-cooled
Armament	one fixed 7.92mm Spandau machine-gun
Maximum Speed	87.5mph (141km/h)
Rate of Climb	656ft (200m)/min
Ceiling	11,500ft (3,505m)
Wing Area	172sq ft (16.0m²)
Weight Empty	880lb (399kg)
Take-off Weight	1,342lb (609kg)
Span	31ft 2¾in (9.52m)
Length	23ft 7½in (7.20m)
Height	7ft 10½in (2.40m)

In the Winter of 1915–16 the Fokker E III mono-planes gained such an ascendancy over the Allied fighter/escorts that they gave rise to the legend of the 'Fokker scourge'. Their pre-eminence was due largely to the provision of gun synchronising gear which allowed a machine-gun to fire through the propeller's disc.

Britain Sopwith 1½-Strutter (1915)

Type	two-seat bomber or single-seat long-range bomber
Engine	110–130hp Clerget or Le-Rhone rotary air-cooled
Armament	(two-seat) 1 Vickers and 1 Lewis machine-gun, plus two 65lb bombs (single-seat) 1 Vickers ma-chine-gun plus four 56lb bombs
Maximum Speed	100mph (160km/h) at 6,500ft (1,980m)
Rate of Climb	750ft (229m)/min
Ceiling	15,500ft (4,725m)
Wing Area	346sq ft (32.14m²)
Weight Empty	1,305lb (592kg)
Take-off Weight	2,150lb (975kg)
Span	33ft 6in (10.21m)
Length	25ft 3in (7.70m)
Height	10ft 3in (3.12m)

The Sopwith Type 9700 was dubbed with the un-official name 1½-Strutter because the outer struts of its central wing bracing looked like half-size interplane struts. It was the first British aircraft fitted with synchronising gear to allow the machine-gun to fire through the propeller disc.

Sopwith 1½-Strutter

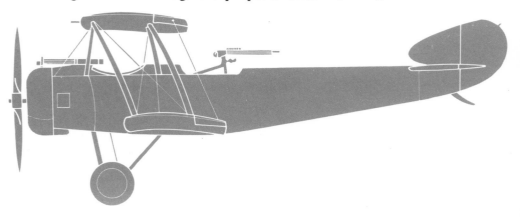

Britain Handley Page 0/100 (1915)

Type	three-seat heavy bomber
Engine	two 266hp Rolls-Royce Eagle II 8-cylinder in-line water-cooled
Armament	three to five machine-guns, plus up to sixteen 112lb bombs
Maximum Speed	85mph (136km/h)
Rate of Climb	310ft (95m)/min
Ceiling	10,000ft (3,050m)
Wing Area	1,648sq ft (153.10m²)
Weight Empty	8,300lb (3,765kg)
Take-off Weight	14,000lb (6,350kg)
Span	100ft (30.48m)
Length	62ft 10¼in (19.16m)
Height	22ft 0in (6.71m)

The Handley Page 0/100 was Britain's first heavy bomber, built to meet an Admiralty requirement of 1914. The specification was amplified by Commodore Murray F Sueter, Director of the Admiralty's Air Department, who requested a 'Bloody paralyser' of an aeroplane.

Albatross D-III

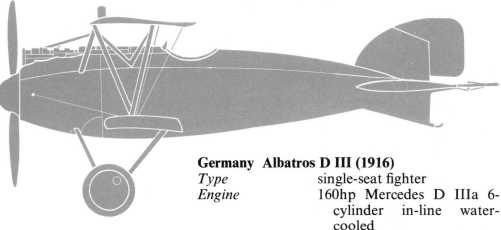

Germany Albatros D III (1916)

Type	single-seat fighter
Engine	160hp Mercedes D IIIa 6-cylinder in-line water-cooled
Armament	two fixed forward-firing 7.92 mm Spandau machine-guns
Maximum Speed	103mph (165km/h)
Rate of Climb	820ft (250m)/min
Ceiling	18,000ft (5,485m)
Wing Area	221sq ft (20.50m²)
Weight Empty	1,457lb (661kg)
Take-off Weight	1,953lb (886kg)
Span	29ft 8¼in (9.05m)
Length	24ft 0½in (7.33m)
Height	9ft 9¼in (2.98m)

The Albatros D III was a developed version of the slightly earlier D Is and D IIs, which sought to adopt some of the design advantages discovered by German examination of captured French Nieuport Scouts. Improvements in wing layout, in particular, to improve visibility made this a most effective fighter.

de Havilland DH4

Britain Sopwith Cuckoo (1916)

Type	single-seat carrier-based torpedo-bomber
Engine	200hp Hispano-Suiza, Sunbeam Arab or Wolseley Viper
Armament	one 18in Mk IX torpedo weighing 1,000lb (453kg)
Maximum Speed	104mph (167km/h) at 2,000ft (610m)
Rate of Climb	415ft (126m)/min
Ceiling	12,100ft (3,690m)
Wing Area	566sq ft (52.58m²)
Weight Empty	2,199lb (997kg)
Take-off Weight	3,883lb (1,761kg)
Span	46ft 9in (14.25m)
Length	28ft 6in (8.69m)
Height	10ft 8in (3.25m)

(Performance and specification with Sunbeam Arab engine.)

The Sopwith Cuckoo is significant for being the world's first carrier-based torpedo-bomber with wheeled landing gear, originating from the far-sightedness of Commodore Murray F Sueter of the British Admiralty. It also had folding wings, to enable it to be accommodated more easily on the carriers of the day, and its single torpedo was mounted beneath the fuselage. The Cuckoo served initially on the aircraft carrier HMS *Argus*, going to sea for the first time on 19 October 1918, but the war ended before the type was used operationally. They served aboard the carriers *Argus*, *Eagle* and *Furious* before their service with the Royal Navy ended in April 1923. The Sopwith Cuckoo was one of the types of aircraft taken to Japan in 1921 by the British Air Mission which was invited by the Imperial Japanese Navy. This Mission, with its British naval aircraft, was responsible for the development of a progressive Naval air service in Japan.

Britain De Havilland DH.4 (1916)

Type	two-seat day bomber
Engine	375hp Rolls-Royce Eagle VIII 8-cylinder in-line water-cooled
Armament	standard armament comprised one fixed forward-firing Vickers machine-gun, one or two Lewis guns on a Scarff ring-mounting, plus two 230lb or four 112lb bombs
Maximum Speed	143mph (229km/h) at sea level
Rate of Climb	1,110ft (338m)/min
Ceiling	22,000ft (6,705m)
Wing Area	434sq ft (40.32m²)
Weight Empty	2,387lb (1,083kg)
Take-off Weight	3,472lb (1,575kg)
Span	42ft 4¾in (12.92m)
Length	30ft 8in (9.35m)
Height	11ft 0in (3.35m)

First British aircraft designed specifically for a day-bomber role, the de Havilland DH.4 was undoubtedly the best light bomber aircraft produced during World War I. It was built in many variants and with a variety of power plants.

Britain Avro 504K (1917)

Type	two-seat trainer
Engine	100–130hp Clerget, Le Rhone or Gnome Monosoupape rotary air-cooled
Armament	(504) up to four 20lb bombs (504C) one Lewis gun (504G) one Vickers machine-gun for the pilot and one Lewis gun
Maximum Speed	95mph (152km/h)
Rate of Climb	700ft (213m)/min
Ceiling	16,000ft (4,875m)
Wing Area	330sq ft (30.66m²)
Weight Empty	1,231lb (558kg)
Take-off Weight	1,829lb (830kg)
Span	36ft 0in (10.97m)
Length	29ft 5in (8.97m)
Height	10ft 5in (3.18m)

Construction of the original Avro 504 prototype, which began in April 1913, and its first flight on 20 September 1913, were important landmarks in British aviation history. Early 504s were used in a bombing and reconnaissance role during 1914–15. In use with the Royal Naval Air Service the Avro made one of the first raids on the zeppelin sheds. The Avro 504K became a superb trainer aircraft, and was to remain in Royal Air Force service until the late 'twenties.

Britain Felixstowe/Porte F.2A (1917)

Type	fighting and reconnaissance flying-boat
Engine	two 345hp Rolls-Royce Eagle VIII 8-cylinder in-line water-cooled
Armament	four to seven Lewis guns and two 230lb bombs
Maximum Speed	95.5mph (153km/h) at 2,000ft (610m)
Rate of Climb	520ft (158m)/min
Ceiling	9,600ft (2.925m)
Wing Area	1,133sq ft (105.26m²)
Weight Empty	7,549lb (3,424kg)
Take-off Weight	10,978lb (4,980kg)
Span	95ft 7½in (29,15m)
Length	46ft 3in (14.10m)
Height	17ft 6in (5.33m)

The Felixstowe/Porte F.2A flying-boat was, in effect, a combination of the aerofoil surfaces of a Curtiss H12 Large America flying-boat with a new hull designed by Squadron Commander John C Porte of the Royal Naval Air Station (RNAS) at Felixstowe, Suffolk. John Porte had discovered certain limitations in the Curtiss flying-boats used operationally by the Royal Navy and had set out to eliminate their shortcomings by the design of a new hull. His work in this connection was so successful that by the war's end the F.2A, and subsequent F.2B and F.2C 'boats, had gained a reputation similar to that which was to attach to the Short Sunderland in World War II. These aircraft were notable for their ability to carry out maritime patrols of up to 6 hours, and especially for operations like that on 4 June 1918 when three F.2As and a Curtiss H12 outfought a force of 14 enemy seaplanes, destroying six for the cost of some damage to one aircraft.

Germany Junkers J I (1917)

Type	two-seat armoured close-support aircraft
Engine	200hp Benz Bz IV 6-cylinder in-line water-cooled
Armament	two fixed forward-firing 7.92 mm Spandau machine-guns and one Parabellum machine-gun in rear cockpit
Maximum Speed	97mph (155km/h)
Rate of Climb	205ft (62m)/min
Wing Area	532sq ft (49.40m²)
Weight Empty	3,893lb (1,766kg)
Take-off Weight	4,797lb (2,176kg)
Span	52ft 6in (16.00m)
Length	29ft 10⅜in (9.10m)
Height	11ft 1½in (3.40m)

The Junkers J I has its place in aviation history as the world's first specially designed armoured ground-support aircraft. Dr. Hugo Junkers had pioneered the construction of all-metal monoplanes, but with the need to cater for a much greater basic weight the J I, which was completed in early 1917, was of biplane configuration. It had a duralumin (aluminium alloy) basic structure, its wings covered with sheets of corrugated light alloy and its fuselage, aft of the armoured capsule for the crew, was fabric covered. The nose capsule was armoured with chrome-nickel sheet steel, a solid bulkhead at the aft end giving the crew protection from the rear. The power plant was also enclosed within this armoured capsule, the engine exhaust discharged vertically upward, and though the aircraft's weight made it difficult to take off and land, it proved popular with crews because of the high degree of protection afforded by its armour.

Britain Vickers Vimy (1917)

Type	twin-engined bomber
Engine	two 200–400hp engines by various manufacturers
Armament	two Lewis guns, eighteen 112lb and two 230lb bombs
Maximum Speed	103mph (165km/h)
Rate of Climb	228ft (69m)/min
Ceiling	7,000ft (2,134m)
Wing Area	1,330sq ft (123.56m²)
Weight Empty	7,101lb (3,220kg)
Take-off Weight	12,500lb (5,670kg)
Span	67ft 2in (20.47m)
Length	43ft 6½in (13.27m)
Height	15ft 3in (4.65m)

(Performance and specification with two Rolls-Royce Eagle VIIIs.)

The prototype of the Vickers FB27, as it was designated originally, first flew on 30 November 1917 powered by two 200hp Hispano-Suiza engines. The Vimy, as it became known when official nomenclatures were issued by the Royal Air Force, entered service too late to be used operationally in World War I. However, unlike its contemporaries, it was to remain in general service with the RAF until the mid-1920s. The definitive version was the Mk IV, powered by two 360hp Rolls-Royce Eagle VIII engines. The Vimy ended its career as a parachute trainer.

France Farman Goliath (1918)

Type	twin-engine civil transport
Engine	two 230hp Salmson Z9 or two 260hp Salmson CM9 9-cylinder radial water-cooled. Engines of other manufacturers were also used
Armament	none
Maximum Speed	(cruising) 75mph (120km/h) at 6,560ft (2,000m)
Ceiling	13,120ft (4,000m)
Wing Area	1,733sq ft (161.00m²)
Weight Empty	5,512lb (2,500kg)
Take-off Weight	10,516lb (4,770kg)
Span	86ft 10in (26.47m)
Length	47ft 0in (14.33m)

Far from beautiful in appearance, the Farman Goliath was evolved late in the war to meet the requirement for a heavy bomber. Like the British Vickers Vimy, it was produced too late to have a military significance, but was to come into its own as a civil airliner. So that the Goliath could fulfil such a task, it was necessary to extend the fuselage nose to provide a forward passenger cabin. The type entered service on the London–Paris route of Cie des Grands Express Aériens on 29 March 1920.

Germany Fokker D VII (1918)

Type	single-seat fighter
Engine	160hp Mercedes D III or 185hp BMW IIIa 6-cylinder in-line water-cooled
Armament	two fixed forward-firing 7.92 mm Spandau machine-guns
Maximum Speed	117mph (187km/h) at 3,280ft (1,000m)
Rate of Climb	1,310ft (400m)/min
Ceiling	22,900ft (6,980m)
Wing Area	221sq ft (20.50m²)
Weight Empty	1,543lb (700kg)
Take-off Weight	1,874lb (850kg)
Span	29ft 2⅜in (8.90m)
Length	22ft 9½in (6.95m)
Height	9ft 0¼in (2.75m)

Undoubtedly the most famous of the fighter scouts to be produced in Germany during World War I, the Fokker D VII was considered to be so important that a special note in the Armistice agreement insisted that all first-line D VIIs should be handed over to the Allies.

Germany Junkers F13 (1919)

Type	four-passenger civil transport
Engine	185hp BMW IIIa 6-cylinder in-line water-cooled. Prototype had 160/170hp Mercedes D IIIa and subsequent variants had engines of up to 310hp
Armament	none
Maximum Speed	(cruising) 87mph (140km/h)
Ceiling	13,125ft (4,000m)
Wing Area	473.6sq ft (44.00m²)
Weight Empty	2,535lb (1,150kg)
Take-off Weight	3,814lb (1,730kg)
Span	58ft 2¾in (17.75m)
Length	31ft 6in (9.60m)

A most important aircraft in German aviation history, the Junkers F13 was the first civil aircraft to be produced by the German aircraft industry in the years immediately following the war. The sale of six of these aircraft to America was negotiated, but was banned initially by the Aeronautical Commission of Control, which had responsibility for supervising Germany's post-war aviation activities. The basis of the ban was that these aircraft could be used in a military role, but this somewhat unrealistic attitude was changed later and the aircraft went to the US. It was an advanced aeroplane of all-metal construction, with cantilever monoplane wings set in a low-wing configuration, and was the world's first aircraft to be fitted with seat belts. It equipped the airline established by the company, known as Junkers-Luftverkehr, which in 1926 amalgamated with Deutsche Aero Lloyd to form the national airline Deutsche Luft Hansa (later Lufthansa).

Spain Cierva Autogiro (1922)

Type	experimental autogiro
Engine	130hp Clerget 9-cylinder rotary air-cooled
Armament	none
Weight Empty	1,490lb (676kg)
Rotor Diameter	36ft 0in (10.97m)
Length	34ft 4in (10.46m)

Juan de la Cierva's first Autogiro was of somewhat mixed parentage, being based on the fuselage of a British Avro 504K and powered by a French Clerget engine. The Spanish rotary wing which de la Cierva had designed, after earlier failures, was the world's first practical single rotor.

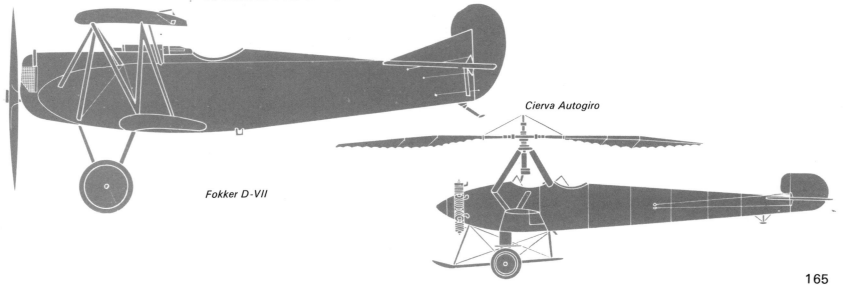

Fokker D-VII

Cierva Autogiro

US Curtiss R-2C1 (1923)

Type	single-seat racing aircraft
Engine	465hp Curtiss D-12A 12-cylinder in-line water-cooled
Armament	none
Maximum Speed	266.6mph (429km/h)
Rate of Climb	2,775ft (846m)/min
Wing Area	148sq ft (13.75m^2)
Weight Empty	1,677lb (761kg)
Take-off Weight	2,150lb (975kg)
Span	22ft 0in (6.71m)
Length	19ft 8½in (6.01m)
Height	6ft 10in (2.08m)

The Curtiss R-2C1 racing biplanes which the US Navy entered in the Pulitzer Trophy race of 1923 had been developed from the CR-1 of 1921. These two R-2C1s took first and second place in the Pulitzer Trophy, at average speeds of 245mph (392km/h) and 242mph (388km/h). Seaplane versions won the Schneider Trophy Contest in the same year at average speeds of 178mph (285km/h) and 174mph (279km/h). The remarkable performance of these aircraft stemmed from the Curtiss power plant, which comprised the advanced D12 engine of very small frontal area, a small-diameter Curtiss-Reed metal propeller, which was efficient at high speeds and eliminated the need for an engine reduction gear, and highly efficient surface radiators that were sufficiently malleable to be formed to the wing section without causing an appreciable change in aerodynamic efficiency.

Britain Supermarine S.4 (1925)

Type	single-seat racing seaplane
Engine	680hp Napier Lion 'broad arrow' 12-cylinder in-line water-cooled
Armament	none
Maximum Speed	232mph (372km/h)
Wing Area	139sq ft (12.91m^2)
Weight Empty	2,600lb (1,179kg)
Take-off Weight	3,191lb (1,447kg)
Span	30ft 7½in (9.33m)
Length	26ft 7¾in (8.12ft)

The impetus of international prestige had, by 1925, begun to speed development of fast, streamlined seaplanes to compete in the Schneider Trophy Contests. From their beginning in 1913 until 1923 Britain had made-do with modifications or developments of existing aircraft. For the 1925 Contest Supermarine, and their chief designer R J Mitchell, had the opportunity to build a new machine from scratch. The resulting Supermarine S.4 was of advanced design and can be regarded as the true ancestor of the Supermarine Spitfire. Construction was almost entirely of wood, the most revolutionary feature being a cantilever monoplane wing, with tail unit and floats completely free from drag-inducing wire bracing. The S.4 flew for the first time on 25 August 1925, and flown by Captain Henri Biard set up a new world speed record for seaplanes on 13 September at 226.6mph (364.6km/h). Unfortunately, the aircraft was destroyed in an accident before it could compete in the 1925 Schneider Trophy Contest.

Britain de Havilland DH Moth (1925)

Type	two-seat light sporting aircraft
Engine	60hp Cirrus 4-cylinder in-line
Armament	none
Maximum Speed	90mph (144km/h)
Wing Area	225sq ft (20.90m^2)
Weight Empty	764lb (347kg)
Take-off Weight	1,250lb (567kg)
Span	29ft 0in (8.84m)
Length	23ft 6in (7.16m)
Height	8ft 7in (2.62m)

The de Havilland Moth was one of the aeroplanes which brought a realisation that flying was not just for supermen, and that even civilians with some essential training could discover the delights of this form of travel. When the Moth was introduced in 1925 it sparked off the flying club movement in Britain, and developed forms of the Moth had a similar effect on a world-wide basis. This was not surprising when one considers that Gipsy-engined Moths proved sufficiently reliable for Francis Chichester (later Sir Francis) and Amy Johnson to make solo flights to Australia, and for C W A Scott to achieve a 9 day 4 hour England-Australia record in 1931. Development of the type continued through a variety of Moths, the Tiger Moth which joined the RAF in 1932 remaining in service with Flying Training Command until 1947, and gaining a reputation as the world's most famous training aircraft.

US Ford Tri-Motor (1926)

Type	three-engine civil transport
Engine	three 235hp Pratt & Whitney Wasp Junior radial air-cooled, and a variety of Pratt & Whitney and Wright radial engines in successive variants
Armament	none
Maximum Speed	130mph (208km/h)
Ceiling	16,500ft (5,030m)
Wing Area	765sq ft (71.07m^2)
Weight Empty	6,500lb (2,948kg)
Take-off Weight	10,130lb (4,595kg)
Span	74ft 0in (22.56m)
Length	49ft 10in (15.19m)
Height	11ft 9in (3.58m)

Evolved from the single-engine Stout Air Pullman of 1924, developed by George Prudden and Bill Stout, the Ford Tri-Motor was designed and built after Henry Ford had acquired the Stout Metal Airplane Company. The prototype, designated 4-AT, flew for the first time on 11 June 1926, being powered by three 200hp Wright J-4 radial engines, and having accommodation for eight passengers. The great reliability of the type was soon apparent, and variants with seating for 11–14 passengers became well used by American airlines. Of all-metal construction, with corrugated light alloy skins of the kind pioneered by Dr. Hugo Junkers in Germany, its structure was to prove most enduring. Perhaps surprisingly, examples of the Tri-Motor are still in regular use, celebrating in 1976 a half-century of valuable service in both cargo and passenger flights.

Britain Hawker Hart (1928)

Type	two-seat day bomber
Engine	525hp Rolls-Royce Kestrel 1B 12-cylinder Vee in-line water-cooled
Armament	1 fixed forward-firing Vickers gun, 1 free Lewis gun on Hawker ring mounting in rear cockpit
Maximum Speed	184mph (295km/h) at 5,000ft (1,525m)
Rate of Climb	1,200ft (366m)/min
Ceiling	22,800ft (6,950m)
Wing Area	348sq ft (32.33m²)
Weight Empty	2,530lb (1,148kg)
Take-off Weight	4,554lb (2,066kg)
Span	37ft 3in (11.35m)
Length	29ft 4in (8.94m)
Height	10ft 5in (3.18m)

An advanced day-bomber, the performance of the Hart was such that it could evade contemporary fighters, thus speeding the development of fighter aircraft capable of speeds in excess of 200mph (320km/h).

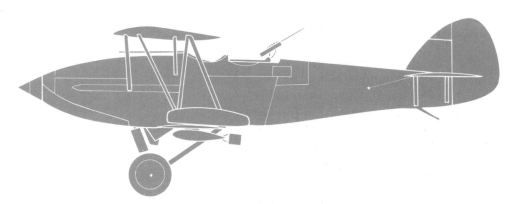

Hawker Hart

Britain Handley Page H.P.42(W) (1930)

Type	four-engined civil transport
Engine	four 555hp Bristol Jupiter 9-cylinder radial air-cooled
Armament	none
Maximum Speed	(cruising) 100mph (160km/h)
Rate of Climb	607ft (204m)/min
Take-off Weight	29,500lb (13,381kg)
Span	130ft 0in (39.62m)
Length	89ft 9in (27.36m)
Height	27ft 0in (8.23m)

There are plenty of people still alive in 1976 who can boast of flying between London and Paris some 40 years ago in the superb Handley Page H.P.42s of Imperial Airways. These were introduced into service on the London-Paris route with the first service being operated by G-AAGX *Hannibal* on 11 June 1931. They provided luxurious four-abreast seating for 38 passengers, 18 being seated in a forward cabin, ahead of the propellers, and 20 in the aft cabin. Between the two passenger cabins was a 250cu ft (7.08m³) mail and baggage compartment on the starboard side, and toilets and a galley on the port side. The aircraft used on the European routes were designated H.P.42(W), those on the long-distance routes to the East H.P.42(E). These latter aircraft had accommodation for only 24 passengers, but had 500cu ft (14.16m³) mail and baggage capacity.

France Pou de Ciel (1933)

Type	ultra-light single-seat monoplane
Engine	17hp Ambier & Dunne 2-cylinder in-line inverted air-cooled. Other engines of similar power output used
Armament	none
Maximum Speed	62mph (99km/h)
Rate of Climb	170ft (52m)/min
Weight Empty	220lb (100kg)
Span	19ft 7in (5.97m)

When Henri Mignet designed and built his first Pou de Ciel in 1933, he had tried to achieve not only a 'Ford car' of the air, which would bring the sport of flying within the reach of vast numbers of people, but also to simplify the system of control to make it easier for people to learn to fly. Moreover, plans and details of how to build it were published in a book, and anyone was free to build one for his own use. The aircraft was controlled in flight by a column which, moved fore and aft, changed the incidence of the wing to control movements in pitch. Moved from left to right it gave directional control by moving the rudder. A large amount of dihedral was intended to take care of lateral stability. Unfortunately, it was found to be unstable in pitch and a number of fatal accidents brought to an end to what were, at that date, quite advanced ideas.

US Boeing Model 247 (1933)

Type	twin-engine civil transport
Engine	two 550hp Pratt & Whitney Wasp 9-cylinder radial air-cooled
Armament	none
Maximum Speed	182mph (292km/h)
Rate of Climb	1,320ft (402m)/min
Ceiling	18,000ft (5,485m)
Wing Area	836.13sq ft (77.68m²)
Take-off Weight	13,650lb (6,192kg)
Span	74ft 0in (22.56m)
Length	51ft 4in (15.65m)
Height	16ft 0in (4.88m)

This classic aeroplane, which first flew on 8 February 1933, was to establish a basic configuration for civil transport aircraft. This was to change little until the introduction of turbojet engines which pushed speeds upwards and brought a fairly general use of swept wings. Prior to the introduction of the Boeing 247, and the aircraft which followed it into airline service, there had been considerable interest in three-engined airliners. In this latter configuration the engine mounted in the fuselage nose was inefficient because of the fuselage bulk immediately behind it, and it was soon realised that the Boeing configuration provided much faster travel for about the same load of passengers as carried by the Junkers FVII-3M and Ford Tri-Motor. Not only was this improvement achieved with one less engine, but range benefited also from operation at a higher altitude.

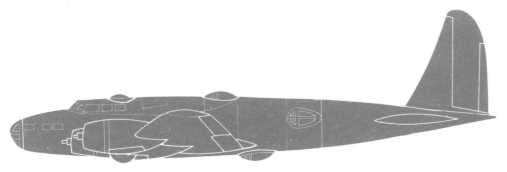

Britain Gloster Gladiator (1934)

Type	single-seat fighter
Engine	840hp Bristol Mercury IX 9-cylinder radial air-cooled
Armament	4 fixed forward-firing Browning machine-guns
Maximum Speed	253mph (406km/h) at 14,500ft (4,420m)
Rate of Climb	2,300ft (701m)/min
Ceiling	33,000ft (10,060m)
Wing Area	323sq ft (30.01m²)
Weight Empty	3,450lb (1,565kg)
Take-off Weight	4,750lb (2,155kg)
Span	32ft 3in (9.83m)
Length	27ft 5in (8.36m)
Height	10ft 4in (3.15m)

Last biplane fighter to serve with the RAF, the Gladiator represented the culmination of biplane fighter development. Fast and highly manoeuvrable, they were soon outdated by such aircraft as the Hurricane, Spitfire and German Me 109.

Germany Junkers Ju 87 (1935)

Type	two-seat dive-bomber and close-support aircraft
Engine	(Ju 87B) 1,200hp Junkers Jumo 211Da 12-cylinder inverted-Vee in-line liquid-cooled
Armament	two fixed forward-firing MG 17 machine-guns, one free 15 machine-gun in rear cockpit. Standard bomb load of one 1,100lb (500kg) under fuselage, or one 550lb (250kg) under fuselage and four 110lb (50kg) bombs beneath the wings. Later variants could carry 4,000lb (1,800kg) beneath the fuselage, including a variety of weapon pods
Maximum Speed	237mph (380km/h) at 13,125ft (4,000m)
Ceiling	26,245ft (8,000m)
Wing Area	343.38sq ft (31.90m²)
Weight Empty	6,063lb (2,750kg)
Take-off Weight	9,370lb (4,250kg)
Span	45ft 3¼in (13.80m)
Length	36ft 1in (11.00m)
Height	12ft 9½in (3.90m)

Junkers Ju 87 Stukas – derived from *Sturzkampffleugzeug*: dive-bomber – were involved in many historic actions in the opening phases of World War I. Much modified they were to serve throughout the war, Ju 87Gs equipped with two 37mm Flak 18 cannon proving potent tank-busters on the Eastern front.

US Boeing B-17 Flying Fortress (1935)

Type	four-engine heavy bomber
Engine	(B-17G) four 1,200hp Wright R-1820 9-cylinder radial air-cooled with exhaust-driven turbocharger
Armament	7 to 13 machine-guns and 4,200lb (1,905kg) to 16,000 lb (7,257kg) bombs according to model
Maximum Speed	287mph (460km/h) at 25,000ft (7,620m)
Rate of Climb	540ft (165m)/min
Ceiling	35,600ft (10,850m)
Wing Area	1,420sq ft (131.92m²)
Weight Empty	36,135lb (16,390kg)
Take-off Weight	65,500lb (29,710kg)
Span	103ft 9in (31.62m)
Length	74ft 9in (22.78m)
Height	19ft 1in (5.94m)

Renowned for its daylight operations against European targets during World War II, the B-17 Flying Fortress was evolved to meet the requirement for a long-range strategic bomber. Envisaged as being essential to USAAF strategy, its procurement was delayed so many times by opposing factions that only 19 were in service when the war began. The Boeing B-29 Superfortress was a development of the B-17.

Germany Messerschmitt Me 109 (1935)

Type	single-seat fighter
Engine	(Me 109G) 1,475hp Daimler-Benz DB 605A 12-cylinder Vee in-line liquid-cooled
Armament	one MK 108 30mm cannon, two MG 131 13mm guns and two MG 151 20mm cannon in Me 109G-6, but an immense variety of weapons in different versions
Maximum Speed	389mph (623km/h) at 22,965ft (7,000m)
Rate of Climb	3,280ft (1,000m)/min
Ceiling	38,550ft (11,750m)
Wing Area	172.77sq ft (16.05m²)
Weight Empty	5,953lb (2,700kg)
Take-off Weight	6,945lb (3,150kg)
Span	32ft 6½in (9.92m)
Length	29ft 7in (9.02m)
Height	11ft 1¾in (3.40m)

The Messerschmitt Me 109 must surely be classed as the most famous German military aircraft ever built. Me 109Bs were first used operationally in the Spanish Civil War, representing the fighter component of the Condor Legion, and many were still in service with foreign air arms 20 years later.

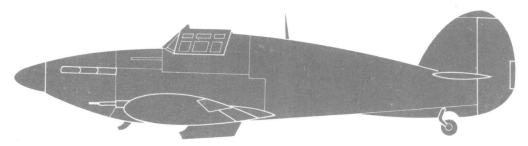

Hawker Hurricane

Britain Hawker Hurricane (1935)

Type	single-seat fighter and fighter-bomber
Engine	(Mk IIB) 1,280hp Rolls-Royce Merlin XX 12-cylinder in-line liquid-cooled
Armament	twelve Browning 0.303in machine-guns, two of which usually removed when carrying bombs, plus bombs or other external stores up to 1,000lb (454kg)
Maximum Speed	340mph (545km/h)
Rate of Climb	2,245ft (684m)/min
Ceiling	36,000ft (10,970m)
Wing Area	257.5sq ft (23.92m²)
Weight Empty	5,640lb (2,558kg)
Take-off Weight	8,250lb (3,742kg)
Span	40ft 0in (12.19m)
Length	32ft 0in (7.75m)
Height	13ft 1in (3.99m)

One of the two eight-gun fighters that served with the RAF during the Battle of Britain, the Hawker Hurricane proved to be a highly adaptable and combat-worthy aircraft. During the period of the Battle, Hurricane pilots were credited with destroying more enemy aircraft than the total achieved by all other types combined.

Britain Short Sunderland (1937)

Type	13-seat maritime patrol and ASW aircraft
Engine	four 1,200hp Pratt & Whitney R-1830 Twin Wasp 14-cylinder radial air-cooled
Armament	8 to 12 0.303in machine-guns, two 0.50in machine-guns and up to 2,000lb (907kg) bombs
Maximum Speed	293mph (470km/h) at 17,390ft (5,300m)
Rate of Climb	840ft (257m)/min
Ceiling	17,900ft (5,455m)
Wing Area	1,487sq ft (138.14m²)
Weight Empty	37,000lb (16,782kg)
Take-off Weight	60,000lb (27,215kg)
Span	112ft 9½in (34.38m)
Length	85ft 4in (26.01m)
Height	32ft 10½in (10.02m)

Probably the finest military flying-boat in aviation history, the Short Sunderland remained in first-line service with the RAF for 17 years after its initial introduction in 1938. Because of its heavy defensive armament it acquired the nickname 'Flying Porcupine' from German pilots.

Junkers Ju 88

Germany Junkers Ju 88 (1936)

Type	three-seat medium bomber
Engine	(Ju 88A-4) 1,340hp Junkers Jumo 211J-1 radial air-cooled
Armament	one MG 81 machine-gun, two MG 131 machine-guns and up to 3,330lb (1,497kg) bombs
Maximum Speed	293mph (470km/h) at 17,390ft
Rate of Climb	771ft (235m)/min
Ceiling	26,900ft (8,200m)
Wing Area	586.65sq ft (54.50m²)
Weight Empty	21,738lb (9,860kg)
Take-off Weight	30,865lb (14,000kg)
Span	65ft 7½in (20.00m)
Length	47ft 3in (14.40m)
Height	15ft 11in (4.85m)

Most versatile bomber aircraft of the German Luftwaffe in World War II, the Ju 88 was used in a variety of roles. These included bomber and reconnaissance aircraft, intruder, torpedo-bomber, night-fighter, and even as the lower, guided component, of the Mistel composite in which the Ju 88 itself became a flying-bomb.

US North American B-25 Mitchell (1939)

Type	3/6-seat medium bomber
Engine	(B-25C) two 1,700hp Wright R-2600 14-cylinder radial air-cooled
Armament	six 0.50in machine-guns and up to 3,000lb (1,361kg) of bombs
Maximum Speed	284mph (455km/h) at 15,000ft (4,570m)
Rate of Climb	910ft (277m)/min
Ceiling	21,200ft (6,460m)
Wing Area	610sq ft (56.67m²)
Weight Empty	20,300lb (9,208kg)
Take-off Weight	34,000lb (15,422kg)
Span	67ft 7in (20.60m)
Length	52ft 11in (16.13m)
Height	15ft 10in (4.83m)

Named after air power protagonist Col. 'Billy' Mitchell, the B-25 was one of the most outstanding bomber aircraft used by the USAAF in World War II. A total of nearly 11,000 were built to meet the needs of the USAAF and its Allies, and it was these aircraft which were used in the famous raid on Japan, led by Lt. Col. 'Jimmy' Doolittle.

Japan Mitsubishi A6M Zero-Sen (1939)

Type	single-seat carrier-based fighter
Engine	(Model 53C) 1,210hp Nakajima NK1P Sakae 31 14-cylinder radial air-cooled
Armament	two 20mm cannon, three 13.2 mm machine-guns, one 7.7 mm machine-gun
Maximum Speed	346mph (555km/h) at 19,680ft (6,000m)
Rate of Climb	3,140ft (957m)/min
Ceiling	35,100ft (10,698m)
Wing Area	229.27sq ft (21.30m²)
Weight Empty	3,920lb (1,778kg)
Take-off Weight	6,026lb (2,733kg)
Span	36ft 1in (11.00m)
Length	29ft 9in (9.07m)
Height	9ft 2in (2.79m)

Japan's famous Zero naval fighter was so named from its military designation of Type 0 Carrier Fighter. At the height of its success in the early days of the Pacific War, it was the world's most formidable carrier-based aircraft, then being superior to any of its land-based opponents. The Zero prototype first flew in April 1939 and was subsequently used as a fighter-bomber. In the last months of the war Zeros were utilized in Kamikaze operations.

Germany Focke-Wulf Fw 190 (1939)

Type	single-seat fighter, fighter-bomber and close-support aircraft
Engine	(Fw 190A-8) 1,700hp BMW 801D-2 14-cylinder radial air-cooled
Armament	four MG 151 20mm cannon and two MG 131 13mm machine-guns
Maximum Speed	408mph (654km/h) at 20,600ft (6,280m)
Rate of Climb	2,350ft (716m)/min
Ceiling	37,400ft (11,400m)
Wing Area	196.98sq ft (18.30m²)
Weight Empty	7,000lb (3,175kg)
Take-off Weight	9,750lb (4,423kg)
Span	34ft 5½in (10.50m)
Length	29ft 0in (8.84m)
Height	13ft 0in (3.96m)

Most advanced fighter aircraft in the world at the time of its introduction in the autumn of 1941, its performance was such that RAF pilots found it necessary to treat this new adversary with respect until the introduction of the Spitfire IX again gave them temporary ascendancy over the Luftwaffe fighters. Almost certainly the finest radial-engined fighter ever built, it was created by the genius of Germany's renowned Kurt Tank. When the prototype flew for the first time it was powered by a 1,550hp BMW 139 radial engine which overheated rapidly unless installed with a cooling fan. It was replaced by a more powerful, newly developed and heavier engine, which required that the cockpit was placed further aft. This became the standard configuration and before the war's end some 20,000 of these aircraft had been built.

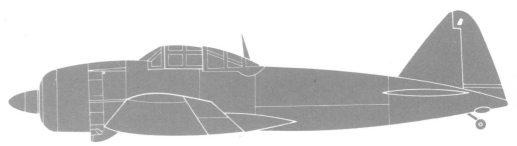

Mitsubishi A6M Zero-Sen

Germany Heinkel He 178 (1939)

Type	turbojet-powered research aircraft
Engine	one 1,100lb (500kg) thrust Heinkel HeS 3 turbojet
Armament	none
Maximum Speed	(cruising) 362mph (580km/h)
Wing Area	97.95sq ft (9.10m²)
Weight Empty	3,572lb (1,620kg)
Take-off Weight	4,405lb (1,998kg)
Span	23ft 7½in (7.20m)
Length	24ft 6½in (7.48m)
Height	6ft 10½in (2.10m)

A very significant aircraft in aviation history, the Heinkel He 178 was the first aircraft in the world to fly solely on the power of a turbojet engine, on 27 August 1939. Its Heinkel HeS 3 engine, developing approximately 1,100lb (500kg) thrust, had been designed by Dr. Hans Pabst von Ohain, quite independently of the work being done by Frank Whittle in Britain.

Heinkel He 178

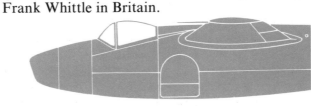

US Vought-Sikorsky VS-300 (1940)

Type	single-seat experimental helicopter
Engine	75hp Lycoming (later 100hp Franklin) 4-cylinder horizontally opposed air-cooled
Armament	none
Maximum Speed	40-50mph (64-80km/h)
Take-off Weight	1,290lb (585kg)
Rotor Diameter	30ft 0in (9.14m)
Length	27ft 10in (8.48m)
Height	10ft 0in (3.05m)

As early as 1909 Igor Sikorsky had been working in his native country of Russia to develop a practical helicopter. He had appreciated the problem posed by torque, and attempted to resolve this by the use of contra-rotating rotors. His second helicopter, built in 1910, succeeded in lifting only itself from the ground. Following the Revolution in 1917, Sikorsky went to America where, in 1923, he established the Sikorsky Aero Engineering Corporation. It was not until 1940 that he had the opportunity to revive his interest in rotary-wing aircraft, building the VS-300 which, in its initial form, had a single main rotor and three auxiliary rotors. One of the auxiliary rotors was to control torque, the other two – mounted on outriggers – were to provide fore-and-aft and lateral control. When flown in December 1941 with a single tail rotor and a main rotor with full cyclic-pitch control, it became the world's first practical single-rotor helicopter.

US North American P-51 Mustang (1940)

Type	single-seat fighter and fighter-bomber
Engine	(P-51D) 1,450hp Rolls-Royce/Packard Merlin V-1650-7 12-cylinder Vee in-line liquid-cooled
Armament	four to six 0.5in Browning machine-guns plus two 1,000lb bombs or ten 5in High Velocity Aircraft Rockets (HVARs)
Maximum Speed	437mph (700km/h) at 25,000ft (7,620m)
Rate of Climb	3,475ft (1,059)/min
Ceiling	40,000ft (12,190m)
Wing Area	233sq ft (21.65m²)
Weight Empty	7,635lb (3,463kg)
Take-off Weight	10,100lb (4,581kg)
Span	37ft 0in (11.28m)
Length	32ft 3in (9.83m)
Height	13ft 8in (4.17m)

The P-51 Mustang, which was undoubtedly the best of all US World War II fighter aircraft, was evolved to meet a British specification for a combat aircraft to replace the Curtiss P-40. As finalised, with a Rolls-Royce engine replacing the original Allison in-line engine, it was an outstanding escort fighter.

Britain de Havilland Mosquito (1940)

Type	multi-purpose military aircraft
Engine	(NF.XIX) two 1,620hp Rolls-Royce Merlin 25 12-cylinder Vee in-line liquid-cooled
Armament	four 20mm cannon
Maximum Speed	378mph (606km/h) at 13,200ft (4,025m)
Rate of Climb	2,700ft (823m)/min
Ceiling	28,000ft (8,535m)
Wing Area	454sq ft (42.18m²)
Weight Empty	15,970lb (7,243kg)
Take-off Weight	20,600lb (9,344kg)
Span	54ft 2in (16.51m)
Length	41ft 2in (12.55m)
Height	15ft 3in (4.65m)

Designed originally as a high-speed unarmed bomber for day or night operation at high or low altitude, the Mosquito was to earn fame also as a photo-reconnaissance aircraft, night-fighter, fighter-bomber, tank and locomotive buster, mine layer, pathfinder, and even as a high-speed military transport. It was the only light bomber in wartime service able to carry a 4,000lb bomb.

Germany Messerschmitt Me 163B (1941)

Type	single-seat rocket-powered fighter
Engine	3,750lb (1,700kg) thrust Walter HWK 109-509-A-2 liquid bi-fuel rocket motor
Armament	two MK 108 30mm cannon
Maximum Speed	596mph (955km/h) at 30,000ft (9,145m)
Rate of Climb	16,000ft (4,875m)/min
Ceiling	54,000ft (16,460m)
Wing Area	211sq ft (19.60m²)
Weight Empty	4,200lb (1,905kg)
Take-off Weight	9,500lb (4,309kg)
Span	30ft 7in (9.32m)
Length	18ft 8in (5.69)
Height	9ft 0in (2.74m)

First rocket-engined combat aircraft to enter operational service with any air force, the Me 163B Komet was also the world's first tailless combat aircraft. Evolved from the research and design work of Alexander Lippisch in the late 1920s, the Komet was built under conditions of great secrecy, although rate of construction was slow, mainly because the project was allocated a low priority basis. When the first prototype flew successfully for the first time on 2 October 1941, the *Reichsluftfahrtministerium* (RLM: German Aviation Ministry) became interested in the project, and immediately ordered a number of prototypes for evaluation. Delays in development of the rocket engine were responsible primarily for the fact that it was not until mid-August 1944 that the first operational sorties were flown by the only Komet-equipped unit, Jagdgeschwader 400. New tactics were necessary to permit the successful deployment of an aircraft with a powered endurance of only 8 to 12 minutes.

Britain Avro Lancaster (1941)

Type	four-engine heavy bomber
Engine	four 1,460hp Merlin 20/22 or 1,640hp Merlin 24 12-cylinder Vee in-line liquid-cooled
Armament	8 to 10 0.303 machine-guns and one 22,000lb (10,000kg) bomb or 14,000lb (6,350kg) of smaller bombs
Maximum Speed	287mph (460km/h) at 11,500ft (3,505m)
Rate of Climb	480ft (146m)/min
Ceiling	24,500ft (7,465m)
Wing Area	1,297sq ft (120.49m²)
Weight Empty	36,457lb (16,536kg)
Take-off Weight	68,000lb (30,844kg)
Span	102ft 0in (31.09m)
Length	69ft 4in (21.13m)
Height	20ft 6in (6.25m)

Known originally as the Manchester III, reflecting its development from the disappointing Manchester, the four-engine Lancaster was the most important bomber aircraft developed in the United Kingdom during World War II. Used primarily on night operations, they carried the 22,000lb Grand Slam bomb and the unique skip-bomb designed by Barnes Wallis.

Avro Lancaster

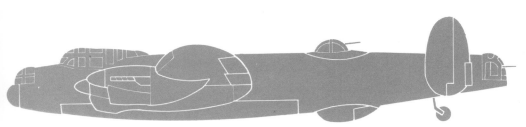

US Boeing B-29 Superfortress (1942)

Type	four-engine heavy bomber
Engine	(B-29A) four 2,200hp Wright R-3350 18-cylinder radial air-cooled
Armament	11 0.5in or 10 0.5in machine-guns and 1 20mm cannon, plus up to 20,000lb (9,072 kg) of bombs
Maximum Speed	358mph (574km/h) at 25,000 ft (7,620m)
Rate of Climb	525ft (160m)/min
Ceiling	31,850ft (9,705m)
Wing Area	1,736sq ft (161.27 m²)
Weight Empty	71,360lb (32,368kg)
Take-off Weight	141,100lb (64,002kg)
Span	141ft 3in (43.05m)
Length	99ft 0in (30.18m)
Height	29ft 7in (9.02m)

The B-29 Superfortress was evolved to provide a 'Hemisphere Defence Weapon', capable of carrying 2,000lb (907kg) of bombs for 5,333 miles (8,549km) at a speed of 400mph (641km/h). The prototype was first flown on 21 September 1942, and B-29s began to enter service with the 58th Very Heavy Bombardment Wing in 1943.

US Bell X-1A (1946)

Type	single-seat rocket-powered supersonic research aircraft
Engine	6,000lb (2,722kg) thrust Reaction Motors E6000-C4 alcohol/liquid-oxygen rocket motor
Armament	none
Maximum Speed	1,650mph (2,655km/h) at 70,000ft (21,335m)
Rate of Climb	13,855ft (4,233m)/min
Ceiling	94,000ft (28,650m)
Take-off Weight	13,400lb (6,078kg)
Span	28ft 0in (8.53m)
Length	31ft 0in (9.45m)

First manned aircraft in the world to exceed the speed of sound in level flight, Bell's X-1 rocket-propelled research aircraft was flown by Captain Charles E. Yeager, USAF, at Mach 1.06 on 14 October 1947. The X-1A flew subsequently, on 12 December 1953, at a speed of Mach 2.42.

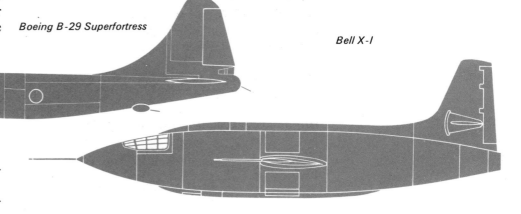

Boeing B-29 Superfortress

Bell X-1

US Bell Model 47 (1946)

Type	two/three-seat utility helicopter
Engine	200hp Lycoming VO-435 6-cylinder horizontally opposed air-cooled
Armament	none
Maximum Speed	100mph (160km/h) at sea level
Rate of Climb	770ft (235m)/min
Ceiling	13,200ft (4,025m)
Weight Empty	1,564lb (709kg)
Take-off Weight	2,450lb (1,111kg)
Rotor Diameter	35ft 1in (10.69m)
Length	27ft 4in (8.33m)
Height	9ft 6in (2.90m)

The Bell Model 47 was the first helicopter in the world to receive a commercial licence, on 8 March 1946. The excellence of its design is emphasised by the fact that it remained in continuous production with Bell for more than 25 years and in 1976 was still being built in other parts of the world. First of the type to be used by the American services was a batch of Model 47As delivered to the USAF in 1947 when the designation YR-13 was allocated. This was changed later to H-13 and subsequently to OH-13 for the US Army and UH-13 for the USAF and USN. Since that time the Model 47 has shown itself to be a robust and reliable vehicle, and served with distinction in the Korean War. It was in this theatre of operations that the value of the helicopter for military usage was highlighted for the first time, casualty evacuation from battlefield areas bringing death from wounds to the lowest figure ever recorded.

Soviet Union Mikoyan MiG-15 (1947)

Type	single-seat jet fighter
Engine	one 6,040lb (2,740kg) thrust RD-45 turbojet
Armament	two 23mm machine-guns, one 37mm cannon
Maximum Speed	666mph (1,068km/h)
Rate of Climb	10,400ft (3,170m)/min
Ceiling	51,000ft (15,545m)
Weight Empty	8,333lb (3,780kg)
Take-off Weight	11,288lb (5,120kg)
Span	33ft 1½in (10.10m)
Length	36ft 5in (11.10m)
Height	11ft 2in (3.40m)

The Mikoyan MiG-15 was first tested in 1947, and delivery of production aircraft began in 1948. When deployed in Korea this Soviet fighter was able to demonstrate performance superior to that of the North American F-86 Sabre, its major opponent. It is believed that more than 15,000 MiG-15s served with the Red Air Force and the air forces of Russian satellite countries.

MiG-15

France Leduc 0-10 (1947)

Type	two-seat ramjet-powered research monoplane
Engine	4,960lb (2,250kg) thrust Leduc thermopropulsive fuselage duct
Armament	none
Maximum Speed	(half power) 500mph (800 km/h)
Take-off Weight	6,172lb (2,800kg)
Span	34ft 6in (10.51m)
Length	33ft 7in (10.24m)

In Chapter 7, brief mention is made of ramjet engines, and their development for aircraft propulsion which was carried out, in the main, in France and Germany, René Leduc in France was responsible for extensive work to demonstrate the suitability of such a power plant for high-speed flight and, as early as 1935, had produced a small ramjet unit. By 1947 he had completed his first ramjet-powered monoplane and to test its aerodynamic characteristics it was air-launched as a glider from a Languedoc four-engined aircraft in October of that year. It was not until 21 April 1949 that the Leduc 0-10 was able to demonstrate the potential of such a power plant when, air-launched again from the Languedoc, it attained a speed of 424mph (680km/h) at a height of 10,000ft (3,050m). The athodyd of the power plant comprised five cylindrical ducts of increasing size, the leading edge of each ringed with fuel injectors to provide a total of 500 fuel burners. One further aircraft was built – the O-21.

Britain Vickers Viscount (1948)

Type	four-turboprop commercial transport
Engine	four 1,740ehp Rolls-Royce Dart R.Da.3 Mk 506 turboprops
Armament	none
Maximum Speed	(cruising) 380mph (609km/h) at 20,000ft (6,095m)
Ceiling	26,700ft (8,140m)
Wing Area	963 sq ft (89.46m²)
Weight Empty	38,358lb (17,399kg)
Take-off Weight	64,500lb (29,257kg)
Span	93ft 8½in (28.56m)
Length	81ft 10in (24.94m)
Height	26ft 9in (8.15m)

The Vickers Viscount has an assured place in aviation history, being the world's first civil transport aircraft with turboprop power plant. It was, incidentally, bought by Trans-Canada Air Lines in 1952, and when the first of their aircraft was delivered in February 1953, the Viscount became the first turbine-powered aircraft to fly the North Atlantic. When they entered service with Trans-Canada they served to introduce the air travellers of North America to the smooth and effortless flight that resulted from turbine power. The aircraft was unique in one other aspect: at the time it entered service it was the only aircraft of its type available to the airlines of the world. As a result more than 60 operators in some 40 countries bought Viscounts, the value of the export sales amounting to about £147 million, and many of these aircraft remain in service in 1976.

Britain English Electric Canberra (1949)

Type	2/3-seat light bomber, photo-reconnaissance and electronic countermeasures aircraft, trainer, radar trainer and night intruder
Engine	(PR7) two 7,500lb (3,402kg) thrust Rolls-Royce Avon 109 turbojets
Armament	bomber can carry 4,000lb (1,814kg) bombs internally, intruder has 4 20mm cannon, plus 2,000lb (907kg) underwing weapons and 3,000lb (1,361kg) bombs internally
Maximum Speed	580mph (930km/h) at 40,000ft (12,190m)
Rate of Climb	3,700ft (1,128m)
Ceiling	48,000ft (14,630m)
Wing Area	960sq ft (89.18m²)
Take-off Weight	49,000lb (22,226kg)
Span	63ft 11½in (19.49m)
Length	66ft 8in (20.31m)
Height	15ft 7in (4.75m)

The English Electric Canberra was the first turbojet-powered bomber aircraft to be built in Britain, as well as the first to enter RAF service, with No. 101 Squadron, in May 1951. Built under licence in America for the USAF by the Glenn L. Martin Company, an advanced high-altitude reconnaissance version was also built by General Dynamics, with a wing span of 122ft 0in (37.19m).

Britain De Havilland Comet I (1949)

Type	four-engine medium-range commercial transport
Engine	four 5,050lb (2,290kg) thrust de Havilland Ghost 50 turbojets
Armament	none
Maximum Speed	(cruise) 490mph (785km/h) at optimum altitude
Ceiling	40,000ft (12,190m)
Wing Area	2,015sq ft (187.19m²)
Take-off Weight	105,000lb (47,627kg)
Span	115ft 0in (35.05m)
Length	93ft 0in (28.35m)
Height	28ft 4½in (8.65m)

The de Havilland Comet I holds a supreme place in the history of civil aviation as the world's first turbojet-powered airliner. For it to have this distinction, it meant that an entirely new type of aeroplane had to be evolved. Not only were the power plants it was to use in the infancy of their development, but the fact that they had to operate at high altitude for reasonable economy meant that the aircraft's cabin had to be pressurised to allow its passengers to travel in complete comfort and well above the worst of the turbulence that often gave a rough ride to the passengers of piston-engined airliners. Metal fatigue of the pressurized cabin structure brought a disastrous end to the Comet I, but examples of the Comet IV, which was developed as a result of this initial experience, were still in service in 1976. The Hawker Siddeley Nimrod has evolved from the de Havilland Comet.

US Bell X-5 (1951)

Type	single-seat variable-geometry research aircraft
Engine	one 4,900lb (2,222kg) thrust Allison J35-A-17 turbojet
Armament	none
Take-off Weight	10,000lb (4,540kg)
Span	(unswept) 32ft 9in (9.98m)
Length	32ft 4in (9.86m)
Height	12ft 0in (3.66m)

Having demonstrated with the X-1 that specially designed aeroplanes could fly faster than the speed of sound, it was necessary to investigate the best means of ensuring that high-performance swept-wing aircraft could be flown and controlled adequately in a low-speed regime for the purposes of take-off and landing. One of the solutions which had been proposed was a variable-geometry – or swing-wing – aircraft which would take off and land with the wings set in a more or less normal configuration for a fixed-wing aircraft. Once airborne the wings could be re-set in flight to an optimum swept position for supersonic speed. The Bell X-5 was built for an evaluation of this concept, thus becoming the world's first manned aircraft with wings which could be swept or extended in flight, and proving the idea to be completely feasible.

US Lockheed F-104 Starfighter (1954)

Type	single-seat supersonic fighter
Engine	(F-104G) one 15,800lb (7,167 kg) thrust – with afterburner – General Electric J79-GE-11A turbojet
Armament	a total of up to 4,000lb (1,815 kg) mixed weapons on under-fuselage and under-wing hardpoints
Maximum Speed	1,450mph (2,324km/h) at 36,000ft (10,975m)
Rate of Climb	50,000ft (15,240m)/min
Ceiling	58,000ft (17,680m)
Wing Area	179sq ft (16.63m²)
Weight Empty	14,300lb (6,486kg)
Take-off Weight	24,500lb (11,113kg)
Span	21ft 11in (6.68m)
Length	54ft 9in (16.69m)
Height	13ft 6in (4.11m)

With an initial rate of climb of approximately 9.5 miles (15km) a minute, and wings which span only 21ft 11in (6.68m), it is not surprising that the Starfighter was often regarded as 'the missile with a man in it'. Built in only limited numbers for the USAF, more than 1,000 examples of the much re-designed F-104G multi-mission version have been produced under an intra-European programme. The Starfighter arms many NATO nations. Its 20-mm Vulcan gun and ability to deploy two or four Sidewinder air-to-air missiles make it a formidable adversary.

US Boeing Model 707 (1954)

Type	four-engined commercial transport
Engine	(707-320B) four 19,000lb (8,618kg) thrust Pratt & Whitney JT3D-7 turbofan engines
Armament	none
Maximum Speed	(cruise) 605mph (973km/h) at 25,000ft (7,620m)
Rate of Climb	4,000ft (1,219m)/min
Ceiling	39,000ft (11,885m)
Wing Area	3,050sq ft (283.40m²)
Weight Empty	141,100lb (64,000kg)
Take-off Weight	333,600lb (151,315kg)
Span	145ft 9in (44.42m)
Length	152ft 11in (46.61m)
Height	42ft 5in (12.93m)

The prototype of this superb commercial transport aircraft, sales of which are approaching 1,000 in 1976, was the first jet transport to be flown in the United States, on 15 July 1954. Pan American introduced the type on its New York-Paris route on 26 October 1958, and they are in use currently with airline operators around the world.

Boeing 707

France Sud-Aviation Caravelle (1955)

Type	twin-jet medium-range commercial transport
Engine	(Series VI-R) two 12,600lb (5,725kg) thrust Rolls-Royce Avon 523R or 533R turbojets
Armament	none
Maximum Speed	(cruise) 527mph (845km/h) at 25,000ft (7,620m)
Wing Area	1,579sq ft (146.70m²)
Weight Empty	57,938lb (26,280kg)
Take-off Weight	110,232lb (50,000kg)
Span	112ft 6¾in (34.30m)
Length	105ft 0¼in (32.01m)
Height	28ft 7¼in (8.72m)

Taking a close look at the turbine-powered commercial transport aircraft being produced in America and Britain, Sud-Aviation concluded that if the power plant could be installed independently of the wing certain advantages would derive. First and foremost, the wing would be able to develop maximum lift, being aerodynamically 'clean' and free from any interference drag imposed by engine nacelles or intakes. They investigated a three-engine layout, with one engine buried in the base of the fin, and one on each side of the rear fuselage. The final decision was for a twin-engine installation, omitting the engine in the base of the fin. The resulting Caravelle prototype flew for the first time on 27 May 1955.

Lockheed F-104 Starfighter

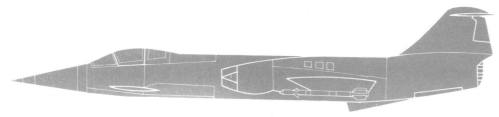

France Dassault Mirage III (1956)

Type	single-seat fighter, fighter-bomber and reconnaissance aircraft
Engine	(III-E) one 13,670lb (6,200kg) thrust Snecma Atar 09C turbojet, and optional jettisonable 3,305lb (1,500kg) thrust SEPR 844 single-chamber rocket motor
Armament	fighter has as standard one Matra R.530 and two Sidewinder air-to-air missiles, plus two 30mm cannon. Ground-attack armament comprises normally two 30mm cannon, two 1,000lb bombs or an AS30 air-to-surface missile under-fuselage, and a 1,000lb bomb beneath each wing
Maximum Speed	873mph (1,400km/h)
Rate of Climb	12,000ft (3,658m)/min
Wing Area	375sq ft (34.84m²)
Weight Empty	15,540lb (7,050kg)
Take-off Weight	29,760lb (14,000kg)
Span	27ft 0in (8.23m)
Length	49ft 3½in (15.02m)
Height	13ft 11½in (4.25m)

Precursor of a family of military aircraft, the Dassault Mirage III is an example of a 'mixed-power' interceptor. Using a conventional turbojet with afterburner as normal power plant, it can use also an auxiliary jettisonable rocket motor to assist take-off or boost its speed when operating as an interceptor.

US General Dynamics B-58 Hustler (1956)

Type	three-seat supersonic medium bomber
Engine	four 15,600lb (7,080kg) thrust General Electric J79 turbojets
Armament	one radar-aimed 20mm Vulcan multi-barrel cannon in fuselage tail cone, plus an under-fuselage mission pod
Maximum Speed	1,385mph (2,220km/h) at 40,000ft (12,190m)
Ceiling	60,000ft (18,290m)
Wing Area	1,542sq ft (143.25m²)
Take-off Weight	163,000lb (73,935kg)
Span	56ft 10in (17.32m)
Length	96ft 9in (29.49m)
Height	31ft 5in (9.58m)

The delta-wing B-58 Hustler was the USAF's, and the world's, first supersonic bomber aircraft to be put into production. The first of these aircraft was flown for the first time on 11 November 1956. A special feature of the design was the use of an external under-fuselage pod to carry fuel for the journey to target as well as a nuclear weapon. It was intended that once the target had been attacked the pod would be jettisoned, and the return to base made on internal fuel. The Hustler also introduced for the first time individual escape capsules for the crew; making ejection possible at supersonic speed.

Britain Short SC1 (1958)

Type	single-seat VTOL research aircraft
Engine	five 2,000lb (907kg) thrust Rolls-Royce RB.108 jet lift engines
Armament	none
Maximum Speed	246mph (394km/h)
Wing Area	141.9sq ft (13.18m²)
Weight Empty	6,000lb (2,722kg)
Take-off Weight	7,700lb (3,493kg)
Span	23ft 6in (7.16m)
Length	29ft 10in (9.09m)

Dr. A A Griffith of Rolls-Royce began to evolve the idea of jet lift as early as 1941, but it was not until March 1952 that the design of a research vehicle to evaluate the concept began. This was the Rolls-Royce TMR (thrust-measuring rig), known far better by the Press-given name of 'Flying Bedstead', which was first demonstrated in free flight on 3 August 1954. Shortly after this flight Rolls-Royce began the design of a small turbojet engine intended to provide jet lift which, designated RB.108, was used to power the Short SC1 VTOL (vertical take-off and landing) research aircraft. One engine provided thrust for conventional flight, supported by the aircraft's wings; the remaining four engines were to provide VTOL capability, and could be tilted fore and aft to permit transition from vertical to horizontal flight, and *vice versa*. The first tethered hovering flight was made on 23 May 1958 and the first free flight on 25 October of the same year. However, the Harrier was developed instead.

Soviet Union Mikoyan MiG-23 (1965)

Type	single-seat variable-geometry tactical fighter
Engine	one turbojet of approximately 20,000lb (9,072kg) thrust, with afterburning
Armament	one twin-barrel 23mm belly-mounted cannon, with a variety of weapons carried on underwing pylons
Maximum Speed	estimated 1,528mph (2,450 km/h) at 36,090ft (11,000 m)
Ceiling	estimated 59,055ft (18,000m)
Take-off Weight	estimated 33,070lb (15,000kg)
Span	estimated 46ft 9in (14.25m)
Length	estimated 55ft 1½in (16.80m)

The prototype of this advanced tactical fighter was seen for the first time in the air during the 1967 Aviation Day Display at Domodedovo airport, Moscow. Its variable-geometry wing was demonstrated in flight, and it was announced that the aircraft had a maximum speed of Mach 2 at altitude, and could fly supersonically at sea level. It is believed that initial deliveries were made to the Red Air Force in 1971, but it seems likely that there were some problems encountered when the type came into service use, for it does not appear to have become fully operational until 1972. Since that time it seems probable that several hundreds of these aircraft have been delivered to the Soviet Air Force, Warsaw Pact air forces and to some countries in the Middle East.

175

Britain Hawker Siddeley Harrier (1967)

Type	single-seat V/STOL close-support and reconnaissance aircraft
Engine	(GR Mk 3) one 21,500lb (9,752kg) thrust Rolls-Royce Bristol Pegasus Mk 103 vectored-thrust turbofan
Armament	a 5,000lb (2,268kg) load of mixed weapons can be carried on under-fuselage and underwing hardpoints
Maximum Speed	more than 700mph (1,122 km/h) at low altitude
Rate of Climb	more than 17,000ft (5,182kg)/min
Ceiling	more than 50,000ft (15,240m)
Wing Area	201sq ft (18.68m^2)
Take-off Weight	more than 25,000lb (11,340 kg) (STOL)
Span	25ft 3in (7.70m)
Length	45ft 6in (13.87m)
Height	11ft 3in (3.43m)

The Hawker Harrier stems from the initial concept demonstrated by the Rolls-Royce TMR and Short SC1, and has been developed from a private-venture design which Hawker Siddeley began in 1957. From this, two prototypes and four development aircraft were ordered under the designation P.1127, and the first of the prototypes began tethered hovering tests on 21 October 1960. The first free hovering flights were made on 19 November 1960 and the first conventional flight trials on 13 March 1961. Shortly after that date the first transitions from vertical to horizontal flight, and *vice versa*, were accomplished. Field-evaluation aircraft of the P.1127 were named Kestrel, and were followed by a new design based on experience with the Kestrel. Known originally as the HS.1127 (RAF), it has since been named Harrier.

Anglo-French Concorde (1969)

Type	four-turbojet supersonic commercial transport
Engine	four 38,050lb (17,260kg) thrust Rolls-Royce/Snecma Olympus 593 turbojets
Armament	none
Maximum Speed	(cruise) 1,354mph (2,179km/h) at 51,300ft (15,635m)
Rate of Climb	5,000ft (1,525m)/min
Ceiling	60,000ft (18,290m)
Weight Empty	(operating) 174,750lb (79,265 kg)
Take-off Weight	400,580lb (181,700kg)
Span	83ft 10in (25.56m)
Length	202ft 3½in (61.66m)
Height	37ft 1in (11.30m)

The first prototype flew for the first time on 2 March 1969, but it was not until 21 January 1976 that Air France and British Airways were able, simultaneously, to introduce these aircraft into service. Type Certification of the Concorde was awarded on 5 December 1975, at which time a total of 5,542 development hours had been flown.

US Boeing Model 747 (1969)

Type	four-turbofan heavy commercial transport
Engine	(747-100) four Pratt & Whitney JT9D-7A or -7AW turbofan engines each of 46,950lb (21,295kg) and 48,570lb (22,030kg) thrust respectively
Armament	none
Maximum Speed	595mph (958km/h) at 30,000ft (9,150m)
Ceiling	45,000ft (13,715m)
Wing Area	5,500sq ft (511.00m^2)
Weight Empty	(operating) 354,061lb (160,600kg)
Take-off Weight	710,000lb (322,050kg)
Span	195ft 8in (59.64m)
Length	231ft 4in (70.51m)
Height	63ft 5in (19.33m)

Preliminary design was initiated in August 1965 and the company made a decision to go ahead with this giant project in March 1966. It was for an airliner with a maximum seating capacity of 500 passengers, and it was proposed that all-passenger, convertible passenger/cargo and all-cargo versions would be made available eventually. When the first aircraft made its first flight, on 9 February 1969, it was quickly dubbed 'Jumbo Jet'.

US General Dynamics F-16 (1976)

Type	single-seat advanced combat fighter
Engine	one 25,000lb (11,340kg) thrust Pratt & Whitney F100-PW-100 turbofan with afterburning
Armament	one M61A-1 20mm multi-barrel cannon, with up to 15,200lb (6,894kg) of mixed weapons carried on external hardpoints
Maximum Speed	more than Mach 2.0 at 40,000 ft (12,200m)
Rate of Climb	42,000ft (12,802m)/min
Ceiling	more than 50,000ft (15,240m)
Wing Area	300sq ft (27.87m)
Weight Empty	14,060lb (6,377kg)
Take-off Weight	33,000lb (14,968kg)
Span	(over missiles) 32ft 10in (10.01 m)
Length	47ft 7¾in (14.52m)
Height	16ft 5¼in (5.01m)

One of the most important fighter aircraft to be developed in the West during recent years, the General Dynamics F-16 originated from the USAF Lightweight Fighter programme. Two prototypes were built by General Dynamics under the designation YF-16 to compete against two YF-17 prototypes designed by the Northrop Corporation. While these aircraft were being built, the USAF changed its programme so that the competitive evaluation was to find a new Air Combat Fighter. The two YF-16 prototypes flew on 20 January and 9 May 1974, and in January 1975 the USAF announced that the General Dynamics contender was the winner.

Civil Aircraft of Today

138

Having taken a fairly extensive look at military aircraft, past and present, it seems desirable to conclude with a brief glimpse of the wide range of civil transport aircraft in use today. After all, it must surely be the hope of all mankind that one day we shall become sufficiently enlightened to dispense with military aviation and weapons of war forever.

One of the most successful small feeder-liner transport aircraft designed and built in Britain in post-war years is the Britten-Norman Islander (138) which was produced originally at Bembridge in the Isle of Wight.

Following acquisition of the assets of the company by the Fairey Group in 1972, a production line was established at Fairey SA's Gosselies, Belgium, factory, eliminating the production hold ups which had presented many problems to Britten-Norman's management over a long period.

With accommodation for a pilot and nine passengers, the rugged and reliable Islander has found buyers all over the world, and its improvement and production seem likely to continue.

139

This page:

In America the Gates Learjet Corporation builds several aircraft of much the same capacity as the Islander, but which are as different as chalk from cheese.

Learjets are luxury executive aircraft powered by twin turbine engines, and emphasis in the company's latest Models 35 and 36 has been to improve comfort and instal turbofan engines to offer greater economy of operation. The Learjet 35 **(139)** has accommodation for a crew of two and from eight to four passengers according to the standards of luxury required. The range of this version with maximum payload is 1,698 miles (2,732 km).

The earlier Learjet 25B **(140)** has similar accommodation, but is powered by turbojet engines.

In June and July of 1976, initial deliveries of the latest aircraft to be produced by Britain's Short Brothers & Harland, their SD3-30 commuter airliner **(141)**, were handed over to Command Airways of America and Time Air of Canada respectively. The only major new British civil aircraft development, other than the Anglo-French Concorde, this 30-passenger airliner benefits from modern technology to ensure quiet and comfortable travel. The initial sales to North America are significant, for the SD3-30 has been designed specifically to comply with the latest requirements of the FAA in relation to commuter airline operations. It could well be that this aircraft may prove important both to Britain and its manufacturers.

141

Following page:
Very similar in appearance to the Lear-jets is the Falcon 20 (142) produced by Dassault-Breguet in France. This has normal accommodation for a crew of two and 8–10 passengers, but it is possible for as many as 14 passengers to be accommodated in reduced-pitch seating and by the elimination of tables.

   Britain's equivalent is the Hawker Siddeley HS125, with a crew of two and a maximum of 12 passengers in the Series 400. Hawker Siddeley and Beech Aircraft Corporation had a marketing agreement, with Beech being responsible for the North American sector of the market. In this area the designation of the Series 400 is BH 125-400 (143), that illustrated being operated in Brazil.

140

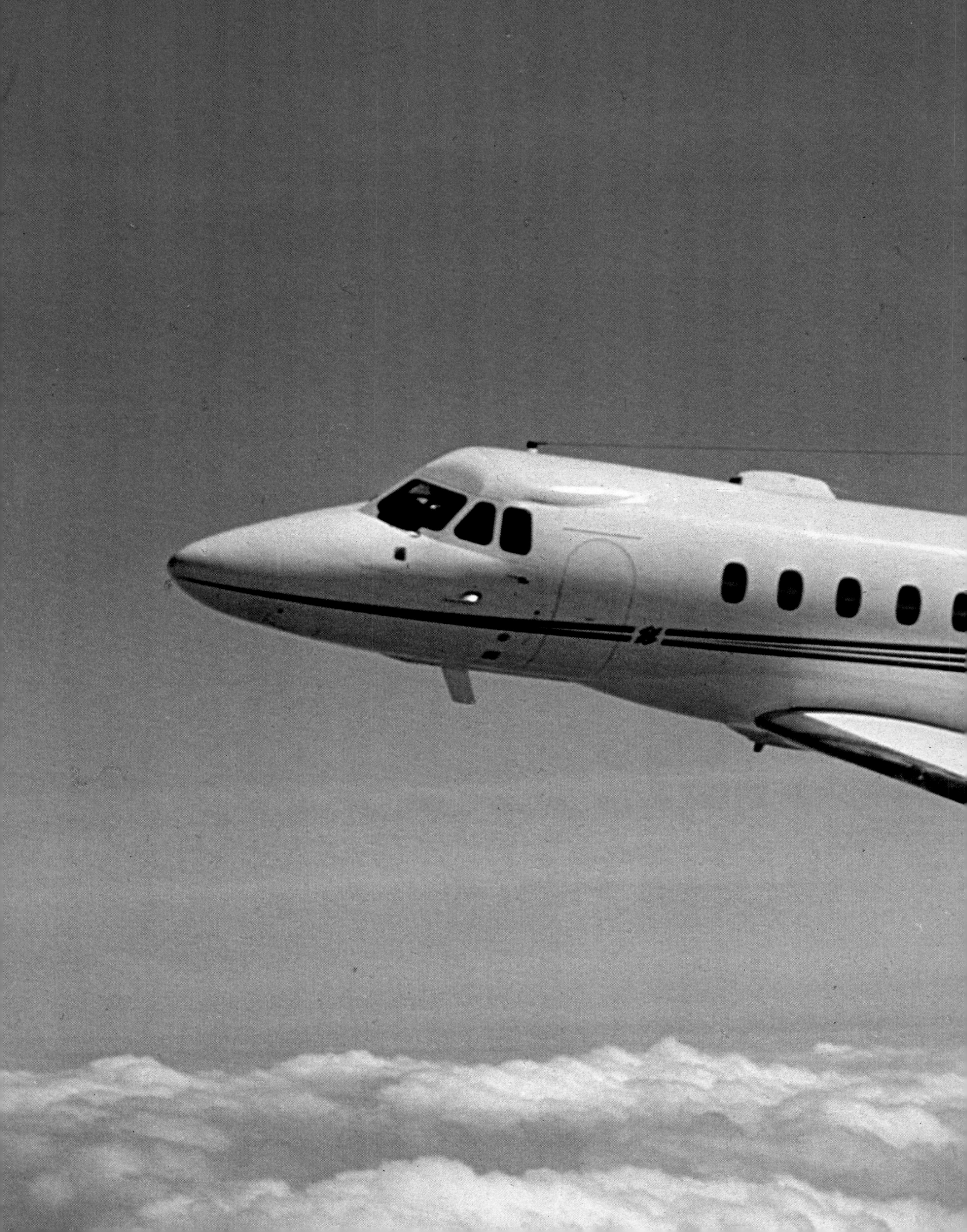

142

PT-DTY

The successful rear-engine installation of the French Caravelle (page 105) was viewed with interest by other manufacturers. Faced with a BEA requirement for a short/medium-range transport, Vickers in Britain investigated, type fuselage with three rear-mounted engines. Finally, BOAC came into the picture, requiring a long-range transport with greater payload, so the choice was made to use four Rolls-Royce Conway turbofan engines, but still in a rear-mounted configuration.

Why rear-mounted for Vickers? The requisite range and payload meant that a thinner-section more efficient wing was desirable. If it was required to serve as the mounting for four engines, then it could not be such an efficient aerofoil. Vickers also favoured the rear-mounted layout to give better airfield performance, lower approach speeds, improved control characteristics, reduced fire hazards in a crash landing, reduced risk of damage from runway debris and, of course, a lower cabin noise level.

The VC10, as the type became named, entered airline service with BOAC on 29 April 1964, proving an immediate success. The 'stretched'-fuselage increased-payload Super VC10 **(55)** began scheduled operations on 1 April 1965. The Super VC10 can carry up to 178 passengers

It is interesting to note how The Boeing Company has followed a logical train of evolution, ranging from the long-range four-engined 707/720, to the short/medium-range 727, and leading to the decision to produce also a twin-engined short-haul version of the same basic configuration, this becoming designated 737 **(145)**.

Since only two engines were required, allowing symmetric disposition, a return to the wing-mounted configuration of the 707 was chosen. And although there has been a reduction in structural weight and overall length, there is still a commonality of components with both the 707 and 727, offering valuable production—and spares stockholding—economies.

The first 737-100 entered service with Lufthansa on 10 February 1968, and a total of 414 had been delivered by 1 June 1975. Some slight measure of Boeing's vast experience in the manufacture of large aircraft is given by the fact that the company's 2,500th commercial jet transport was delivered—to Transavia of the Netherlands—on 17 May 1974.

145

146

148

This page:

The Netherland's best seller has been the Fokker-VFW F.27 Friendship, a medium-range turboprop-powered airliner which has accommodation for a crew of two and a maximum of 48 passengers in all but the Mk 500 version, which has an optional high-density seating arrangement for 56 passengers. Well over 600 of these aircraft have been sold, and the very colourful example illustrated is a Mk 400/600 in the service of Royal Air Inter **(146)**. Britain also has a successful turboprop airliner in much the same size category, namely the Hawker Siddeley 748, with normal accommodation for 40–58 passengers. Like the Friendship, it is powered by two of the reliable and economical Rolls-Royce Dart turboprop engines which have contributed so much to the success of many other aircraft.

Just the right combination of engine and airframe is, so often, the key to an airliner's popularity with operators and, more importantly, the passengers. A good example is British Aircraft Corporation's One Eleven, its various series powered by two rear-mounted Rolls-Royce Spey turbofan engines. Illustrated is a Series 500 of British Caledonian **(147)**, which accommodates a maximum of 119 passengers. Well over 200 of these aircraft have been sold, and utilization of the type by operators such as Allegheny, Braniff and American Airlines speaks much for the competitive performance it has to offer.

In the largest category of airliners pride of place is taken by the current Queen of the Air, the magnificent Boeing 747 which—whether Boeing like it or not—will be remembered as *the* Jumbo jet.

The first of the world's wide-body large-capacity commercial transports, it heralded a new age of air travel, and on 1 June 1975, almost 5½ years after the 747's introduction into airline service, Boeing could announce that the combined fleet of these aircraft had carried more than 90 million passengers, and that they had flown more than 1,420 million miles (2,286 million km). This picture of a Boeing 747B of South African Airways, ready for take-off on a night flight, depicts the grace—and glamour—of these wonderful aeroplanes **(148)**

It seemed logical that a freighter version of the Boeing 747 would appeal to many operators, leading to the 747F. This ground shot of the nose loading door **(149)** gives a good impression of the aircraft's size, particularly when it is pointed out that the height of the nosewheel tyres in the foreground is 4 ft 1 in (1.24 m).

It was a foregone conclusion that, so far as American manufacturers of commercial transport aircraft were concerned, the Boeing Company could not be allowed to have a monopoly of the market for wide-body jet airliners. The first to follow Boeing's lead was the Douglas Aircraft Company, a division of the McDonnell Douglas Corporation, whose three-engine DC-10 Series 10 made its first scheduled passenger flight on 5 August 1971. Illustrated **(150)** is a DC-10 Series 30 before delivery to Union de Transports Aériens (UTA).

Last of the three big wide-body jets into service was Lockheed Aircraft Corporation's L-1011 TriStar, powered by the advanced technology RB.211 turbofan engine developed by Rolls-Royce. First revenue-earning flight of the TriStar **(151)** was made by Eastern Air Lines on 15 April 1972.

149

150

151

153

Neither could one approach the conclusion of this history without mention of that other remarkable product of international co-operation, the Anglo-French Concorde supersonic transport aircraft.

So much has been written about Concorde that comment seems almost superfluous. The two pictures (**152** in British Airways insignia and **153** in Air France insignia) must serve to illustrate the graceful lines of this aircraft of tomorrow.

Simultaneous take-offs by Concordes of Air France and British Airways were made on 21 January 1976, marking the beginning of supersonic air travel for ordinary fare paying passengers.

As these words were being written,

in early 1976, there was still great uncertainty about operation of Concordes into the American international airports at New York and Washington, although there had been an earlier announcement of a 16-month trial period. Despite this, environmentalists and anti-Concorde groups seemed determined to fight this approval of a trial period by all possible means. Almost simultaneously with the appearance of this news, Air France announced that it had recorded a 66.9 per cent load factor on the first 17 Concorde flights from Paris to Rio de Janeiro and 58.3 per cent on the return flights. These figures must be regarded as highly satisfactory for these pioneering services, for the break-even load factor has been quoted as 55 per cent.

Index

Acknowledgments

The publishers would like to thank the following individuals and organizations for their kind permission to reproduce the photographs in this book:

Air BP 4 below left, 7 below, 8, 34–35 above, 97 below; Air France 105 centre, 188–189; Air Portraits 44 below, 53 below; Beech Aircraft Corporation 113; Bell Helicopter Company 124–125; Lewis Benjamin 177; Boeing Company 4–5 above, 36–37 above, 38 above, 39, 42–43, 43, 46–47, 46 inset, 47 inset, 48, 48–49, 70 above, 97 above, 98–99, 106–107 148 below, 183, 186; British Aircraft Corporation 4 above left, 45, 79 inset, 100 above and below, 120 below, 182, 184; British Airways 189; K J A Brookes 104 above; Daily Telegraph Colour Library 1; Dassault-Breguet Aviation 76 left, 76–77, 156–157, 157, 159 below, 181 inset; Douglas Aircraft Company 36–37 below, 51 above, 54 below, 55, 63, 64–65; Don Downie 116; Fokker-VFW 101; M Fricke 126 above; Gales Learjet Corporation 178 above; General Dynamic Corporation 146–147; Arthur Gibson 2–3; James Gilbert 10–11, 11 inset; Grumman Aerospace Corporation 158 above and below; Handley Page 102–103; Hawker Siddeley Aviation Ltd. 104 below, 150, 154–155 below, 180–181; Leslie Hunt 41, 50 above and below, 51 below; International Civil Aviation Organization 114–115; Howard Levy 8–9, 12 below, 13, 14 above, 16, 74, 74–75, 110, 112 below, 123 above and below; Lockheed Aircraft Corporation 159 above, 187 below; LTV Aerospace Corporation 66 above, 66–67, 68; Glenn Martin Company 58 above; Ministry of Defence 72–73, 78–79, 153 above, 154–155 above, 160; David Mondey 68–69, 178–179; McDonnell Aircraft Company 65, 146; Kenneth McDonough 33 below; H McDougall 34–35 below; Northrop Company 60–61, 145, 148 above; Popperfoto 70–71; N B Rivett 14–15; Rockwell International Corporation 60 inset, 149; Saab-Scania Aktiebolag 151 above and below; K Sissons 34 above, 102, 109, 185 above; South African Airways 185 below, John W R Taylor 4 above centre, 4 below right, 5 below, 7 above, 12 above, 14 below left, 33 above, 38 below, 40 above, centre and below, 44 above, 52–53, 56 above, 56–57 below, 59 below, 62 above and below, 76 above, 80, 105 above and below, 107 above, 108–109, 110–111, 112 above, 115, 116–117, 120 above, 126 below, 127, 128, 152–153, 179 above; Norman E Taylor 54 above; Teledyne Ryan Aeronautical 118, 119 above and below; United States Air Force 73 inset; Mick West 34 below; Westland Helicopters Ltd. 121, 122; Gordon Williams 57 above, 58 below, 59 above, 61 inset.

192